Julia Keese Colles

Authors and writers associated with Morristown

With a chapter on historic Morristown

Julia Keese Colles

Authors and writers associated with Morristown
With a chapter on historic Morristown

ISBN/EAN: 9783337203191

Printed in Europe, USA, Canada, Australia, Japan

Cover: Foto ©Thomas Meinert / pixelio.de

More available books at **www.hansebooks.com**

OLD MORRISTOWN.

Painted by CHARLES WETMORE. 1815.

Owned by HON. AUG. W. CUTLER.

Pen and ink sketch by Miss S. Howell, from original painting.

AUTHORS AND WRITERS

ASSOCIATED WITH

MORRISTOWN

WITH A CHAPTER ON

HISTORIC MORRISTOWN

BY

JULIA KEESE COLLES

1893
VOGT BROS.
MORRISTOWN, N. J.

DEDICATION.

TO THE MEN AND WOMEN, OF EARLY AND OF LATER YEARS, WHO HAVE SCATTERED THEIR PEARLS OF BEAUTY AND OF WISDOM ALONG THE DUSTY PATHS OF OUR HISTORIC CITY, THESE PAGES ARE INSCRIBED WITH AFFECTIONATE ADMIRATION BY
THE AUTHOR.

PREFACE.

This long-promised volume, the first of its kind, so far as known, ever given to the world, is now offered to the public. It is the result of a lecture given about three and a half years ago, which was repeated by request, and finally promised for publication, with the endorsement of one hundred and fifty subscribers.

No effort has been spared to have every statement in the book accurate; nor has any name been omitted which has presented a title to notice, in spite of the fact that the number of "Authors and Writers," has nearly doubled since the work of publication was undertaken. Any suggestion or criticism, however, will be gladly received by the author, as having a bearing on possible future work in this direction.

Morristown, New Jersey, February, 1893.

PREFACE.
POEM—MORRISTOWN.
HISTORIC MORRISTOWN.
GEORGE WASHINGTON.
POETS— PAGE.
    WM. AND STEPHEN V. R. PATERSON 33
    MRS. ELIZABETH CLEMENTINE KINNEY 40
    ALEXANDER NELSON EASTON 42
    FRANCIS BRET HARTE 45
    MRS. M. VIRGINIA DONAGHE MCCLURG 48
    CHARLTON T. LEWIS, LL. D. 54
    MISS EMMA F. R. CAMPBELL 58
    MRS. ADELAIDE S. BUCKLEY 63
    REV. OLIVER CRANE, D. D., LL. D. 63
    REV. J. LEONARD CORNING, D. D. 68
    MRS. MARY LEE DEMAREST 69
    HON. ANTHONY Q. KEASBEY 72
    MAJOR LINDLEY HOFFMAN MILLER 76
    MISS HENRIETTA HOWARD HOLDICH 79
    WILLIAM TUCKEY MEREDITH 81
    MISS HANNAH MORE JOHNSON 84
    MISS MARGARET H. GARRARD 87
    MISS JULIA E. DODGE 89
    CHARLES D. PLATT 90
    MRS. JULIA R. CUTLER 96
    MISS FRANCES BELL COURSEN 99
    MISS ISABEL STONE 100
    REV. G. DOUGLASS BREWERTON 102
    MRS. ALICE D. ABELL 104
    GEORGE WETMORE COLLES, JR. 105
HYMNODIST—
    JOHN R. RUNYON 107
NOVELISTS AND STORY WRITERS—
    FRANCIS RICHARD STOCKTON 109
    FRANCIS BRET HARTE 118
    MISS HENRIETTA HOWARD HOLDICH 131

>   Mrs. Miriam Coles Harris . 141
>   Miss Maria McIntosh . . 146
>   Mrs. Maria McIntosh Cox . 149
>   David Young . . . 155
>   Mrs. Nathaniel Conklin . 165
>   Mrs. Catharine L. Burnham . . 171
>   Hon. John Whitehead . . . 179
>   Mrs. Georgeanna Huyler Duer . . 181
>   Madame de Meissner . . 186
>   Miss Isabel Stone . 188
>   Augustus Wood . . 193
>   Charles P. Sherman . 193
>   Miss Helen M. Graham . . 193
>   Other Novelists and Story Writers 195

TRANSLATORS—
>   Mrs. Adelaide S. Buckley 197
>   Miss Margaret H. Garrard 202
>   Other Translators . 203

LEXICOGRAPHER--
>   Charlton T. Lewis, LL. D. 205

HISTORIANS AND ESSAYISTS—
>   William Cherry, Ancient Chronicler . 207
>   Rev. Joseph F. Tuttle, D. D. . . 209
>   Hon. Edmund D. Halsey . . . 215
>   Hon. John Whitehead . . . 218
>   Bayard Tuckerman . . . 221
>   Loyal Farragut 227
>   Josiah Collins Pumpelly . . 229
>   Miss Hannah More Johnson . 233
>   Mrs. Julia McNair Wright . 237
>   Mrs Edwina L. Keasbey . . 239
>   Mrs. Marian E. Stockton . . . 243

TRAVELS AND PERSONAL REMINISCENCES—
>   Marquis de Chastellux . . . 247
>   Rev. John L. Stephens 254
>   Hon. Charles S. Washburne . . . 255
>   General Joseph Warren Revere . . 257
>   Henry Day 260

THEOLOGIANS—

Rev. Timothy Johnes, D. D.	264
Rev. James Richards, D. D.	270
Rev. Albert Barnes	271
Rev. Samuel Whelpley	275
Stevens Jones Lewis	278
Rev. Rufus Smith Green, D. D.	279
Rev. Wm. Durant	282
Rev. J. Macnaughtan, D. D.	286
Rev. C. DeWitt Bridgman	291
Rev. J. T. Crane, D. D.	293
Rev. H. A. Buttz, D. D., LL.D.	296
Rev. J. K. Burr, D. D.	297
Rev. J. E. Adams	299
Rev. James M. Buckley, D. D., LL. D.,	300
Rev. James M. Freeman, D. D.	308
Rev. Kinsley Twining, D. D., LL. D.,	310
Rev. Theodore L. Cuyler, D. D.	314
Rt. Rev. Wm. Ingraham Kip, D. D., LL. D.	319
Rev. William Staunton, D. D.	323
Rev. Arthur Mitchell D. D.	327
Rev. Charles E. Knox, D. D.	332
Rev. Albert Erdman, D. D.	334
Rev. Joseph M. Flynn, R. D.	337
Rev. George H. Chadwell	338
Rev. William M. Hughes, S. T. D.	345

PUBLIC SPEAKERS AND LAWYERS—

Hon. Jacob W. Miller	351
Hon. William Burnet Kinney	355
Hon. Theodore F. Randolph	358
Hon. Edward W. Whelpley	360
Hon. Jacob Vanatta	362
Hon. George T. Werts	364
Joseph F. Randolph	365
Edward Q. Keasbey	367

SCIENTISTS—

Samuel F. B. Morse, LL. D.	368
Alfred Vail	371
William Graham Sumner, LL. D.	376

Elwyn Waller, Ph. D.	380
George W. Maynard, Ph. D.	382
Emory McClintock, LL. D.	383
Andrew F. West, LL. D.	384
Senor Jose Gros	386

MEDICAL AUTHORS AND WRITERS—

Condict W. Cutler, M. S., M. D.	388
Phanet C. Barker, M. D.	390
Horace A. Buttolph, M. D., LL. D.	392

AUTHORS AND WRITERS ON ART—

Thomas Nast	395
Rev. Jared Bradley Flagg, D. D.	398
Rev. J. Leonard Corning, D. D.	400
George Herbert McCord, A. N. A.	401

DRAMATIST—

William G. Van Tassel Sutphen	403

ILLUSTRATIONS.

	PAGE.
FRONTISPIECE—OLD MORRISTOWN.	
ORIGINAL FIRST PRESBYTERIAN CHURCH, 1738,	17
OLD ARNOLD TAVERN,	25
FIRST PRESBYTERIAN CHURCH,	97
WASHINGTON HEADQUARTERS,	209
PLAN OF FORT NONSENSE,	305
SPEEDWELL IRON WORKS,	369
OLD FACTORY AT SPEEDWELL,	377

POEM.

BY WILLIAM PATERSON.

MORRISTOWN, NEW JERSEY.

These are the winter quarters, this is where
   The Patriot Chieftain with his army lay,
When frosty winds swept down and chilled the air,
   And long, cold nights closed out the shorter day.

The bell still rings within the white church spire,
   Rising toward heaven upon the village green,
Whose chimes then called the people, pastor, choir,
   To praise and pray each Sabbath morn and e'en.

And there with them, the Christian soldier sealed
   The common covenant which a dying Lord,
To those who broke bread with him last revealed,
   And bade them ever thus His love record.

A country hamlet then, nor did it lose
   Its rural charms and beauties for long years;
The stranger would its quiet glories choose,
   Far from the toils and strifes of daily cares.

The people, too, were simple in their ways,
   And dwelt contented in their humble sphere,
The morning and the evening of their days,
   Passing the same with every closing year.

There were the Deacons, solemn, sober, staid,
    Beneath the pulpit each Communion Sunday,
They never smiled, but sung there psalms and
    prayed ;
    And then made whiskey at the still on Monday.

Perhaps you smile just here, I only say,
    Men did not deem it then a heinous crime ;
Such was the common custom of the day,
    As those can tell who recollect the time.

For further proof of this, look up the tract
    Of Deacon Giles and his distillery,
Where you will find that for this very fact,
    He was set up high in the pillory.

Young life for me began its early spring,
    Here in the freshness of the Mountain air,
When nature seemed in fullest tune to sing,
    And all the world was beautiful and fair.

And Death Who stays to think of him, till age
    Comes stealing on with sure and silent tread ?
Nor even then can he the thoughts engage,
    Till his cold fingers touch the dying bed.

He called one then in withered leaf and sere,
    And sent a warning, so wiseacres said,
By causing apple blossoms to appear
    In winter, and the old man soon was dead.

The Guinea Chieftain too, a century old,
    Born a young Prince beneath his native sky,
Who with his banjo sang rare tales of gold—
    I saw him strive and struggle, gasp and die.

A child was brought one evening, lived, and died,
    Almost before its eyes beheld the day ;
The infant and the old men, side by side,
    Were in the quiet churchyard laid away.

I learned of Life and Death, but know no more
    Of their mysterious secrets now than then ;
No sesame can open wide the door,
    That veils those mysteries from the light of men.

Upon the summit of the rock-bound hill
    That looks down on the lowland plains afar,
Are seen the outlines of the earthworks still
    Remaining there, rude vestiges of war.

That was a day to be remembered long,
    When crowds were gathered on the village green,
To welcome with warm hearts and floral song,
    Him who a friend in war's dark hour had been.

And not while nature's suns shall pour their light,
    Will Freedom's sons that honored name forget,
Nor cease to, until worlds shall pass from sight,
    Keep green the memory of Lafayette.

Hark, on the air tolls out the passing bell.
    Fourscore and ten and yet again fourscore :
Tread lightly now, it is the parting knell
    For two great spirits gone out evermore.

Together they had lived, together died
    As Freedom's Bell rang in her natal day,
And what than this could be more mete beside
    That twinned in death, their souls should pass
        away !

There comes a memory of the bugle horn,
    Winding a blast, as with their daily load,
The prancing coach-steeds dashed out in the morn
    To run the toll-gates of the turnpike road.

Behold the change! now brakes are whistled down,
    And screaming engines wake the Mountain air;
There is no longer, as of old, a Town
    Committee, but a Council and a Mayor.

Go where the lake sleeps in the summer night,
    Kissed by the winds that on its bosom play,
When the round moon sends down her fullest light,
    And evening glories in soft splendor lay.

And you can almost fancy then that over,
    The moonlit mirror of the tranquil tide,
You see the water spirits rise and hover,
    And on the sheen in laughing lightness glide.

And I have seen those waters as they flow,
    Down on their course past bridge and wheel and mill,
Where we as boys would " in-a-swimming go ; "
    Do the boys swim in "Sunnygony" still?

Oh, fellow scholar who along with me
    Learned the first rudiments of ball and book
Within the grounds of the Academy,
    In vain for that old landmark now you look.

Gone with the Master, yet a memory lingers,
    And will forever consecrate the spot,

Nor can the power of Time's effacing fingers,
  While life shall last, the recollection blot.

Teacher and pupils, few remain, and they
  Far on in years, lean on a slender staff;
The school-house, all you see of that to-day
  Is shown you there upon its photograph.

Change is on all things, and I see it here;
  Land that then grew the turnip and "potater,"
Now blooms in flowers and costs exceeding dear,
  Bringing some thousand dollars by the acre!

And villas crown the rising hill-tops round,
  And stately mansions stand adorned with art,
And liveried coaches roll with rumbling sound
  Where once jogged on the wagon-wheel and cart.

Hail to the future, ages come and go,
  And men are borne upon the sweeping tide;
Wave follows wave in ever ceaseless flow,
  The present stays not by the dweller's side.

I stand to-day far down the farthest slope,
  And up the lengthened pathway turn and look,
Where on the summit once stood Youth and Hope,
  Now soon to turn the last leaf of the Book.

And I am glad that while there come to me
  These fragrant memories of life's early scene,
That still in robes of purest white I see
  The Church Spire rising on the village green.

HISTORIC MORRISTOWN.

Throughout our country, there is no spot more identified with the story of the Revolution, and the personality of Washington, than Morristown. Nestled among its five ranges of hills, its impregnable position no doubt first attracted the attention of the commander-in-chief and that of his trusted quartermaster, General Nathaniel Greene. Besides, the enthusiastic patriotism of the men and women of this part of New Jersey was noted far and wide, and the powder-mill of Col. Jacob Ford, Jr., on the Whippany river, where "good merchantable powder," was in course of manufacture,—some of which had probably already been tested at Trenton, Princeton and elsewhere,— was also among the attractions.

It was on December 20th, 1776, that Washington wrote to the President of Congress: "I have directed the three regiments from Ticonderoga, to halt at Morristown, in Jersey (where I understand about eight hundred Militia have collected) in order to inspirit the inhabitants and as far as possible to cover that part of the country."

(Quoted by Rev. Dr. Tuttle in his paper on "Washington in Morris County," in the Historical Magazine for June 1871.)

These were regiments from New England.

The British, who were always trying to gain "the pass of the mountains," had made an attempt on the 14th of December, but had been repulsed by Col. Jacob Ford, Jr., with his militia, at Springfield.

At this time the village numbered about 250 inhabitants with a populous community of thriving farmers surrounding it. To the north of the town were the estates of the Hathaway and Johnes families; to the east, those of the Fords, who had just erected the building now known as the Headquarters; to the south, those of General John Doughty and to the west, those of Silas Condict and his brothers.

Morris county was settled "about 1710," by families of New England ancestry, who were attracted by the iron ore in the mountains round about and who came from Newark and Elizabethtown. The Indian name for the country round, seems to have been "Rockciticus" as late as the arrival of Pastor Johnes in 1742, according to the traditions in his family. The original name of the settlement of Morristown was West Hanover, and in court records this name is found as late as 1738. It was also called New Hanover. The present name was adopted when the county court held its first meeting here at the house of Col. Jacob Ford, on March 25th, 1740. The town was named for the county and the county was named for Governor Lewis Morris, who was Governor of New Jersey from

1738 to 1740. Evidently this was to be the county town of Morris County.

At the time of the Revolution the church, the "Court House and Jail" and the Arnold Tavern were the most important buildings. The Magazine also, a temporary structure, stood on South street, near the "Green". To it casks of power were constantly taken and sometimes casks of *sand* to deceive the spies who were always hanging about. The "Court House and Jail" was famous as the common prison of Tories caught in Morris and the adjoining counties. It was built in 1755 and stood on the northwest corner of the village "Green" as shown in the picture of Old Morristown. It was a plain wooden structure with a cupola and bell. Its sides and roof were shingled.

One of the illustrations of this book is of the Arnold Tavern, as it appeared in Washington's time. The picture is from a pen-and-ink sketch by Miss S. Howell, made originally and recently for the Washington Association of N. J., under careful direction from study of the time, by one of its members. Taverns were dotted all about the country in those days and most of the public meetings were held in their spacious rooms. Whether it was this fact or because of certain qualities possessed by the early proprietors of taverns, we find that many of them eventually became the most eminent men of the community.

The erection of the First Church building was begun in 1738 and finished in 1740, although the organization had existed from 1733. The first pastor, Rev. Timothy Johnes found it ready for his reception on his arrival in 1742 and for his installation, the following year. We are indebted to our young artist, Miss Emma H. Van Pelt, for a painting of this early church, from the only outline that remains to us, and to Miss S. Howell, for the pen-and-ink sketch, from the painting, for this book. This outline was embroidered upon a sampler owned by Miss Martha Emmell, and, according to family history, is a faithful representation of the building and the only suggestion other than traditional of Morristown's first place of worship. Miss Van Pelt's picture of the old church also follows in all respects her own, and the study of others, from the ancient records of the time. The structure stood about a rod east of the present building, facing upon Morris street and was always known as the " Meetin' House." It was originally of a somewhat plain and barn-like exterior, nearly square, with shingled sides, and windows let into the sloping roof. It was twice altered. In 1764, it was enlarged and two other entrances, besides the main entrance, were provided. A steeple also was erected in which was hung the bell in use at the present time. This bell was a gift, according to traditional history from the King of Great

Britain to the church at Morristown. It had upon it the impress of the British crown and the name of the makers, "Lister & Pack, of London *fecit*." It was re-cast about thirty years ago. This early church and the Baptist church, which stood on the site occupied by the one quite recently removed, (because of the fine new building in course of erection), have honorable record for unselfish devotion to the cause of the patriots. Both buildings were nobly given up for the use of the soldiers, suffering with small-pox, in the terrible winter of 1777.

Washington first came to Morristown, with his staff and army, three days after the battle of Princeton, on January 7th, 1777, and remained until May of that year. He made his Headquarters at the Arnold Tavern, then kept by Colonel Jacob Arnold, a famous officer of the "Light Horse Guards", whose grandsons are now residents of Morristown. This historic building stood on the west side of the Green, where now, a large brick building, "The Arnold", has been erected on its site. The old building with its many associations was about to be destroyed, when it was rescued, at the suggestion of the author of this book, and restored upon its present site on the Colles estate, on Mt. Kemble avenue, the old Baskingridge road of the Revolution. It has recently been purchased and occupied for a hospital by the All Souls' Hospital Association. Though extended and enlarged, it is still the same building and retains many of the distinctive features which characterized it when the residence of Washington. Here is still the bedroom which Washington occupied, the parlor, the dining-room and the ball-room where he received his generals, Greene, Knox, Schuyler, Gates, Lee, de Kalb, Steuben, Wayne, Winds, Putnam, Sullivan and others, besides distinguished visitors from abroad, all of whom met here continually during the winter of 1777. One of these visitors and one of our authors, the Marquis de Chastellux, gives an interesting account of his experience and impressions. In one of the bedrooms of this old house, has been seen within a few years, between the floor and the ceiling below, a long case for guns, above which was painted on the floor, in very large squares, covering the entire opening, a checkerboard about which, in an emergency, evidently the soldiers expected to sit and so conceal from the enemy the trap door of their arsenal. About this ancient building many traditions linger and from it have gone forth Washington's commands and some of his most important letters.

The road taken by Washington and his army, on coming first to Morristown, was, according to Dr. Tuttle, "through Pluckamin, Baskingridge, New Vernon, thence by a grist mill near Green Village, around the corner and thence along the road leading from Green Village to Morristown and over the ground which had been selected for an encampment in the valley bearing the beautiful Indian name of Lowantica, now called Spring Valley." It was here that the terrible scourge of small-pox broke out among the soldiers.

One cannot but wonder continually at Washington's courage and serenity in the midst of such overwhelming difficulties. He had hardly entered his winter home, in the Arnold Tavern, when the loss was announced to him of the brave and noble Col. Jacob Ford, Jr., his right-hand man, upon whom he had depended. He was buried, by Washington's orders, with the honors of war, and the description of that funeral cortege is one of the most picturesque pages out of traditional history. Then came the alarm about small-pox, the first death occurring on the same day as Col. Ford's funeral. Washington himself was taken ill, says tradition, with quinsy sore throat, and great fears were felt for his life. It is interesting to know that being asked who should succeed him in command of the army, should he not recover, he at once pointed to Gen. Nathaniel Greene. It was during this time of residence at the Arnold Tavern, that Washington joined Pastor Johnes and his people in their semi-annual communion after receiving the good pastor's assurance : "Ours is not the Presbyterian table, but the Lord's table, and we give the Lord's invitation to all his followers of whatever name." This is said to be the only occasion in his public career, when it is certainly known that Washington partook of the Sacrament. The hollow is still shown behind the house of Pastor Johnes, on Morris street, (purchased Feb. 3rd, 1893, of Mrs. Eugene Ayers, for the Morristown Memorial Hospital,) where a grove of trees then stood, when this historic event took place in the open air, while the church building was taken up with the soldiers sick of small-pox. Of this fact, in addition to the confirmation of Rev. Timothy Johnes's granddaughter, now living, Mrs. Kirtland, we have the following from Mr. Frederick G. Burnham, who says, (Oct 12th, 1892); "My Aunt, Huldah Lindsley, sister of Judge Silas Condict, and born in Morristown, gave me, in the most distinct and definite manner an account of General Washington's having communed with the Presbyterian Church on the occasion of the encampment in Morristown. My aunt told me that the congregation sat out of doors, even in the winter, but were shielded from the severe winds by surrounding high ground, that benches were placed in a circular position, that the pastor occupied a central point and that it was in this out-of-door place, muffled in their thickest clothing and many of them warmed by foot-stoves and other arrangements for keeping the feet warm, with nothing overhead but the wintry sky, that the congregation, among them General Washington, partook of the Lord's Supper."

Early in December 1779, came Washington once more, with his army, to Morristown, and remained until the following June, the guest of Mrs. Theodosia Ford, widow of the gallant Col. Jacob Ford, Jr., at her home now known as the "Headquarters." The story of the purchase and preservation of this building for the state and country, by the Washington Association of New Jersey, is given farther on. "It is still," says the orator of Fort Nonsense (the Rev. Dr. Buckley), "the most charming residence which Morristown contains and historically inferior only in interest to Mount Vernon and far superior to it in beauty of location and surrounding scenery." Among the treasures of the Headquarters is the original Commission to Washington, as Commander-in-chief of the Army.

At the opening ceremonial of the Washington Headquarters on July 5th, 1875, Governor Theodore F. Randolph, in an eloquent address, said as follows:

"Under this roof have been gathered more characters known to the Military history of our Revolution than under any other roof in America. Here the eloquent and brilliant Alexander Hamilton lived during the long winter of 1779--'80 and here he met and courted the lady he afterwards married -the daughter of General Schuyler. Here too was Greene—splendid fighting Quaker as he was and the great artillery officer, Knox, the stern Steuben, the polished Kosciusko, the brave Schuyler, gallant Light-horse Harry Lee, old Israel Putnam, "Mad Anthony" Wayne, and, last to be named of all, that brave soldier, but rank traitor - Benedict Arnold."

Many authenticated stories are extant of Washington, himself, and of the other distinguished inmates of the Headquarters during this memorable winter. Of the women of Morris County too, and the country round, many historic tales are told. If possible, they seem to have been even more patriotic than the men, whom, on several occasions, they upheld when wavering with doubt or fear. They had knitting and sewing circles for the soldiers in camp upon the Wicke Farm. These were presided over by Mrs. Ralph Smith, on Smith's Hummock, by Mrs. Anna Kitchell at Whippany, and by Mrs. Counselor Condict and Mrs. Parson Johnes, in Morristown.

In all this sympathetic work, Martha Washington led, and we hear of her that after coming through Trenton on December 28th, in a raging snow storm, to spend New Year's Day in the Ford Mansion, some of the grand ladies of the town came to call upon her, dressed in their most elegant silks and ruffles, and "so", says one of them, " we were introduced to her ladyship, and don't you think we found her with a *speckled homespun*

apron on, and engaged in knitting a stocking! She received us very handsomely and then again resumed her knitting. In the course of the conversation, she said, very kindly to us, whilst she made her needles fly, that 'American ladies should be patterns of industry to their countrywomen * * * * we must become independent of England by doing without these articles which we can make ourselves. Whilst our husbands and brothers are examples of patriotism, we must be examples of industry'. 'I do declare,' said one of the ladies afterwards, 'I never felt so ashamed and rebuked in my life!'"
(Rev. Dr. Tuttle.)

The "Assembly Balls," a subscription entertainment, no doubt arranged to keep up the spirits of the army officers, were held that winter at the O'Hara Tavern, says Dr. Tuttle, a house facing the Green and on or adjoining the lot where now stands Washington Hall,—and probably also at the Arnold Tavern.

In the meadow, in front of the headquarters, Washington's body-guard was encamped, originally a select troop of about one hundred Virginians.

Martha Washington was a fine horsewoman and the General a superb horseman, as are all Virginians of the present day. Many were the rides they took together over the country, one of the most frequent, being to a certain elevation on the

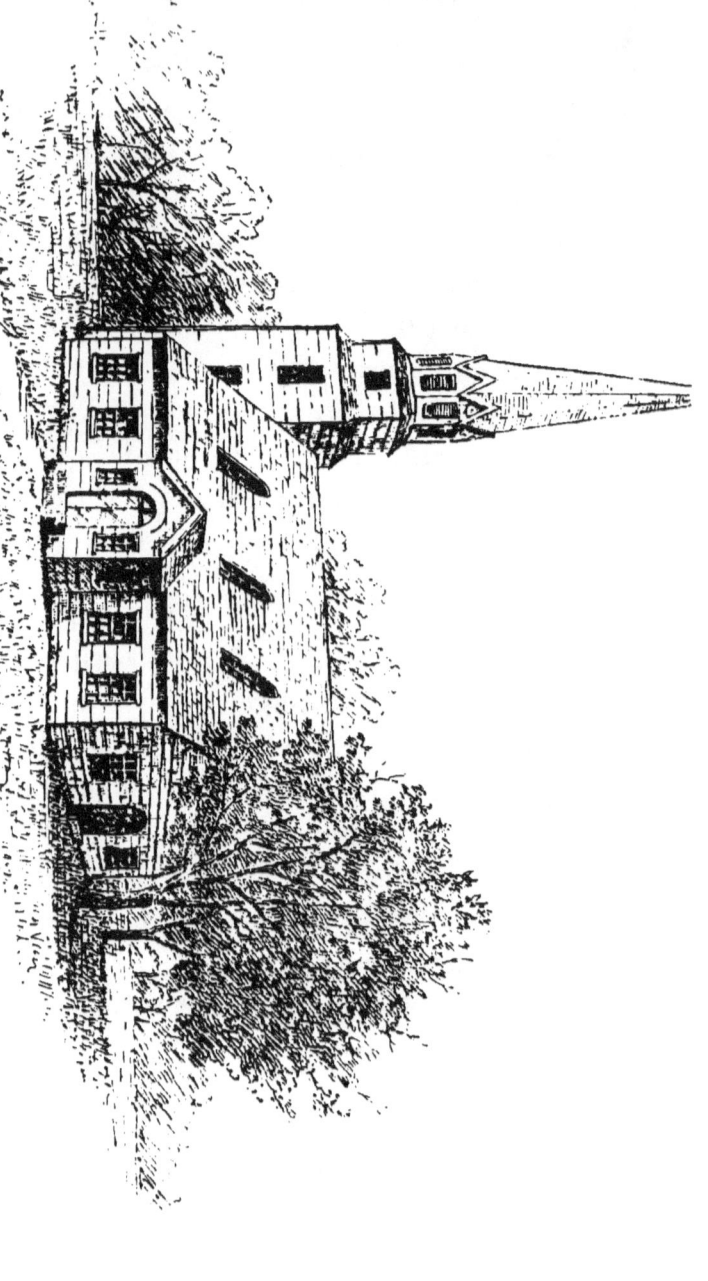

Short Hills, from which the General with his glass could see every movement of the enemy. Here was stationed the giant alarm-gun, an eighteen-pounder, and here was the main centre of the system of beacon-lights on the hills around. From this point can be seen the entire sea-board in the vicinity of New York City, which was of great importance when it was not known whether Howe would move towards West Point or Philadelphia. There is also a view of the entire region west of the mountain, "to the crown of the hills which lie back of Morristown, and extending to Baskingridge, Pluckamin and the hills in the vicinity of Middlebrook on the South, and over to Whippany, Montville, Pompton, Ringwood, and, across the State-line among the mountains of Orange County, N. Y., on the north." On our road to Madison, we may call up in imagination, the vision, which in those days was no unusual sight, says Dr. Tuttle, of "Washington and his accomplished lady, mounted on bay horses and accompanied by their faithful mulatto, 'Bill,' and fifty or sixty mounted Life-guards, passing on their way to or from their quarters in Morristown. At these times "the 'star spangled banner' was sure to float from the village liberty-pole, while our ancestors congregated along the highway where he was to pass and around the village inn, to do honor to the man to whose fidelity and martial skill all eyes were turned for the salvation of our country."

Sometimes this cavalcade would pass along the Baskingridge Road, (now Mt. Kemble Avenue), perhaps stop at General Doughty's house, or, galloping on, stop at the Kemble mansion, (afterwards the Hoyt residence and now that of Mr. McAlpin), four miles from town, or turning the corner up Kemble Hill to the Wicke farm, and Fort Hill, to view the soldiers' encampment, they would clatter back again, down the precipitous Jockey Hollow road, past the Hospital-field, or burial place of the soldiers, stopping at the Headquarters of General Knox, off the Mendham road, about two miles from town, for Mrs. Knox and Mrs. Washington were close friends. Returning, they might slacken rein at the house of Pastor Johnes, (Mrs. Eugene Ayers') on Morris Street, where a ring still remains at the side of the piazza, to which Washington's horse was tied, under an elm tree's shade; or, they would stop at Quartermaster Lewis's (Mr. Wm. L. King's) where they would find Lafayette, after his return from France, if he happened to be in Morristown,—then at Dr. Jabez Campfield's house, on Morris Street, the east corner of Oliphant Lane,—the Headquarters of General Schuyler.

Again the General, with his Life-guards, would set out to attend some appointed meeting of the "Council of Safety" at the house of its president,

Silas Condict. This was about a mile out on the Sussex Turnpike, where the house still stands, on the west side of the old cross-road leading from that turnpike to Brant's paper-mill. Here he would meet the high-minded and dauntless Governor Livingston and perhaps his son-in-law, Judge Symmes, who lived near by, and whom the Governor frequently visited ; all were men whose lives were sought for, by the British. Nearly all these homes are standing now and representatives of these families remain with us. Stories and traditions also relating to these homes and people have come down to us.

Silas Condict, the bold, the brave, the honored patriot, member of the Provincial Legislature and of the Continental Congress besides filling other high places of trust, is represented by his great-grand-son, Hon. Aug. W. Cutler, who now occupies the second house this ancestor built.

General John Doughty's interesting old house, with its curious interior, and many a secret closet, stands as of old, on Mt. Kemble Avenue, at the head of Colles Avenue. "He might be called," says Mr. Wm. L. King, "the most distinguished resident of Morristown, at whose house Washington was a frequent visitor and no doubt often dined." He is represented by a great-nephew, Mr. Thomas W. Ogden, who has written an important paper on General Doughty, for the Washington Association, which is published by them. General Doughty was the third in command of the American Army, and succeeded General Knox.

A descendant of General Knox is with us,— Mr. Reuben Knox, of Western Avenue.

General Schuyler's Headquarters has a romantic interest as the scene of the courtship between Miss Elizabeth Schuyler and Alexander Hamilton.

Of Pastor Johnes descendants, three generations are now with us to some of whom we have referred in the sketch of this distinguished man.

Out on the Wicke farm, stands the house as it was in those old days when Tempe Wicke took her famous ride ahead of the pursuing soldiers and saved her favorite horse by concealing him for three weeks in the guest chamber, until every man of the army had gone to fight his country's battles on the banks of the Hudson. This house is near Fort Hill from which is the magnificent view which embraces Schooley's Mountain to the westward and a line of broken highlands to the South, among which is the town of Baskingridge where General Lee was captured. On the northern slope of this hill, as late as 1854, 66 fireplaces of the encampment were counted in regular rows and in a small space were found 196 hut chimneys.

Going up a long, high street, not far from the Park, gradually ascending over rocks, and rough winding pathways, we come upon an open plateau on which is "Fort Nonsense," so named, on leaving it, by Washington, says tradition, because the soldiers had here been employed in constructing an octagonal earthwork, only to occupy them and to keep them from that idleness which was certain to breed discontent when added to their poverty, poor shelter, hopelessness, and homelessness. Here, on a bright afternoon of April, 1888, a monument to commemorate the site, was unveiled with appropriate ceremonies by the Washington Association. Long will be remembered the strange and startling effect upon those who sat waiting, as the procession drew near at a quickstep, up the hill, and led by the Fairchild Continental Drum Corps, in characteristic dress. Nearer and nearer came the tramp of many feet, to the sound of fife and drum playing Yankee Doodle, and, as they emerged from the trees upon the hill, it seemed as if Time's clock had been turned back more than a hundred years. Standing upon the stone, the orator of the occasion, Rev. Dr. Buckley, made a memorable address, in the course of which he mentioned that this monument, though small, is higher, measured from the level of the sea, than the great Washington Monument, which is declared to be the wonder of the world. The plan of the Fort, drawn by Major J. P. Farley, U. S. A., is now at the Headquarters and the illustration in this volume, is given from an engraving of the Messrs. Vogt, by their kind permission.

Probably no Author will again record the presence of the second "First Church", which has measured its hundred years and more, in its old familiar place upon the Park. Soon it will be replaced by a modern structure. In October, 1891, prolonged and interesting services were held to celebrate the centennial of its erection. Closely involved with all the history of Morristown, the influences of this old church are felt and shown all through this book. The picture we give of it and the Soldiers' Monument, is as we look upon both to-day. (For the use of the engraving, we are again indebted to the Messrs. Vogt). Sorrowfully, we note the passing of the old church building and number it among the things we would not lose, but which soon shall be no more. Behind it, is the old historic cemetery, where have been laid to rest the forms of many of the patriots and honored dead of the century gone by.

The "Old Academy" was an outcome of the First Church organization, and its early history is recorded in the "Trustees Book," of the church. Its centennial was observed on February 13th, 1891, on which occasion, among others, Hon. John Whitehead, of Morristown, and Judge William Paterson, of Perth Amboy, told its story, and the "Old Bell", placed upon the stage, was rung by Mr. Edward Pierson, who attended the Academy in 1820.

In 1825, Lafayette came again, from France, to revisit the scenes of the Revolution. It was on July 14th, about six o'clock in the evening, that coming from Paterson, he arrived at Morristown. The Morris Brigade under General Darcy was paraded on the Green and the firing of cannon and ringing of church bells announced his coming. General Doughty was Grand Marshal of the day and an eloquent address was made, in behalf of the town, by Hon. Lewis Condict. Lafayette dined at the Ogden House, the home of Jonathan Ogden, a large brick building, corner of Market street and the Green (shown in the picture). He attended a ball given in his honor, at the Sansay House (now Mrs. Revere's, on DeHart street), and stayed over night with Mr. James Wood, in the white house, corner of South and Pine streets. Two of Morristown's citizens have given their reminiscences of this event to the author of this book, as follows :

Mr. Edward Pierson, January 10th, 1893, says : " I remember well each member of the Committee who received Lafayette, but two. I remember very well the visit of General Lafayette to Morristown, in the year 1825. There was a delegation went from Morristown, in carriages and on horseback, to meet him beyond Morristown and escort him here. They came in by the Morris street road, past the Washington Headquarters. At that time there was only one small house on the north side of the street, below the present Manse of the First Church to the foot of the hill. The ground sloped from the graveyard to the street and was filled with people to see the procession come in. A reception was given and Lafayette was taken to the James Wood house (white house on the east corner of Pine and South streets, opposite my residence), to spend the night. I well remember the next morning seeing them start off with the General and his party in a four-horse carriage."

Mr. A. H. Condict, well-known as a resident of Morristown, writes from Mansfield, Ohio, (January 12th, 1893): "My eldest sister has related to me that when I was about a year old, General Lafayette was given a public reception at Morristown, in an elegant brick building then standing on the corner of the Park and Market street; that suitable addresses were made on the occasion and that while he was being observed by the great crowd of people, she held me up and that I looked at him. This would fix the time in the Summer of 1825, which corresponds with my notes gathered from the various histories."

Morristown has always been a centre, not only geographically, but a centre of influence from the time when it received its name. We have seen how, midway between West Point and Philadelphia, with roads radiating in every direction and with high hills well fitted for beacon-lights and commanding far-reaching views, Washington soon

THE ORIGINAL ARNOLD TAVERN.
FROM PEN AND INK SKETCH BY MISS S. HOWELL.

discovered it was the point for him to select for watching the movements of Lord Howe in New York, who might at any moment start up the Hudson for West Point, or Southwards, for Philadelphia.

In the early religious movements of the country, Morristown was conspicuous, having among its theologians some of the most brilliant thinkers of the period. Recently we find, in the published minutes of the Synod of New Jersey, Oct. 1892, the significant fact recorded that after the division of the Presbytery of New York, into that of New York and of New Jersey, the "Presbytery of Jersey at its first meeting in Morristown, April 24th, 1810, did appoint supplies for fourteen Sabbaths from May to September, to the pulpit of the vacant Brick Church in the City of New York".

One of the first Sunday Schools, if not the first, in New Jersey was started here, by Mrs. Charlotte Ford Condict of Littleton, the grandmother of Henry Vail Condict, now a resident of Morristown, and this was said to be the beginning of the great revival under Albert Barnes.

In a scientific direction, Morristown was the cradle of perhaps the greatest invention of the age, the electric telegraph. Also at the Speedwell Iron Works were manufactured the first tires, axles and cranks of American locomotives and a part of the machinery of the "Savannah," the first steamship that crossed the ocean.

Morristown also reflected the superstitions of the period; the people largely believed in witchcraft in those early days, and here was enacted, for about a year, the most remarkable ghostly drama that was ever published to the world, or influenced the best citizens of a community. The story of the Morristown Ghost will go down to future ages.

For philanthropy, from Revolutionary times, Morristown has been famed, since Martha set the example of knitting the stockings for the needy soldiers and good Hannah Thompson voiced the hearts of her sisters round about, when she gave food to a starving company of them, saying: "Eat all you want; you are engaged in a good cause, and we are willing to share with you what we have as long as it lasts." This old centre of patriotism and Revolutionary enthusiasm has radiated philanthropic movements which influence not only the conditions of the whole State but the welfare of humanity. Here was commenced that voluntary work of the State Charities Aid Association, which considers, and practically carries out, through its counselors, measures for reform among the pauper and criminal classes in the State institutions, and out of them, and which will undoubtedly influence for good all future generations. This work is on much the same plan that was originally thought out and organized by Miss Louisa Lee Schuyler, of New York, the great-grand-daughter of General

Philip Schuyler whose noble devotion to his Commander-in-chief is memorable during those days in Morristown. So we see how the old life of the Revolutionary period connects itself with the new life of progression. The principles then so nobly maintained take new forms in new projects.

Everywhere, we find the old and the new combined, for even the streets bear the names, with those of Schuyler, Hamilton and Washington, of Farragut and McCullough. In the Park there stands a granite shaft surmounted by a full length figure of a Morris County Volunteer, commemorating the lives of the noble men who fell in those hard-won fields, fighting to preserve the nationality which had been secured by their forefathers. Everything is significant of either noble deeds in the past or of honored names of later day and of private citizens whose personal influence has added moral dignity to this City of many associations.

George Washington.

Among the first notable writings associated with Morristown are the letters of Washington written from the old Arnold Tavern, and from the Ford Mansion, during the two memorable winters of 1777 and of 1779-'80. These noble letters are acknowledged on all sides to have been supremely efficient in promoting our national independence, filled as they are with the personality of Washington himself. They are very numerous. Many of them are published ; some are in our "Headquarters", and many still are scattered over the Country, in the possession of individuals. All are interesting and none appear to reveal what we would wish had not been known, as in the case of so many other published letters.

Of the man himself, our authors speak, here and there, throughout this volume. It is certain that no name, no face or character is more familiar to us than that of Washington, and no name in history has received a greater tribute than to be called, as he was, by the nation, at the end of his very difficult career, the "Father of his Country."

Here is Lafayette's first impression, as he attends a dinner in Philadelphia, given by Congress in honor of the Commander-in-Chief. He says : "Although surrounded by officers and citizens, Washington was to be recognized at once by the majesty of his countenance and his figure." And this is Lafayette's tribute to Washington, when the two men have parted : "As a private soldier, he would have been the bravest ; as an obscure citizen, all his neighbors would have respected him. With a heart as just as his mind he always judged himself as he judged circumstances. In creating him expressly for this revolution, Nature did honor to herself ; and to show the perfection of her work, she placed him in such a position that each quality must have failed, had it not been sustained by all the others."

(Quoted by Bayard Tuckerman in his " Life of Lafayette.")

In the portrait of Washington which Chastellux gives us, occur these words : "His strongest characteristic is the perfect union which reigns between the physical and moral qualities which compose the individual. one alone will enable you to judge of all the rest. If you are presented with medals of Cæsar, Trajan or Alexander, on examining their features, you will still be led to ask what was their stature and the form of their persons ; but if you discover, in a heap of ruins, the head or the limb of an antique Apollo, be not anxious about the other parts, but rest assured that they all were conformable to those of a God. * * * This will be said of Washington, '*At the end of a long civil war, he had nothing with which he could reproach himself.*' "

Thatcher, in his Military Journal, speaks of Washington as he appeared at a great entertainment given by General Knox, in celebration of the alliance with France : "His tall, noble stature and just proportions, his fine, cheerful countenance, simple and modest deportment, are all calculated to interest every beholder in his favor and to command veneration and respect. He is feared even when silent and beloved even while we are unconscious of the motive."

The first French minister, M. Gerard, tells us, referring to Washington: "It is impossible for me briefly to communicate the fund of intelligence which I have derived from him. I will now say only that I have formed as high an opinion of the powers of his mind, his moderation, patriotism and of his virtues, as I had before from common report conceived of his military talents, and of the incalculable services he had rendered to his country."
(Quoted by A. D. Mellick in his "Story of an Old Farm.")

We see the General in his evening dress of "black velvet, with knee and shoe buckles and a steel rapier; his hair thickly powdered, drawn back from his forehead and gathered in a black silk bag adorned with a rosette" walking gracefully and with dignity through the figures of a quadrille. We see him devoted to his wife and courteous to every woman, high and low. Greene writes from the Headquarters: " Mrs. Washington is extremely fond of the General and he of her; they are happy in each other." We see him, with his tender sympathy among the soldiers and so find the key to the wonderful devotion of the soldiers to their chief, and his influence over them. As an old soldier tells the story to the Rev. O. L. Kirtland: " There was a time when all our rations were but a single *gill of wheat* a day. Washington used to come round and look into our tents, and he looked so kind and he said so tenderly. 'Men, can you bear it?' 'Yes, General, yes we can,' was the reply; 'if you wish us to act give us the word and we are ready!'" Many were the letters he wrote in their behalf to Congress, who neglected them, and to Lord Howe in New York, because of his cruelty to the prisoners in his power.

Another key we have to his calm and self-reliant bearing, even in his darkest hours, so that, says Tuttle, "there seemed to be something about this man, which inspired his enemies, even when victorious, with dread." It is expressed in a letter of Washington when heartsick at the round of misfortunes at the outset of the Revolution, and after the capture of Fort Washington by the enemy. He writes: "It almost overcomes me to reflect that a brother's sword has been sheathed in a brother's breast and that the once happy and peaceful plains of America are either to be drenched in blood or inhabited with slaves. Sad alternative! But can a virtuous man hesitate in his choice?"
(Quoted by Dr. Tuttle from Sparks.)

A touching letter is written on the 8th of January, 1880, from the Ford Mansion, to the Morris County authorities, about the hungry, destitute soldiers, to which he receives at once so warm and generous a response that he writes again: "The exertions of the magistrates and inhabitants of the State were great and cheerful for our relief."
(Quoted by Dr. Tuttle from Sparks.)

Though a warm Episcopalian, his broad Christian feeling is shown when he says : " Being no bigot, myself, I am disposed to indulge the professors of Christianity in the Church with that road to heaven which to them shall seem the most direct, the plainest and easiest and least liable to objections."
(Dr. Tuttle, quoted from Sparks.)

And again, in reply to the Address of the Clergy of different denominations, in and about Philadelphia ; " Believing as I do, that *Religion and Morality are the essential* pillars of society, I view with unspeakable pleasure, that harmony and brotherly love which characterize the clergy of different denominations, as well in this, as in other parts of the United States, exhibiting to the world a new and interesting spectacle, at once the pride of our Country and the surest basis of universal harmony."
(Quoted by Dr. Tuttle from Dr. Green's Autobiography.)

What man, after arriving at such a height of power and influence over men, has been able to take up, with content again, his life of a country gentleman ? Wonderfully appropriate were the last words that fell from his lips : " It is well."

Of Washington it may be said as of no other, in the words of Henry Lee, in his Eulogy of December 26th, 1799 : " To the memory of the man, first in war, first in peace, and first in the hearts of his countrymen."

POETS.

William and Stephen V. R. Paterson.

A curious circumstance surrounds the poetic work of the two Paterson brothers William and Stephen Van Rensselaer Paterson and gives it a unique interest apart from its especial merits. The survivor of the two brothers says, in the short and highly interesting introduction to their poems, published in 1882 and called "Poems of Twin Graduates of the College of New Jersey":

"The title explains itself, and shows that the writers were born under the sign of the Gemini. They lived under that sign for rising fifty years, when one was taken and the other left. Two of us came into existence within the same hour of time, and passing through the early part of education together, entered the world-life as twin graduates of the collegiate institution bearing the name of the State of which they were natives. This dual species of psychology was something of a curiosity because outside of common experience. Pleasure and pain seemed to flow like electric currents from the same battery. In a certain sense, we could feel at once, and think at once and act at once. It is problematical whether this proceeded from a real elective affinity, or was mechanical. It was most marked, however, at first, and particularly in the beginning or rudiments of learning. Both then went along exactly at the same rate, and one never was in advance of the other. Both always worked and played together, and whichever discovered something new, would communicate it in an untranslatable language to his companion.

"This dual character, to a greater or less extent, pervaded the joint lives of the writers of these pieces. Not that the similarity extended to the business or pursuits, the tastes or habits of life, for in many respects they were different and apart as those bearing a single relation. Still the influence of the mystic tie, whatever it was or may have been, remained till nature loosed, as it had woven, the bond."

Although Judge William Paterson was born in Perth Amboy and now resides there, his associations with Morristown, as related in a letter under his signature, are those of early boyhood passed on the farm, now occupied by Mrs. Howland. "Morristown was then but a village hamlet," he says, and "the old Academy and the Meeting House on the village green were the only places in which services were held." Still, we gather, that at Morristown, the two poets received their "scholastic and agricultural training." Here, too, was laid the foundation of their "political and religious faith," the latter under the administration of Albert Barnes, and, what may be a noted event in their lives, they heard Mr. Barnes preach the sermon on the "Way of Salvation," which caused the division of the Presbyterian Church.

Judge Paterson is a graduate of Princeton, which is in a double sense his Alma Mater, inasmuch as members of his family were among the first graduates, soon after the removal of the College from Newark and "when that village, then a hamlet amid the primeval forests had become the permanent site for the Academy incorporated by royal charter."

Various positions of importance in the community have been held by Judge Paterson. In 1882, he was made Lay Judge of the Court of Errors and Appeals of the State; he was also Mayor of Newark for ten years, at different times from 1846 to 1878, filling important and non-important municipal and county offices. Thus his work has been mostly legal and political, save, when he has made dashes into the more purely literary fields, rather, perhaps, through inspiration and for recreation from the dry details of practical work.

More than once has Judge Paterson told to amused and interested audiences in Morristown his recollections of boyhood and youth spent here. Notably, many remember his recent graphic address on the occasion of the Centennial of the Morristown Academy.

In 1888, our author published a valuable "Biography of the Class of 1835 of Princeton College," the class in which he graduated. The "Poems" were published in 1882. Looking through the latter volume, which contains many treasures, we wonder how, many of the poems—written as they were under the influence of a higher inspiration than ordinary rythmic influences—should not earlier have found their way, in book form, from the writer's secret drawers to the readers of the outside world. Many of these poems are connected with experiences and memories of Academic days in Princeton and, among them all we would mention "The Close of the Centennial;" "Living on a Farm," which refers to Mrs. Howland's farm, long the poet's home in boyhood; "14th February, 1877;" "The Hickory Tree," and "Polly," in which the writer has caught wonderfully the bright, playful spirit of the child. The poem "Morristown," a pictorial reminiscence, we have selected to open this book.

Quite recently, (in September, 1892) has been published and bound in true orange color, *An Address*, read before the New York Genealogical and Biographical Society, on February 12th, 1892, on the life and public services of *William Paterson*, his honored grandfather, who was "Attorney-General of New Jersey during the Revolution, a framer of the Federal Constitution, Senator of the United States from New Jersey, Governor of that State, and an Associate Justice of the Supreme Court of the United States at the time of his death, September 9th, 1806." "He was the first Alumnus of Princeton," says the writer, "who was tendered a place in the Cabinet or on the Federal Judiciary, the Attorney-General, the first one being William Bradford, also an Alumnus, a classmate of Madison, and Collegemate of Burr, then not constituting part of the Executive household." "He began the study of legal science and practice under the instruction of Richard Stockton, who was an Alumnus of the first Class that went forth from the College of New Jersey, then located in Newark, and who, though young, comparatively, was rising fast to the forefront of his profession, and, afterward, to become of renowned judicial and revolutionary fame."

The publication is full of interest, graphic description and notice of men and events of the period. Here is a letter to Aaron Burr, between whom while a student in the College at Princeton, and Mr. Paterson, then established in the practice of his profession, had sprung up a strong friendship which continued during life :

"Princeton, January 17th, 1772. DEAR BURR : I am just ready to leave and therefore cannot wait for you. Be pleased to accept of the enclosed notes on *dancing.* If you pitch upon it as the subject of your next discourse, they may furnish you with a few hints, and enable you to compose with greater facility and despatch. To do you any little service in my power, will afford me great satisfaction, and I hope you will take the liberty— it is nothing more, my dear Burr, than the freedom of a friend—to call upon me whenever you may think I can. Bear with me when I say, *that you cannot speak too slow.* Every word should be pronounced distinctly ; one should not be sounded so highly as to drown another. To see you shine as a speaker, would give great pleasure to your friends in general and to me in particular. You certainly are capable of making a good speaker.

"Dear Burr, adieu. WM. PATERSON."

The writer pays a beautiful tribute to Ireland, the land of his ancestors : "Irish Nationality," he says, "is no empty dream ; it goes back more than two thousand years, is as old as Christianity, and is attested by the existence of towers and monuments, giving evidence of greater antiquity than is to be found in the annals of any other country in all Europe. For centuries, Ireland sent missionaries of learning throughout the continent to herald the advent of civilization and stay the advance of barbarism, and her story is one running over with great deeds and glorious memories, with associations of poetry and art and bards, and a civilization, ante-dating that of almost any other Christian community. It cannot be claimed that the rude exploits of her early inhabitants are classic in story or in song. They acquired no territory; their island domain is but a spec of green verdure amid the waste of ocean waters, and the flash of an electric light, located on the hills where stood the ancient psaltery, could be sent throughout its length and breadth. They conquered no worlds. No manifest destiny led them to seek for wealth, applause or gain, beyond the limits of their narrow bounds. They did not so much as pass over the seas that wash their either shore. But yet in the absence of all the achievements that can gratify ambition, with no record of pomp or pageantry or power, her people bear a character more like a dream of fancy than a thing of real life, and to-day they stand as remnants of national greatness, though you may look in vain in their annals or traditions for any evidence of usurpation or of subjugation by sceptre or by sword."

Mrs. Elizabeth Clementine Kinney.

Mrs. Kinney, the mother of the poet, Edmund Clarence Stedman, and daughter of David L. Dodge of New York city, was for several years a resident of Morristown, and will long be remembered with interest and affection by her many friends. Her husband, Mr. William Burnet Kinney, not only resided here in later years, but was born at Speedwell, then a suburb of Morristown, and passed a part of his early boyhood there. To him we shall refer, in the grouping of *Editors and Orators*.

Mr. Kinney was a brilliant literary man and about this home in Morristown unusual talent and genius naturally grouped themselves. To it came and went the poet Stedman: in the group, we find two gifted women, daughters of Mrs. Kinney, and later on, the same genius developing itself in the son of one of these, the boy Easton, of the third generation.

Mrs. Kinney published in 1855, "Felicita, a Metrical Romance;" a volume of "Poems" in 1867; and, a few years later, a stirring drama, a tragedy in blank verse, entitled "Bianco Cappello." This tragedy is founded upon Italian history and was written during her residence abroad in 1873. While abroad, Mrs. Kinney's letters to *The Newark Daily Advertiser* gave her a wide reputation and were largely re-copied in London and Edinburgh journals from copies in the New York papers.

Among the "Poems," the one "To an Italian Beggar Boy" is perhaps most highly spoken of and has been chosen by Mr. Stedman to represent his mother in the "Library of American Literature." A favorite also is the "Ode to the Sea." Both pieces are strong and dramatic. The poem on "The Flowers" has been translated into three languages. It opens:

> "Where'er earth's soil is by the feet
> Of unseen angels trod,
> The joyous flowers spring up to greet
> These messengers of God."

Mrs. Kinney's sonnets are peculiarly good. Her sonnet on "Moonlight in Italy," which we give to represent her, was written at ten o'clock at night in Italy by moonlight, and has been much praised. Mr. Kingston James, the English translator of Tasso, repeated it once at a dinner table, as a sample of "in what consisted a true sonnet."

MOONLIGHT IN ITALY.

There's not a breath the dewy leaves to stir ;
  There's not a cloud to spot the sapphire sky ;
All nature seems a silent worshipper :
  While saintly Dian, with great, argent eye,
Looks down as lucid from the depths on high,
  As she to earth were Heaven's interpreter :

Each twinkling little star shrinks back, too shy
  Its lesser glory to obtrude by her
Who fills the concave and the world with light ;
  And ah ! the human spirit must unite
In such a harmony of silent lays,
  Or be the only discord in this night,
Which seems to pause for vocal lips to raise
  The sense of worship into uttered praise.

Alexander Nelson Easton.

In the third generation in the line of Mrs. Kinney, appears a boy, now seventeen years of age, of unusual promise as a poet—Alexander Nelson Easton, grandson of William Burnet and Elizabeth C. Kinney. He has written and published several poems. He took the $50 prize offered by the *Mail and Express* for the best poem on a Revolutionary incident, written by a child of about twelve years. It was entitled " Mad Anthony's Charge."

Young Easton was born in Morristown, and spent his early years in this place, in the house on the corner of Macculloch Avenue and Perry Street, belonging to Mrs. Brinley. He began to write at eight years when a little prose piece called " The Council of the Stars," found its way into print, out in California. His next was in verse, written at ten years on "The Oak." That was also published and copied. A "Ballad" followed "A Scottish Battle Song," written in dialect, which was published also. Then came the prize poem, "Mad Anthony's Charge," above referred to. He has composed two stories since, one of which, "Ben's Christmas Present," has been accepted by the New York *World* and is to appear with a sketch of this young writer, in their Christmas number. At twelve years, he wrote a monody on "The Burial of Brian Boru," which is given below.

The literary efforts of Easton, so far, have been spontaneous and spasmodic, but contain certain promise for the future. After studying for some time at the Morristown Academy, Easton went as a student to the Bordentown Military Institute from which he has graduated and has now passed on to Princeton College. At Bordentown he won golden opinions, and gave the prize essay at the June Commencement. This was an oration of considerable importance on "The Value of Sacrifice," but withal his gifts are essentially poetic.

THE BURIAL OF BRIAN BORU.

Slowly around the new-made grave
  Gathers the mourner throng ;
Women and children, chieftains brave,
  Numb'ring their hundreds strong.

Glitter beneath the sun's bright ray
  Helmet and axe and spear;
Sadness and sorrow reign to-day,
  Dark is the land and drear!

Yesterday leading his men to fight,
  Now lies he beneath their feet,
Clad in his armor, strong and bright,
  'Tis his only winding sheet.

Close to his grave stand his warriors grim,
  Bravest and best of his reign;
They, who through danger have oft followed him,
  Mourn the wild "Scourge of the Dane."

Look! from the throng with martial stride
  Steps an old chief of his clan,
Pauses and halts at the deep grave's side,
  Halts as but warriors can.

White is the hair beneath his cap,
  Withered the hand he holds on high;
Standing, beside the open gap,
  Speaks he without a pause or sigh.

> "*Brian Boru* the brave!
>   *Brian Boru* the bold!
> Lay we thee in thy grave;
>   Deep is it, dark and cold.
>
> Bravest of ev'ry chief
>   Erin has ever known;
> Hurling the foes in grief,
>   Fiercest of Danes o'erthrown.

Youth and old age alike
  Found thee in war array;
Wielding the sword and pike,
  E'er in the thick o' the fray!

Erin is freed and blest,
  Freed by thy mighty arm;
Well hast thou earned thy rest,
  Take it! secure from harm.

Friend of our hearts! Our king!
  Generous, kind and true!
Out let our praises fling—
  Shout we for *Brian Boru*."

Bursts the wild song from a thousand throats,
  Sounding through wood and plain,
While the mountains echo the dying notes,
  Ringing them out again.

Francis Bret Harte.

As a poet, we represent Bret Harte by his "Plain Language from Truthful James," better known as "The Heathen Chinee." The main reference to his writings follows, in the next classification of *Novelists and Story Writers*.

PLAIN LANGUAGE FROM TRUTHFUL JAMES,

BETTER KNOWN AS "THE HEATHEN CHINEE."

TABLE MOUNTAIN, 1870.

Which I wish to remark,—
  And my language is plain,—
That for ways that are dark,
  And for tricks that are vain,
The heathen Chinee is peculiar.
  Which the same I would rise to explain.

Ah Sin was his name ;
  And I shall not deny
In regard to the same
  What that name might imply,
But his smile it was pensive and child-like,
  As I frequent remarked to Bill Nye.

It was August the third ;
  And quite soft was the skies ;
Which it might be inferred
  That Ah Sin was likewise ;
Yet he played it that day upon William
  And me in a way I despise.

Which we had a small game,
  And Ah Sin took a hand :
It was Euchre. The same
  He did not understand ;
But he smiled as he sat by the table,
  With the smile that was child-like and bland.

Yet the cards they were stocked
  In a way that I grieve,
And my feelings were shocked
  At the state of Nye's sleeve :
Which was stuffed full of aces and bowers,
  And the same with intent to deceive.

But the hands that were played
  By that heathen Chinee,
And the points that he made,
  Were quite frightful to see,—
Till at last he put down a right bower,
  Which the same Nye had dealt unto me.

Then I looked up at Nye,
  And he gazed upon me ;
And he rose with a sigh,
  And said, "Can this be ?
We are ruined by Chinese cheap labor,"—
  And he went for that heathen Chinee.

In the scene that ensued
  I did not take a hand,
But the floor it was strewed
  Like the leaves on the strand
With the cards that Ah Sin had been hiding,
  In the game "he did not understand."

In his sleeves, which were long,
  He had twenty-four packs,—
Which was coming it strong,
  Yet I state but the facts ;
And we found on his nails, which were taper,
  What is frequent in tapers—that's wax.

Which is why I remark,
And my language is plain,
That for ways that are dark,
And for tricks that are vain,
The heathen Chinee is peculiar,—
Which the same I am free to maintain.

Mrs. M. Virginia Donaghe McClurg.

Mrs. McClurg, the niece of our honored townsman, Mr. Wm. L. King, is better known to us by her maiden name of M. Virginia Donaghe. Although endowed with varied gifts, having been editor, newspaper correspondent, story-writer, biographer and local historian, her talent is essentially poetic, therefore we place her among our poets.

A proud moment of Mrs. McClurg's life was, when a child, she received four dollars and a half from *Hearth and Home* for a story called "How did it Happen," written in the garret, the author tells us, without the knowledge of any one. Next, were written occasional letters and verses and short stories for the New York *Graphic*, including some burlesque correspondence for a number of papers, one of which was the *Richmond State*. The writer then went to Colorado for her health and accepted the position of editor on the *Daily Republic* of Colorado Springs, for three years. She wrote a political leader for the paper every day. It happened that many distinguished men died during those years, and she did in consequence biographical work. She also wrote book reviews, dramatic and musical reviews, condensed the state news every day from all the papers of the state and edited the Associated Press dispatches. In addition, all proofs were brought to her for final reading. For the first year she had private pupils and broke down with brain fever.

In 1885, she went into the Indian country to explore the cliff-dwellings of Mancos Cañon, in the reservation of the Southern Utes. They were only known through meagre accounts in the official government reports, and Miss Donaghe was the first woman who ever visited them, so far as known. On this occasion, she had an escort of United States troops and spent a few days there. She however made a second visit, fully provided for a month's trip, the result of which was a series of archaeological sketches contributed to a prominent paper, the *Great Divide*, under the title of "Cliff-Climbing in Colorado." These ten papers gave to Miss Donaghe a reputation in the west as an archaeologist.

The following year she published, in the *Century*, one of the best of her sonnets, "The Questioner of the Sphinx," afterwards contained in her book, "Seven Sonnets of Sculpture."

The same year she published her first book, "Picturesque Colorado," also a popular sonnet called "The Mountain of the Holy Cross." The Colorado mountain of the Holy Cross has crevices filled with snow which represent always on its side a cross. The little sand lily of Colorado blossoms at the edges of the highways in the dust, in the Spring, and looks like our star of Bethlehem. Of these sand lilies an artist friend made a picture which harmonized with the sonnet referred to. These were published together as an Easter card and a large edition sold. The sonnet begins:
"In long forgotten Springs, where He who taught
Amid the olive groves of Syrian hills."—

And ends:
"The lilies bloom upon the prairie wide
A stainless cross is reared by nature's hand,
And plain and height alike keep Easter-tide."

In 1887, the *Century* published a "Sonnet on Helen Hunt's Grave," with a picture of the grave. About this time Miss Donaghe was writing a series of letters which were published in a Southern newspaper, *The Valley Virginian*, and were widely copied. These were on Utah, when the Mormon hierarchy was in its power. Then appeared a book on "Picturesque Utah," making one of a group with "Picturesque Colorado" and "Colorado Favorites." The last is made up of six poems on Colorado flowers, illustrated by water colors of the blossoms, by Alice Stewart, and was the first book published.

The author was married to Mr. Gilbert McClurg of Chicago, one of the family of the publishing house of that name, in Morristown, on June 13th, 1889. Since then Mrs. McClurg has been both editor and newspaper correspondent, and, within the last two years, a valuable assistant to her husband in the preparation of his department of the official history of Colorado, which included several county histories.

In the *Cosmopolitan* of June, 1891, a sonnet appeared, "The Life Mask," and was reprinted in the *Review of Reviews*. Two of Mrs. McClurg's songs were set to music by Albert C. Pierson in the summer of 1890; "Lithe Stands my Lady"; "Je Reste et Tu T'en Vas"; the latter with a French refrain, the rest in English.

The last poem of Mrs. McClurg was published in the *Banner*, of Morristown, Dec. 24th, 1891, written to Mr. William L. King on his 85th Thanksgiving Day, and based on the Oriental salutation, "O King! Live forever".

Among the writings of Mrs. McClurg are also two articles on the Washington Headquarters of Morristown; being "quotations, comments and descriptions on two Order Books of the Revolution, daily records of life in camp and at Headquarters, in the year 1780." A passage from this is given in the opening chapter of this book.

The "Seven Sonnets of Sculpture" came out in 1889 and 1890. This book was widely and favorably noticed by some of the largest and most important journals. Says the writer in the Chicago *Daily News*: "It was a happy inspiration that led Mrs. McClurg to the idea realized in the publication of her latest volume 'Seven Sonnets of Sculpture'. The work is artistic from cover to cover, but the conception of equipping each one of the stanzas it contains with a photograph of the piece of sculpture which suggested it, was unique. * * To translate a work of art from its original form to another, to find the hidden sense of a conception imbedded in stone and revive it in words, to endue marble with speech, is in its nature a delicate task and one that demands the keenest of perceptions and sensibilities." The author says, in her dedication that seven was a Hebrew symbol of perfection.

The sonnet we select from these, to represent Mrs. McClurg, is " The Questioner of the Sphinx ". This sonnet was written from the impression received from Elihu Vedder's engraving of the Sphinx and the artist expressed in a letter to the author, his appreciation of the fidelity of the interpretation in verse of his picture. His criticism is perhaps the best that could be given.

"I think it," he wrote, "good and strong and shall treasure it among the few good things that have been suggested by my work. My idea in the Sphinx was the hopelessness of man before the cold immutable laws of nature. Could the Sphinx speak, I am sure its words would be, 'look within,' for to his working brain and beating heart man must look for the solution of the great problem."

THE QUESTIONER OF THE SPHINX.

(SUGGESTED BY ELIHU VEDDER'S PICTURE.)

Behold me! with swift foot across the land,
While desert winds are sleeping, I am come
To wrest a secret from thee; O thou, dumb,
And careless of my puny lip's command.
Cold orbs! *mine* eyes a weary world have scanned,
Slow ear! in *mine* rings ever a vexed hum
Of sobs and strife. Of joy mine earthly sum
Is buried as thy form in burning sand.
The wisdom of the nations thou has heard;
The circling courses of the stars hast known.
Awake! Thrill! By my feverish presence stirred,
Open thy lips to still my human moan,
Breathe forth one glorious and mysterious word,
Though I should stand, in turn, transfixed,—a stone!

Charlton T. Lewis, LL. D.

A sketch of Dr. Lewis will be found under the grouping of *Lexicographer*.

The poem from which we select (reluctantly we take a part instead of the whole, for lack of space), is an embodiment of the story taken from Theodoret. The poet has found in the beautiful tradition, meagre though it is, a lovely theme for his divine song of spiritual love and Christian martyrdom.

The following is the translation of the Greek passage which heads the poem:

"A certain Telemachus embraced the self-sacrificing life of a monk, and, to carry out this plan, went to Rome, where he arrived during the abominable shows of gladiators. He went down into the arena, and strove to stop the conflicts of the armed combatants. But the spectators of the bloody games were indignant, and the gladiators themselves, full of the spirit of battle, slew the apostle of peace. When the great Emperor learned the facts he enrolled Telemachus in the noble army of martyrs, and put an end to the murderous shows.
Theodoret. Eccl. Hist. v. 26.

The scene is Rome,—the place the Coliseum. It is the time of the games. There, are the crowds of eager people; the Emperor Honorius; the horri-

ble Stilicho. Lowly and beautiful in his great love
for Christ, Telemachus follows onward to the
Coliseum to meet his sorrowful fate; holding in
his voice the power that "stilled the fire and dulled
the sword and stopped the crushing wine-press."
He followed, silently, consecrated and alone, to
"do the will of God."

TELEMACHUS.

I mused on Claudian's tinseled eulogies,
And turned to seek in other dusty tomes,
Through the wild waste of those degenerate days,
Some living word, some utterance of the heart;
Till as when one lone peak of Jura flames
With sudden sunbeams breaking through the mist,
So from the dull page of Theodoret
A flash of splendor rends the clouds of life,
And bares to view the awful throne of love.

The bishop's tale is meagre, but as leaven,
It works in thoughts that rise and fill the soul.
   *   *   *   *   *   *
He felt the soil, long drenched with martyr's blood,
Send healing through his feet to all his frame.
He drank the air that trembled with the joys
Of opening Paradise, and bared his soul
To spirits whispering, "Come with us to-day!"
The longings of his life were satisfied,
He stood at last in Rome, Christ's Capital,
The gate of heaven and not the mouth of hell.

Suddenly, rudely, comes disastrous change.
He starts and gazes, as the glory of the saints

Fades round him and the angel songs are stilled :
A world of hatred hides the throne of love ;
Hell opens in the gleam of myriad eyes
Hungry for slaughter, in a hush that tells
How in each heart a tiger pants for blood.
Into the vast arena files a band
Of Goths, the prisoners of Pollentia,—
Freemen, the dread of Rome, but yesterday,
Now doomed as slaves to wield those terrible arms
In mutual murder, kill and die, amid
The exultation of their nation's foes.
Pausing before the throne, with well-taught lips
They utter words they know not ; but Rome hears:
" Cæsar, we greet thee who are now to die ! "
Then part and line the lists ; the trumpet blares
For the onset, sword and javelin gleam, and all
Is clash of smitten shields and glitter of arms.

Without the tumult, one of mighty limb
And towering frame stands moveless ; never yet
A nobler captive had made sport for Rome.
Throngs watch that eye of Mars, Apollo's grace.
The thews of Hercules, in cruel hope
That ten may fall before him ere he falls.
They bid him charge ; he moves not ; shield and
    sword
Sink to his feet ; his eyes are filled with light
That is not of the battle. Three draw near
Whose valor or despair has cut a path
Through the thick mass of combat, and their
    swords,
Reeking with carnage, seek a victim new
The glory of whose death may win them grace
With that fierce multitude. Telemachus

Gazes, and half the horror turns to joy
As the fair Goth undaunted bares his breast
Before the butchers, and awaits the blow
With peaceful brow, a firm and tender lip
Quivering as with a breath of inward prayer,
And hands that move as mindful of the cross.
And with a mighty cry, "Christ! he is thine!
He is my brother! Help!" The monk leaps forth,
Gathers in hands unarmed the points of steel,
Throws back the startled warriors, and commands,
" In Christ's name, hold! Ye people of Rome give
    ear!
God will have mercy and not sacrifice.
He who was silent, scourged at Pilate's bar,
And smitten again in those he died to save,
Is silent now in his great oracles.
The throne of Constantine and Peter's chair,
Speaks thus through me :—' In Rome, my capital,
Let love be Lord, and close the mouth of hell.
I will have mercy and not sacrifice.' "

The slaughter paused, he ceased, and all was still,
But baffled myriads with their cruel thumbs
Point earthward, and the bloody three advance :
Their swords meet in his heart. Honorius
Cries "Save,"—too late, he is already safe,—
And turns, with tears like Peter's, to proclaim,
The festival dissolved : nor from that hour
Ever again did Rome, Christ's capital,
Make holiday with blood, but hand in hand
The throne of Constantine and Peter's chair
Honored the martyr—Saint Telemachus,
And love was Lord and closed the mouth of hell.

Miss Emma F. R. Campbell.

In our midst is a quiet, gentle woman who passes in and out among us without noise or ostentation. Yet upon her has fallen the great honor of being the author of an immortal hymn.

In the *Canada Presbyterian* of Feb. 9th, 1887, appeared an article entitled "A Great Modern Hymn." Also, it is said, that in a volume soon to be published on "The Great Hymns of the Church" will appear a paper on "Jesus of Nazareth Passeth By." From the first named, we cannot do better than quote:

"Among all the hymns used in recent revivals of religion, none has been more honored and owned by God, than this—none so often called for, none so inspiring, none bearing so many seals of the divine approval. This is the testimony of the great evangelist of these days, Mr. Moody, and this testimony will surprise no one who has ever heard it sung by his companion in the ministry, Mr. Sankey, who, under God, has done so much to send forth light and truth into dark minds and break up the fountains of the great deep, amid the masses of godless men.

* * *

"As to the origin of the hymn—the circumstances of its birth—we have to invite the reader to go back some twenty-three years, to the Spring of 1864—to a great season of religious awakening in the city of Newark, N. J. The streets were crowded from day to day and the largest churches were too small to contain the growing numbers. Among those most deeply moved by the impressive scenes and services was a young girl, a Sabbath School teacher, one who for the first time realized the powers of the world to come, and the grandness of the great salvation. As descriptive of what was passing around her but with no desire for publicity, still, with the great desire of reaching some soul unsaved, especially among her youthful charge, she wrote the lines beginning with, 'What means this eager, anxious throng?'"

The hymn was first published under the signature "Eta", the author having sometimes appended to her writings the Greek letter, using that character instead of her English name. We quote again from the same source :

"Soon it rose into popularity and it is spreading still, not only in the English language, but in other languages—even the languages of India— (think of a recent account of an assembly of 500 Hindus enthusiastically using this hymn in the Mahrati and the Syrian children singing it in their own vernacular)—as the author thinks of all these things, she can only say with a thankful and an adoring heart: 'It is the Lord's doing and it is marvellous in mine eyes!'"

Miss Campbell has also written many other poems of beauty and articles in prose, which however, are all so eclipsed by this "Great Hymn" that perhaps they are not known or noticed as they otherwise would be. One in particular, we would mention, "A New Year Thought," published December, 1888.

Miss Campbell belongs also in the group of *Novelists, Story-Writers, and Moralists.* She has written a number of books for the young, among which are "Green Pastures for Christ's Little Ones"; "Paul Preston"; "Better than Rubies"; and "Toward the Mark".

Miss Campbell wrote by request, at the time of the Centenial Celebration of the First Presbyterian Church in October, 1891, a beautiful hymn for the occasion which was read by Mr. James Duryee Stevenson.

"JESUS OF NAZARETH PASSETH BY."

What means this eager, anxious throng,
Pressing our busy streets along,
These wondrous gatherings day by day,
What means this strange commotion, pray?
Voices in accents hushed reply
    "Jesus of Nazareth passeth by!"

E'en children feel the potent spell,
And haste their new-found joy to tell;
In crowds they to the place repair
Where Christians daily bow in prayer,
Hosannas mingle with the cry
    "Jesus of Nazareth passeth by!"

Who is this Jesus? Why should He
The city move so mightily?
A passing stranger, has He skill
To charm the multitude at will?
Again the stirring tones reply
    "Jesus of Nazareth passeth by!"

Jesus! 'tis He who once below
Man's pathway trod mid pain and woe;
And burdened hearts where'er He came
Brought out their sick and deaf and lame.
Blind men rejoiced to hear the cry
    "Jesus of Nazareth passeth by!"

Again He comes, from place to place
His holy footprints we can trace.
He passes at *our* threshold—nay
He enters,—condescends to stay!
Shall we not gladly raise the cry—
    "Jesus of Nazareth passeth by?"

Bring out your sick and blind and lame.
'Tis to restore them Jesus came.
Compassion infinite you'll find.
With boundless power in Him combined.
Come quickly while salvation's nigh.
    "Jesus of Nazareth passeth by!"

Ye sin-sick souls who feel your need,
He comes to you, a friend indeed.
Rise from your weary, wakeful couch.
Haste to secure His healing touch ;
No longer sadly wait and sigh.—
    " Jesus of Nazareth passeth by !"

Ho all ye heavy-laden, come !
Here pardon, comfort, rest, a home
Lost wanderer from a Father's face,
Return, accept his proffered grace.
Ye tempted, there's a refuge nigh
    Jesus of Nazareth passeth by !

Ye who are buried in the grave
Of sin, His power alone can save.
His voice can bid your dead souls live,
True spirit-life and freedom give.
Awake ! arise ! for strength apply,
    Jesus of Nazareth passeth by !

But if this call you still refuse
And dare such wondrous love abuse,
Soon will He sadly from you turn
Your bitter prayer in justice spurn.
" Too late ! too late !" will be your cry.
    " Jesus of Nazareth has passed by !"

Mrs. Adelaide S. Buckley.

Mrs. Buckley will appear again among *Translators*. The following verses were inspired by a painting of Cornelia and the Gracchi:

    Purest pearls from the sea,
        Diamonds outshining the sun,
    Sapphires which vie with heaven,
        With pride to Cornelia are shown.

    Clasping her dark-eyed boys,
        Fairer could be no other,
    "These my jewels are"
        Said the noble Roman mother.

Rev. Oliver Crane, D. D., LL. D.

Before coming to Morristown, in 1871, Dr. Crane's life had been a very active one, including extensive traveling in Turkey, Europe, Egypt and Palestine. Twice he had been a missionary in Turkey acquiring the Turkish language and doing efficient work there, first for five years, then for three. In the seven years interval of his return he accepted two pastorates in this country.

On coming to Morristown, having resigned his ministerial charge at Carbondale, Pennsylvania, he devoted himself mainly to literary work, and with General H. B. Carrington wrote the "Battles of the Revolution" which has since become a standard work. Nine years later as secretary of his college class, he prepared an exhaustive biographical record of every member of the class. The book was a pioneer in this class of publications.

In 1888, he published his translation of Virgil's Æneid and the following year a small volume of poems entitled "Minto and Other Poems", in which the "Rock of the Passaic Falls" is conspicuous as relating to Washington and Lafayette "who," says the poet, "visited together these Falls while their troops were stationed at Totawa (as the spot was then called) in the Winter of 1780. The initials G. W. are still to be seen cut in the rock below the cataract."

The *Translation of Virgil's Æneid*, "literally, line by line into English Dactyllic Hexameter," is Dr. Crane's great work and has absorbed much of his time for years. It is a singular fact that, although for more than four hundred years the learned have been giving to the English reader, through the press, specimen translations of this old classic, this is the first complete version in the original measure.

In the very interesting preface, Dr. Crane gives

a careful review of the translations of Virgil, noticing the singular and severe prejudice that has always debarred any desire to render this classic in the metre of the original, and discussing the advantage of translating in the style of verse chosen by the author himself. In fact, he tells us, Longfellow had, from his own admirable translations, become thoroughly convinced of its utility, if not of its indispensability in giving the classic epics a fitting setting in English.

The following is an extract taken from Book X., lines 814 to 842 of Dr. Crane's literal English translation of *Virgil's Æneid*, which describes the hand to hand contest of Æneas with the youth Lausus, who insists upon fighting Æneas in opposition to his father's wishes and in the face of every effort made by Æneas to avoid the conflict :

TRANSLATION
OF
VIRGIL'S ÆNEID.

BOOK X, LINES 814 TO 842.

The destinies now are for Lausus the last threads
815 Gathering in; for Æneas his powerful scimitar ruthless
Drives through the midst of the youth, and buries it wholly within him.
Right through the menacer's targe, and his delicate armor, the keen blade
Passed through the tunic his mother had woven in tissue of gold thread
For him, and blood filled all of his bosom; then life on the breezes
820 Mournful withdrew to the shades, and abandoned his body untimely.
But as the son of Anchises in truth on the visage and features
Gazed of the dying — the features becoming amazingly pallid —
Pitying deeply he sighed and instinctively tendered his right hand.
Fresh as the image recurred to his mind of regard for a father:
825 "What to thee now, O pitiable boy, for these laudable efforts,

"What shall the pious Æneas, befitting such nobleness render?
Keep it—thine armor, in which thou rejoicest, and I to thy parents'
Shades and their ashes, if this could be any requital, remit thee;
Yet thou in this, though unlucky, canst solace thy sorrowful exit,
830 That by the hand of the mighty Æneas thou fallest." Abruptly
Chides he his faltering comrades, as gently from earth he uplifts him,
Soiling his ringlets with blood, that were combed in the comeliest fashion.
 Meanwhile, his father was down by the wave of the stream of the Tiber
Staunching his wound with its waters, and resting his body, reclining
835 Close by the trunk of a tree. At a distance his coppery helmet
Hangs on its boughs, and at rest on the sod is his cumbersome armor;
Standing around are his warriors chosen; he sickly and panting
Eases his neck, as his out-combed beard streamed down on his bosom;
Often he asks after Lausus, and many a messenger sends he
840 Back to recall him, and bear him his sorrowful parent's injunctions:
But on his armor his comrades were weepingly bearing the lifeless
Lausus away—a hero o'ercome by the wound of a hero.

Rev. J. Leonard Corning, D. D.

Dr. Corning, who, with his family, was for some years a resident of Morristown and is now abroad, is represented later in the volume, among the writers on Art. We give here his beautiful poem, "The Ideal".

THE IDEAL.

Awake, asleep, in dreams, amid the din of mortal
    striving,
I feel thee ever near, vision of fancy's sweet contri-
    ving ;
The setting sun and twilight glow
Thou art the music sweet and low.

When on the sands, at dead of night,
Dark waves are breaking in their might.
While, through the billowy crests, the wild winds
    roar,
Thou art the gull who over all dost soar.

Amid the storm and lightning flash,
The pelting rain and thunder crash,
When faces blanch, and none can will,
Thou, heavenly bow, art faithful still.

'Tis not the kiss, the touch, the sigh,
That bringeth love from earth to sky ;
For motions strange about the heart
Reveal the inner nature of thy part.

Mrs. Mary Lee Demarest.

Mrs. Augustus W. Cutler has kindly given us the following monograph:

"In a Memorial of the late Mrs. Mary Lee Demarest occurs the following passage: 'For two hundred and fifty years, the English readers of the Bible were obliged to content themselves with the phrase, 'They seek a country'. It was not the whole thought. It was reserved for a corps of learned revisers to light upon the happy phrase, 'They are seeking a country of their own'.' But a score of years before the wise grammarians reached this line, a youthful poetess, seeing and greeting the Heavenly promise from afar, wrote simply and sweetly:

" 'I'll ne'er be fu' content, until mine een do see
The shining gates o' Heaven, an' *my ain countree*'.

"This youthful poetess was Mary Lee, afterwards Mrs. T. F. C. Demarest.

"Before her marriage, in 1870, she spent several years in Morristown and became identified with the place and its interests; and there are many persons living here who remember her sweet face and gentle ways.

"A taste for the Scotch dialect is said to have been acquired from an old Scotch nurse who lived a long time in the family, when the children were young. The girl caught it so completely, that when deeply moved, she was wont to drop into it, for the more vigorous expression of her feelings. 'Somehow', said she, 'the Scotch is more homely, less formal to me'. Thus, in the poem alluded to, could the thoughts contained in it, have been expressed as beautifully and tenderly in the mother tongue?

"Again, there is a little poem in the same dialect, entitled 'My Mither', which appeals to every heart.

"Though many of her poems and prose writings are of a devotional character, yet she had a keen sense also of the humorous side of life as the verses entitled 'Allen Graeme', will testify.

"Mrs. Demarest traveled extensively throughout our own country, and also abroad. Two volumes of her writings have been published—one entitled 'Gathered Writings', a collection of short stories, fragments of foreign travel and reflections".

MY AIN COUNTREE.

I am far frae my hame, an' I'm weary afterwhiles,
For the langed-for hame-bringing an' my Father's
    welcome smiles ;
I'll ne'er be fu' content, until mine een do see,
The shining gates o' heaven an' my ain countree.
The earth is fleck'd wi' flowers, mony tinted fresh
    and gay,
The birdies warble blithely, for my Father made
    them sae ;

But these sights an' these soun's will as naething
 be to me,
When I hear the angels singing in my ain countree.

I've His gude word o' promise that some gladsome
 day, the King
To his ain royal palace His banished hame will
 bring ;
Wi' een an' wi' hearts running owre, we shall see
The King in His beauty, in our ain countree;
My sins hae been mony, an' my sorrows hae been
 sair,
But there they'll never vex me, nor be remembered
 mair ;
His bluid has made me white—His hand shall dry
 mine e'e,
When he brings me hame at last, to mine ain coun-
 tree.

Sae little noo I ken, o' yon blessed, bonnie place,
I ainly ken its Hame, whaur we shall see His face ;
It wud surely be eneuch forever mair to be
In the glory o' His presence in our ain countree.
Like a bairn to its mither, a wee birdie to its nest,
I wad fain be ganging noo, unto my Saviour's
 breast,
For he gathers in His bosom witless, worthless
 lambs like me,
An' carries them Himsel', to His ain countree.

He's faithfu' that has promised, He'll surely come
 again,
He'll keep his tryst wi' me, at what hour I dinna
 ken ;

But he bids me still to wait, an' ready aye to be
To gang at ony moment to my ain countree.
So I'm watching aye, and singing o' my hame as I
　　wait,
For the soun'ing o' His footfa' this side the gowden
　　gate,
God gie His grace to ilk ane wha' listens noo to me,
That we a' may gang in gladness to our ain coun-
　　tree.

Hon. Anthony Q. Keasbey.

We cannot do better than quote the words of Dr. Thomas Dunn English, the well-known author of "Ben Bolt", now living in Newark, N. J.,—with regard to Mr. Keasbey.

"Here, in Newark", says he, "we have a lawyer of distinction, Anthony Q. Keasbey, who occasionally throws off some polished verses, as he excuses them, by way of 'safety plugs for high mental pressure,' and these are always smooth and scholarly. They are mostly privately printed for the amusement of the poet and a few chosen friends. One of these, however, has such a vein of tenderness and so much heart music that it deserves to become public property and to remain as much the favorite with others as it is with me." The poem referred to is, "My Wife's Crutches."

"Unquestionably", continues Dr. English, "Mr. Keasbey stands well in his profession, and for years, under several Federal administrations, filled the office of United States District Attorney with credit to himself and advantage to the public ; but this little tender poem does more honor to his intellect than his legal acquirements, however eminent they may be, and gives him a still stronger claim to the regard of his many friends."

Among Mr. Keasbey's published collected poems are "Palm Sunday", of which Mr. Stedman once said he had put it away among some fine hymns ; also "May", published in England and set to music by Faustina Hodges. These verses were inspired by the falling of the cherry blossoms on the grave of little May, and are most sweet and touching. One of the best is "The Dirge for Old St. Stephen's", written while they were demolishing the church built on Mr. Keasbey's ground, where now a "mart and home" have taken its place as was anticipated by the poet.

Mr. Keasbey has published numberless papers in prominent journals and magazines. Some of these are to be collected and published in book form. His address on "The Sun : How Man has Regarded it in Different Ages", is well worthy of preservation in more permanent form than that in which it appears at present; also "The Sale of East New Jersey at Auction", an address delivered February 1st, 1862, before the New Jersey Historical Society at Trenton, on the Bi-Centennial of the Sale. This is full of interesting information, told in a charming way and is valuable for reference.

The paper on "The Sun", was inspired by Mr. Keasbey's reading with great interest, the papers of Professor Norman Lockyer, the great astronomer, describing his researches into the constitution of the sun, through the medium of the spectroscope and the photograph. Mr. Keasbey had been interested in observing the extent to which modern science had reached with respect to the actual condition of the sun and the materials of which it is composed. This led him to the thoughts of how very recent had been any such attempts to understand its true nature and, from that reflection, he was led to consider, as a subject of a paper, how human eyes in all ages have looked upon the sun and in what manner they have regarded it. This published address was delivered before the Brooklyn Historical Society, a brilliant audience present, and Rev. Dr. Storrs, presiding.

A book on Florida, "From the Hudson to the St. John's", describing a month's journey to Florida and the St. John's River was published in 1875; also, more recently, a small book on "Isthmus Transit by Chiriqui and Golfo Dulce", with a view of describing the Chiriqui mountain rib or back bone of Darien and all the executive and legislative action, with respect to the region between Panama and Nicaragua, with reference to railroad communication across the isthmus from the harbor of Chiriqui on the coast to the Pacific.

In the *Hospital Review*, of July, 1882, is a very striking and powerful paper on the "Tragedy of the Lena Delta", where De Long and his companions so heroically met their fate in the Arctic snows.

Below is the favorite of Dr. English among the Poems :

MY WIFE'S CRUTCHES.

" Ye solemn, gaunt, ungainly crutches,
    That serve her frame such slippery tricks,
Were you within my lawful clutches,
    I'd fling you back in River Styx.

Ye grew beside the Boat of Charon,
    In murky fens of Stygian gloom,
Nor ever, like the rod of Aaron,
    Shall your grim spindles burst in bloom.

Your reeds were tuned for groans rheumatic,
    And croaking sighs from gouty man ;
Nor e'er shall thrill with tones ecstatic,
    As did the pipes of ancient Pan.

Avaunt you, then, ye helpers dismal !
    Offend my eyes and ears no more ;
Go stalking back to realms abysmal
    And guide the ghosts on Lethe's shore.

But see! while yet my words upbraid them,
  Her crutches bud with blossoms fair,
And Patience, Love and Faith have made them
  Than Aaron's rod, more rich and rare.

And hark! from out their hollows slender,
  No dismal groans or sighs proceed,—
But tones of joy more sweet and tender
  Than swelled from Pan's enchanted reed.

Then stay! your use her worth discloses,
  Your ghastly frames her worth transmutes,
From withered sticks, to stems of roses—
  From creaking reeds, to magic flutes.

Major Lindley Hoffman Miller,

Major Miller, a brother of our well-known townsman, Henry W. Miller, was among the first of the 7th Regiment of New York City, who answered the call of the government to march to Washington for the protection of the Capitol. He served in that regiment through the riots in New York, and afterwards joined a Colored Regiment and was promoted to the rank of Major. He served in this position at Memphis and elsewhere through the South. In this campaign he lost his health and came home to die. He died in June, 1864, and was laid in old St. Peter's churchyard.

Mr. Miller was a man of brilliant mind and unusual genius. His fugitive poems are very beautiful. They were published in various journals of the time, and one we will add to this short sketch of his brief but valuable life, "The Skater's Song", full of spirit and dash, and gay with the heart of youth.

THE SKATER'S SONG, BY MOONLIGHT!

Come away, from your blazing hearths !
  Come away, in the gleaming night,
Where the radiant sky is peering down
  With a million eyes of light !
Heigho ! for the glancing ice,
  For the realm of the old Frost King !
We'll shake the chain of the bounding stream
  Till all its fetters ring !
    Then away ! my boys, away !
      Far over the ice we'll sweep,
    And wake the slumbering echo's voice
      From the gloom of its winter sleep !

Come away, from your cheerless books !
  Come away, in the clear, cold air !
And read in the deeps of the starry night
  God's endless volume there.
Ho ! now we're flashing along,
  At the snow-flake's drifting rate !
Did ever anything stir the pulse
  Like a glimmering moonlight skate !

Then away,! my boys, away !
　Far over the ice we 'll sweep,
And wake the slumbering echo's voice
　From the gloom of its winter sleep !

Come away, from the ball-room's glare !
　Come away, to a merrier dance,—
To a hall, whose floor is the flashing ice,
　Whose light is the stars' pure glance !
Now we 're watching the moon in her dreams,
　Now we dash at our speed again ;
While the stream groans under the icy links
　Which the frost has forged for his chain !
Then away ! my boys, away !
　Far over the ice we 'll sweep,
And wake the slumbering echo's voice
　From the gloom of its winter sleep !

Come away, each lady fair !
　Come, add to the magical sight !
And mingle the silvery tones of your words
　With the echoing "voices of night" !
Heigho ! for the frozen plain !
　Here's a glancing mirror, I ween,
Reflecting all the beautiful forms
　That move in our fairy-like scene.
Away ! my lady, away !
　Far over the ice we 'll sweep,
And wake the slumbering echo's voice
　From the gloom of its winter sleep !

Come away, from your sorrow and grief,
　All you that are gloomy and sad !
Unwrinkle your brows to the whistling wind,

Till your hearts grow merry and glad!
Ho! Hark! how the laughter in peals,
　Is shaking the tides of the air,
And shouting aloud to drown with its joy
　　The muttering murmurs of care!
　　　Then away! my boys, away!
　　　　Far over the ice we'll sweep,
　　　And wake the slumbering echo's voice
　　　　From the gloom of its winter sleep!

Come, one and all, then, away!
　Come, cheerily join in our song,
And mingle with music the ring of the steel,
　Keep in time, as we're sweeping along!
Heigho! for the throne of the Frost!
　We'll frighten the phantoms of night,
And serenade, far under the depths,
　The river's listening sprite!
　　　Then away! my boys, away!
　　　　Far over the ice we'll sweep,
　　　And wake the slumbering echo's voice
　　　　From the gloom of its winter sleep!

Miss Henrietta Howard Holdich.

Miss Holdich, poetess and story-writer, has been a resident of Morristown, since 1878, and has written at various periods since she was seventeen years of age. Her poems, stories, and other writings have appeared from time to time in *Harper's Magazine* and other important publications. We would like to give Miss Holdich's beautiful and thoughtful poem, "In Holy Ground", suggested by a Russian Legend, but, as we give her Centennial story entire, our space does not allow. She is represented, instead, by a few lovely lines written for a golden wedding and sent to the happy pair with a basket of flowers and fruit.

LINES
WRITTEN FOR A GOLDEN WEDDING.

Orange buds a maiden wears
   On the blissful wedding morn ;
Snowy buds on golden hair
   Tell of love and faith new born.

Ripened now the perfect fruit,
   Fifty sunny years have passed ;
Golden fruit on snowy hair
   Tells of love and faith that last.

William Tuckey Meredith.

Mr. Meredith, a Philadelphian by birth, and also a banker in New York City, is also one of our summer residents, his main interest in Morristown coming, as he says, from the fact that his grandmother was a Morristown Ogden. He served as an officer in the United States Navy with Farragut at the battle of Mobile Bay and was afterwards his secretary.

Mr. Meredith is perhaps best known by his spirited poem, entitled "Farragut", which appeared in *The Century*, in 1890, and heads the group of "Various Poems" in Stedman and Hutchinson's Library of American Literature.

Besides this, Mr. Meredith has written for *The New York Times* and other journals and publications at various times. He wrote for *The Century* a War article on "Farragut's Capture of New Orleans", which may be found in Volume IV of the published series. A novel appeared with his name, in 1890, entitled "Not of Her Father's Race", in which the "Fox Hunt" is, the author tells us, a study of a bag chase in which he took part some years ago near Morristown, although he has laid the scene in Newport. We give the poem, "Farragut".

FARRAGUT.

MOBILE BAY, 5 AUGUST, 1864.

Farragut, Farragut,
   Old Heart of Oak,
Daring Dave Farragut,
   Thunderbolt stroke,
Watches the hoary mist
   Lift from the bay,
Till his flag, glory-kissed,
   Greets the young day.

Far, by gray Morgan's walls,
   Looms the black fleet.
Hark, deck to rampart calls
   With the drum's beat!
Buoy your chains overboard,
   While the steam hums;
Men! to the battlement,
   Farragut comes.

See, as the hurricane
   Hurtles in wrath
Squadrons of cloud amain
   Back from its path!
Back to the parapet,
   To the guns' lips,
Thunderbolt Farragut
   Hurls the black ships.

Now through the battle's roar
   Clear the boy sings,
"By the mark fathoms four,"
   While his lead swings.

Steady the wheelmen five
  " Nor' by East keep her,"
"Steady" but two alive ;
  How the shells sweep her !

Lashed to the mast that sways
  Over red decks,
Over the flame that plays
  Round the torn wrecks,
Over the dying lips
  Framed for a cheer,
Farragut leads his ships,
  Guides the line clear.

On by heights cannon-browed,
  While the spars quiver ;
Onward still flames the cloud
  Where the hulks shiver.
See, yon fort's star is set,
  Storm and fire past.
Cheer him, lads —Farragut,
  Lashed to the mast !

Oh ! while Atlantic's breast
  Bears a white sail,
While the Gulf's towering crest
  Tops a green vale ;
Men thy bold deeds shall tell,
  Old Heart of Oak,
Daring Dave Farragut
  Thunderbolt stroke !

Hannah More Johnson.

Miss Johnson, the niece of Mr. J. Henry Johnson, one of Morristown's old residents, and the last preceptor of the old Academy, will be found again among "Historians". She has written and published a large number of poems, besides, and from them we select the following :

THE CHRISTMAS TREE.

Shall I tell you a story of Christmas time?
   Of what Nellie found by her Christmas tree?
If I tell it at all, it must be in rhyme
   For it seems like a song to Nellie and me
That ripples along to a breezy tune,
Like a brook that sings through the woods in June;
   And yet it was dark November weather
   When song and story began together.

"Papa", said Nellie, with wistful tone,
   "When God sends little children here,
Do beautiful angels flutter down
   As once when they brought our Saviour dear?
Don't they sing in the sky, where we can't see
   And listen up there to Harry and me?
'Cause I prayed last night for the bestest things
   Heavenly Father sends us, and Harry said
I might ask for a sister who had n't wings
   A dear little sister to sleep in my bed ;
For my other one went away, you know,

To sing with the angels long ago,
   And I want another to stay with me
   A dear little sister like Daisy Lee.
So high, Papa ! Look, do n't you see ?
   Just up to my chin. Heavenly Father knows
'Bout her dress and her shoes and her curly hair
   'Cause I told him all, and so I s'pose
The first little sister He has to spare
   He 'll send her down here, oh won't she be
A dear little sister for Harry and me !"

"Yes, my Nellie", her father said,
   One gentle hand on the curly head
With tender caress and whispered word
   Too low for her ear, 'though a Bright-one heard
And passed it up, meet signal given
   From love on earth to love in heaven ;
"Yes, my Nellie, wait and see !
   We are all in our Heavenly Father's care
And He 'll send what is best for you and me
   When we look to Him with a loving prayer".

The days passed on. 'Twas that happy time
When bells ring out with their Christmas chime ;
   There were people at work all over the land
   Busy for Santa Claus, heart and hand,
And some in cabin and work-shop dim
Who would n't have work if it was n't for him ;
And Harry and Nellie ?—There were none
   In that Christmas time had a gayer tree.
Papa was at work at early dawn
   And the children all tip-toe to see ;
But the dark December day wore on

E'er the door was opened noiselessly,
And the light streamed out in the dusky hall
From a beautiful cedar bright and tall.
   Starry tapers were gleaming there,
   Toy and trumpet and banner fair,
The topmost flag on the ceiling bore
While the laden branches swept the floor ;
   While gay little Rover frisking in,
   Led the children in frolic and din
As they spied each treasure and in their glee
Shouted with joy round the Christmas tree,
While Papa stood back in a corner to see.

"Oh ! Harry", said Nellie, "I do declare
   Here 's a basket for me !" She opened the lid
And pulled back the blanket folded there
   And what d'ye think was safely hid
But a dear live baby so fast asleep
   That it never waked up with the children's shout
Till Nellie asked, "is it ours to keep ?"
   And kissed its hand as she stood in doubt.

"Of course," said Harry, "do n't angels know
When God has told them which way to go ?
That 's our little sister we wanted so !"

"Little sister", said Nellie, "I'm very glad,
I know you 're the best Heavenly Father had
   And now you 're ours and you 're going to stay
   'Cause the angels have left you and gone away".
"No, my Nellie", a voice replied,
As Papa drew near to Nellie's side.
   "Let us pray they may watch over this little one

Day by day, till life is done,
That she may be glad through eternity
She was ever left 'neath our Christmas tree".

Miss Margaret H. Garrard.

Our gifted young townswoman, Miss Garrard, who has often entertained us with her rare dramatic talent, has contributed, for a number of years, articles in prose and verse to well-known magazines and journals, notably to *Lippincott's Magazine* and *Life*. In *Lippincott* for June, 1890, we find a very pretty poem embodying a clever thought and entitled "A Coquette's Motto". In a previous number appears "A Trip to Tophet", which is a sparkling and graphic description of a descent into a silver-mine at Virginia City, California. In it occurs the following picture of the visitor's surroundings:

"The next few minutes will always be a haunting memory to me. The long, dark passages, the burning atmosphere, the scattered lights, the weird figures of the miners appearing, only to vanish the next moment in the surrounding gloom, all recur like some infernal dream".

We select to represent Miss Garrard, the first poem she published in *Life:*

THE PLAQUE DE LIMOGES.

You hang upon her boudoir wall,
    Plaque de Limoges!
She prizes you above them all
    Plaque de Limoges!
Yet do your blossoms never move,
Although she looks on them with love,
And treasures your hard buds above
The gathered bloom of field and grove,
    Insensate, cold Limoges!

Brilliant in hue your every flower,
    Plaque de Limoges!
Copied from some French maiden's bower,
    Plaque de Limoges!
But still you let my lady stand—
The fairest lady in the land—
Caressing you with her soft hand,
Nor breathe, nor stir at her command,
    Cold-hearted clay—Limoges!

Would that I in your place might be,
    Plaque de Limoges!
That she might stand and gaze on me,
    Plaque de Limoges!
I'd live in love a little space,
Then—fling my flowers from their place,
At her dear feet to sue for grace,
Until she'd raise them to her face,
    Happy, but crushed Limoges!

Miss Julia E. Dodge.

Though Miss Dodge finds her place naturally and kindly in the society of our poets, all readers of *The Century* will remember a charming prose paper of hers called "An Island of the Sea", beautifully illustrated by Thomas Moran and published in 1877. Before and since that time, her pen has not been idle, for short prose articles have been scattered here and there, in various periodicals, and it is difficult to select from the number of thoughtful and delicate poems now before us, one to represent her. The poem, "A Legend of St. Sophia in 1453", is full of spirit and fire. It was written in 1878, when the advance of the Russian forces towards Constantinople seemed to point to the fulfillment of ancient prophecy and the restoration of Christian dominion over the stronghold of Islam. The poem entitled "Satisfied" was first published in *The Churchman* and afterwards placed, without the author's knowledge, in a collection called "The Palace of the King", published by Randolph & Co. Among the other poems are: "Our Daily Bread", "Spring Song", "Telling Fortunes", "September Memories", and "To a Night-Blooming Cereus", which last we give principally because, besides being a beautiful expression of a beautiful thought, it was written under the inspiration of a flower sent to the writer from an ancient plant in a Morristown conservatory.

TO A NIGHT-BLOOMING CEREUS.

O fleeting wonder, glory of a night,
  Only less evanescent than the gleam
    That marks the lightning's track, or some swift dream
That comes and, vanishing, eludes our sight !
How canst thou be content, thy whole rich stream
  Of life to lavish on this hour's delight,
  And perish ere one morning's praise requite
Thy gift of peerless splendor ? It doth seem
Thou art a type of that pure steadfast heart
  Which hath no wish but to perform His will
  Who called it into being, no desire
But to be fair for Him ; no other part
  Doth choose, but here its fragrance to distil
For one brief moment ere He bid "Come higher"!

Charles D. Platt.

Mr. Platt, the faithful principal of our Morris Academy, has of late, "at odd moments and in vacations," as he says, written verses of local reference and others, upon various subjects, which have been published in our local papers and elsewhere.

Born at Elizabeth, N. J., Mr. Platt lived there until 1883. He was graduated at Williams' College in 1877, taught in the Rev. J. F. Pingry's School in Elizabeth for six years, came to Morristown and took charge of the Morris Academy in 1883, and has retained that position to the present time.

Among the poems which refer to local interests are "Fort Nonsense," which we give in the opening chapter on "Historic Morristown"; "The Old First Church"; "The Lyceum" and "The Washington Headquarters", which last will follow this short sketch, as embodying so much that is interesting of that historic building and its surroundings.

Other of the poems might, perhaps, for some special qualities, better represent Mr. Platt than this; there is the excellent and gay little parody, which we would like to give, of "That Old Latin Grammar". "The Wild Lily" is charming. Then there are "Memorial Day"; "Easter Song"; "Modern Progress"; "A Myth"; and "John Greenleaf Whittier", the last written and published upon the occasion of the poet's death September 16th, 1892. Besides these, there are the "Ballads of the Holidays" which form a series by themselves, dealing in part with the subject of popular maxims, and including poems for Christmas, New

Year's Day, Discovery Day and other holidays.
We give

THE WASHINGTON HEADQUARTERS, MORRISTOWN, NEW JERSEY.

What mean these cannon standing here,
   These staring, muzzled dogs of war?
Heedless and mute, they cause no fear,
   Like lions caged, forbid to roar.

This gun* was made when good Queen Anne
   Ruled upon Merry England's throne ;
Captured by valiant Jerseymen
   Ere George the Third our rights would own.

"Old Nat",† the little cur on wheels,
   Protector of our sister city,
Was kept to bite the British heels,
   A yelping terror, bold and gritty.

That savage beast, the old "Crown Prince",‡
   A British bull-dog, glum, thick-set,
At Springfield's fight was made to wince,
   And now we keep him for a pet.

---

   *Inscription on this Cannon:—
    Gun made in Queen Anne's time. Captured with a British vessel by a party of Jerseymen in the year 1780, near Perth Amboy. Presented by the township of Woodbridge, New Jersey, in 1874.
   †Inscription on " Old Nat :".-
    This cannon was furnished Capt. Nathaniel Camp by Gen George Washington for the protection of Newark N J , against the British. Presented to the Association by Mr. Bruen H. Camp, of Newark, N. J.
   ‡The inscription upon it is as follows :—
    The " Crown Prince Gun." Captured from the British at Springfield. Used as an alarm gun at Short Hills to end of Revolutionary War. Given in charge by General Benoni Hathaway to Colonel Wm. Brittin on the last training at Morristown, and by his son, Wm. Jackson Brittin, with the consent of the public authorities, presented to the Association in the year 1890.

Upon this grassy knoll they stand.
  A venerable, peaceful pack ;
Their throats once tuned to music grand,
  And stained with gore their muzzles black.

But come, that portal swinging free,
  A welcome offers, as of yore,
When, sheltered 'neath this old roof-tree,
  Our patriot-chieftain trod this floor.

And with him in that trying day
  Was gathered here a glorious band ;
This house received more chiefs, they say,
  Than any other in our land.*

Hither magnanimous Schuyler came,
  And stern Steuben from o'er the water ;
Here Hamilton, of brilliant fame,
  Once met and courted Schuyler's daughter.

And Knox, who leads the gunner-tribes,
  Whose shot the trembling foeman riddles,
A roaring chief,† his cash subscribes
  To pay the mirth-inspiring fiddles.‡

The "fighting Quaker", General Greene,
  Helped Knox to foot the fiddlers' bill :

---

*The list of officers of the Revolutionary army mentioned in the poem is taken from a printed placard which hangs in the hall of the Headquarters.

†Knox is called a roaring chief because when crossing the Delaware with Washington his "stentorian lungs" did good service in keeping the army together.

‡The reference to the fiddlers is based upon an old subscription paper for defraying the expenses of a "Dancing Assembly," signed by several persons, among them Nathaniel Greene and H. Knox, each $400, PAID.

This paper may be seen in the collection made by Mrs. J. W. Roberts.

And here the intrepid "Put." was seen,
   And Arnold—black his memory still.

And Kosciusko, scorning fear,
   Beside him noble Lafayette ;
And gallant "Light Horse Harry" here
   His kindly chief for counsel met.

"Mad Antony" was here a guest,—
   Madly he charged, but shrewdly planned ;
And many another in whose breast
   Was faithful counsel for our land.

Among these worthies was a dame
   Of mingled dignity and grace ;
Linked with the warrior-statesman's fame
   Is Martha's comely, smiling face.

But look around, to right to left ;
   Pass through these rooms, once Martha's pride,
The dining hall of guests bereft,
   The kitchen with its fire-place wide.

See the huge logs, the swinging crane,
   The Old Man's seat by chimney ingle,
The pots and kettles, all the train
   Of brass and pewter, here they mingle.

In the large hall above, behold
   The flags, the eagle poised for flight ;
While sabres, bayonets, flint-locks old,
   Tell of the struggle, and the fight.

Old faded letters bear the seal
   Of men who battled for a stamp ;
A cradle and a spinning-wheel
   Bespeak the home behind the camp.

Apartments opening from the hall
   Show chairs and desks of quaint old style,
And curious pictures on the wall
   Provoke a reverential smile.

Musing, we loiter in each room
   And linger with our vanished sires ;
We hear the deep, far-echoing boom
   That spoke of old in flashing fires.

But deepening shadows bid us go,
   The western sun is sinking fast;
We take our leave with footsteps slow,
   Farewell, ye treasures of the past.

A century and more has gone,
   Since these old relics saw their day ;
That day was but the opening dawn
   Of one that has not passed away.

Our banner is no worthless rag,
   With patriot pride hearts still beat high;
And there, above, still waves the flag
   For which our fathers dared to die.

Mrs. Julia K. Cutler.

Mrs. Cutler's graceful pen has already contributed to this volume the sketch of Mrs. Mary Lee Demarest and also another to follow of Mrs. Julia McNair Wright. Her pen has been busy at occasional intervals from girlhood, when as a school-girl her essays were, as a rule, selected and read aloud in the chapel, on Friday afternoons, and a poem securing the gold medal crowned the success.

Living since her marriage, in the old historic house of Mr. Cutler's great-grandfather, the Hon. Silas Condict, fearless patriot of the Revolution, and President of the Council of Safety during the whole of that period that "tried men's souls", it is little wonder that the traditions of '76 clinging about the spot should nurture and develop the poetic spirit of the girl. It was in 1799, after Mr. Condict's return from Congress that he built the present house familiar to us all, but the old house stands near by, full of the most interesting stories and traditions of revolutionary days.

Mrs. Cutler has written many articles, often by request, for papers or magazines, and verses prompted by circumstances or surroundings, or composed when strongly impressed upon an especial subject.

FIRST PRESBYT
SESSION H(
MORRIS COUNTY S(

Before us lies a lovely poem of childhood, entitled "Childish Faith", founded on fact, but we select from the many poems of Mrs. Cutler, the Centennial Poem given below, and written on the occasion of the Centennial of the old First Church.

CENTENNIAL FIRST PRESBYTERIAN CHURCH.

The moon shines brightly down, o'er hill and dale
As it shone down, One Hundred years ago,
On these same scenes. The stars look down from Heaven
As they did then, as calm, serene, and bright—
Fit emblems of the God, who changes not.
Only in him can we find sure repose
'Mid change, decay and death, who is the same
To-day as yesterday, forevermore.
    Through the clear air peal forth the silvery notes,
Of thy old Bell, thou venerable pile,
Thou dear old Church, whose birthday rare,
We come to celebrate with tender love.
    One Hundred years! How long; and yet, how short
When counted with the centuries of the past
That help to make the ages of the world:
How long when measured by our daily cares,
The joys, the sorrows that these years have brought
To us and ours. "Our fathers, where are they?"
The men of strength, one hundred years ago,
As full of courage, purpose, will, as we,
Have gone to join the "innumerable throng"

That worship in the Father's House above.
Their children, girls and boys, like the fair flowers,
Have blossomed, faded, and then passed away,
Leaving their children and grandchildren, too,
To fill their places, take their part in life.
      How oft, dear Church, these walls have
        heard the vows
That bound two hearts in one. How oft the tread
Of those that bore the sainted dead to rest.
How oft the voices, soft and low, of those
Who, trusting in a covenant-keeping God
Gave here their little ones to God. A faith
Which He has blessed, as thou canst truly tell,
In generations past, and will in days to come.
How many servants of the most high God,
Beneath thy roof have uttered words divine,
Taught by the Spirit, leading souls to Christ
And reaping, even here, their great reward.
Many of these have entered into rest
Such as remains for those who love the Lord.
Others to-day, have gathered here to tell
What God has done in years gone by, and bear
Glad testimony to the truth, that in this place
His name has honored been.—'Tis sad to say
Farewell. But 'tis decreed, that thou must go.
Time levels all ; and it will lay thee low.
But o'er thy dust full many a tear shall fall,
And many a prayer ascend, that the true God,
Our Father's God, will, with their children dwell,
And that the stately pile which soon shall rise,
Where now, thou art, a monument shall be
Of generations past, recording all
The truth and mercies of a loving God.
    Oct. 14th, 1891.

Miss Frances Bell Coursen.

The rythmic, airy verses of Miss Coursen, full of the spirit of trees, flowers, the clouds, the winds and the insinuating and lovely sounds of nature, charm us into writing the author down as one of Morristown's young poets. The verses have attractive titles which in themselves suggest to us musical thoughts, such as "To the Winds in January"; "June Roses"; "In the Fields"; and "What the Katydids Say". We quote the latter for its bright beauty.

WHAT THE KATYDIDS SAY.

"Katy did it!" "Katy did n't!"
  Does n't Katy wish she had?
"Katy did!" that sounds so pleasant,
  "Katy did n't" sounds so bad.

Katy did n't—lazy Katy,
  Did n't do her lessons well?
Did n't set her stitches nicely?
  Did n't do what? Who can tell?

But the livelong autumn evening
  Sounds from every bush and tree,
So that all the world can hear it,
  "Katy did n't" oh dear me!

Who would like to hear forever
    Of the things they had n't done
In shrill chorus, sounding nightly,
    From the setting of the sun.

But again, who would n't like it
    If they every night could hear,
" Yes she did it, Katy did it",
    Sounding for them loud and clear ?

So if you 've an "awful lesson",
    Or "a horrid seam to sew ",
Just you stop and think a minute,
    Do n't decide to "let it go".

In the evening, if you listen,
    All the Katydids will say
" Yes she did it, did it, did it !"
    Or, "she did n't". Now which way ?

Miss Isabel Stone.

Miss Stone, long a resident of Morristown, has published many poems in prominent journals and magazines, also stories, but always under an assumed name. She will take a place in another group, that of *Novelists and Story-Writers*. She is represented here by her poem on "Easter Thoughts".

EASTER THOUGHTS.

Sometimes within our hearts, the good lies dead,
   Slain by untoward circumstances, or by our own
      free will,
And through the world we walk with bowèd head;
   Or with our senses blinded to our choice,
Thinking that " good is evil—evil good ;"
   Or, with determined pride to still the voice
That whispers of a " Resurrection morn."
   This is that morn—the resurrection hour
Of all the good that has within us died,
   The hour to throw aside with passionate force
The cruel bonds of wrong and blindness—pride—
   And rise unto a level high of power,
Of strength—of purity—while those we love rejoice
   With "clouds of angel witnesses" above,
And all the dear ones, who before have gone.

And we ascend, in the triumphant joy
   And peace, and rapture of a changèd self
That now transfigured stands—no more the toy
   Of circumstance—or pride, or sin, to blight—
   Until we reach sublimest heights—
   And stand erect, eyes fixed upon the Right—
Strong in the strength that wills all wrong to still,
   Will—pointing upwards to th' ascended Lord,
Bless, aye, thrice bless, this fair, sweet Easter Dawn.

Rev. G. Douglass Brewerton.

The Rev. Mr. Brewerton was pastor of the Baptist Church in Morristown in 1861, and during the early years of our Civil War. He was very patriotic and public-spirited and founded a Company of boy Zouaves in the town, which is well remembered, for at that time the war-spirit was the order of the day. He wrote a number of poems which were published in the Morristown papers and others. Of these, the following is one, published January 30, 1861.

OUR SOLDIERS WITH OUR SAILORS STAND.

A NATIONAL SONG

RESPECTFULLY DEDICATED TO THE VOLUNTEERS OF BOTH SERVICES, BY ONE WHO ONCE WORE THE UNIFORM OF THE FEDERAL GOVERNMENT.

Our soldiers with our sailors stand,
  A bulwark firm and true,
To guard the banner of our land,
  The Red, the White, the Blue.

The forts that frown along the coast,
  The ramparts on the steep,
Are held by men who never boast,
  But true allegiance keep.

While still in thunder tones shall speak
  Our giants on the tide,
Rebuking those who madly seek
  To tame the eagle's pride.

While breezes blow or sounding sea
  Be whitened by a sail,
The banner of the brave and true
  Shall float, nor fear the gale.

While Ironsides commands the fleet,
  Shall patriot vows be heard,
Where pennants fly or war drums beat,
  True to their oaths and word.

Then back, ye traitors ! back, for shame !
  Nor dare to touch a fold ;
We 'll guard it till the sunshine wane
  And stars of night grow old.

Thus ever may that flag unrent
  At peak and staff be borne,
Nor e'er from mast or battlement
  By traitor hands be torn.

Mrs. Alice D. Abell.

Mrs. Abell has for several years contributed poems and articles to various papers and magazines. From the poems we select the following, which was copied in a Southern paper as well as in two others, from *The New York Magazine* in which it first appeared:

BEHIND THE MASK.

Behind the mask—the smiling face
  Is often full of woe,
And sorrow treads a restless pace
  Where wealth and beauty go.

Behind the mask—who knows the care
  That grim and silent rests,
And all the burdens each may bear
  Within the secret breast?

Behind the mask—who knows the tears
  That from the heart arise,
And in the weary flight of years
  How many pass with sighs?

Behind the mask—who knows the strain
  That each life may endure,
And all its grief and countless pain
  That wealth can never cure?

Behind the mask—we never know
　How many troubles hide,
And with the world and fashion show
　Some spectre walks beside.

Behind the mask—some future day,
　When all shall be made plain ;
Our burdens then will pass away
　And count for each his gain.

George Wetmore Colles, Jr.

The following is by one of the young writers of Morristown, written at Yale University and published in the *Yale Courant* of February, 1891 :

TO A MOUNTAIN CASCADE.

To him who, wearied in the noontide glare,
　Seeks cool refreshment in thy quiet shade,
　In all thy beauteous rainbow tints arrayed,
How sweet ! O dashing brook, thy waters are !

Sure, such a glen fair Dian with her train
　Chose to disport in, when Actæon bold

That sight with mortal eyes dared to behold
Which mortals may not see and life retain.

To such a glen I, too, at noonday creep,
   Leaving the dusty road and haunts of men,
   To quaff thy purling, sparkling ripples ; then
To plunge within thy clear, cold basin deep.

Alone in Nature's lap (this mossy sod)
   I lie ; feel her sweet breath upon me blow ;
   Hear her melodious woodland voice, and know
Her passing love, the eternal love of God !

HYMNODIST.

John R. Runyon.

Our fellow townsman of old New Jersey name, whose enthusiastic love for music, and especially for church music, is well known, has manifested his interest in this direction by compiling a collection of hymns known as "Songs of Praise. A Selection of Standard Hymns and Tunes". It is published by Anson D. F. Randolph & Company, and "meets", says the compiler, "a universally acknowledged want for a collection of Hymns to be used in Sunday Schools and Social Meetings".

Says Charles H. Morse in *The Christian Union* of August 20th, 1892 : "If music is a pattern and type of Heaven, then, indeed, are those whose mission is to provide the music for our worship burdened with a weight of responsibility and called to a blessed ministry second only to that of the pastor who stands at the desk to speak the words of Life".

To compile from various sources a collection of hymns acceptable to varied classes of minds, requires much discernment, great care and large range of knowledge on the subject, as well as a comprehension of what is needed which comes from long and wide experience, study and observation, in addition to natural genius.

NOVELISTS
AND
STORY-WRITERS.

Francis Richard Stockton.

Although born in Philadelphia, Mr. Stockton belongs to an old and distinguished New Jersey family, and he has, after many wanderings, at last selected his home in the State of his ancestors.

Within a few years he has purchased and fitted up a quaint and attractive mansion in the suburbs of Morristown, overlooking the beautiful Loantika Valley, where in the Revolutionary days the tents of the suffering patriots were pitched or their log huts constructed for the bitter winter. Beyond the long and narrow valley, the homes of prominent residents of Morristown appear on the Western limiting range of hills, and are charmingly picturesque.

This home Mr. Stockton has named "The Holt" and his legend, taken from Turberville, an old English poet, is painted over the fire-place in his Study which is over the Library on the South corner of the House :

> " Yee that frequent the hilles
> and highest holtes of all,
> Assist me with your skilful
> quilles and listen when I call."

Mr. Stockton and Richard Stockton, the signer of the Declaration of Independence, are descended from the same ancestor, Richard Stockton, who came from England in 1680 and settled in Burlington County, New Jersey.

Much fine and interesting criticism from various directions, has been called out by Mr. Stockton's works.

Edmund Gosse, the well-known Professor of Literature in England, said just before leaving our shores :

"I think Mr. Stockton one of the most remarkable writers in this country. I think his originality, his extraordinary fantastic genius, has not been appreciated at all. People talk about him as if he were an ordinary purveyor of comicality. I do not want to leave this country without giving my *personal tribute*, if that is worth anything, to his genius."

"More than half of Mr. Stockton's readers, without doubt", says another critic. "think of him merely as the daintiest of humorists; as a writer whose work is entertaining in an unusual degree, rather than weighed in a critical scale, or considered seriously as a part of the literary *expression* of his time".

It is acknowledged that Americans are masters, at the present day, of the art of writing short stories and these, as a rule, are like the French, distinctly realistic. In this art Mr. Stockton excels. Among his short stories, "The Bee Man of Orn" and "The Griffin and the Minor Canon" represent his power of fancy. "The Hunting Expedition" in "Prince Hassak's March" is particularly jolly, and in "The Stories of the Three Burglars", we find a specimen of his realistic treatment. In the last, he makes the young house-breaker, who is an educated man, say: "I have made it a rule never to describe anything I have not personally seen and experienced. It is the only way, otherwise we can not give people credit for their virtues or judge them properly for their faults." Upon this, Aunt Martha exclaims: "I think that the study of realism may be carried a great deal too far. I do not think there is the slightest necessity for people to know anything about burglars." And later she says, referring to this one of the three : "I have no doubt, before he fell into his wicked ways, he was a very good writer and might have become a novelist or a magazine author, but his case is a sad proof that the study of realism is carried too far."

No critic seems to have observed or noticed the very remarkable manner in which Mr. Stockton renders the negro dialect on the printed page. In this respect he quite surpasses Uncle Remus or any other writer of negro folk-lore. He spells the words in such a way as to give the sense and sound to ears unaccustomed to negro talk as well as to those accustomed to it. This we especially realize in "The Late Mrs. Null".

But besides the qualities we have noticed in Mr. Stockton's writings, there is a subtle fragrance of purity that exhales from one and all, which is in contrast to much of the novel-writing and story-telling of the present day. We have reason to welcome warmly to our homes and to our firesides, one who, by his pure fun and drollery, can charm us so completely as to make us forget, for a time, the serious problems and questions which agitate and confront the thinking men and women of this generation.

So varied and voluminous are the writings of Mr. Stockton, they may be grouped as *Juveniles, Novels, Novelettes* and *Collected Short Stories*. Besides, there are magazine stories constantly appearing, and still to be collected. Most prominent among the volumes are "The Lady or The Tiger?"; "Rudder Grange" and its sequel, "The Rudder Grangers Abroad"; "The Late Mrs. Null"; "The Casting Away of Mrs. Lecks and Mrs. Aleshine"; "The Hundredth Man"; "The Great War Syndicate"; "Ardis Claverden"; "Stories of the Three Burglars"; "The House of Martha" and "The Squirrel Inn".

After considering what Mr. Stockton has accomplished and the place which by his genius and industry he has made for himself in Literature, we do not find it remarkable that in July, 1890, he was elected by the readers of *The Critic* into the ranks of the *Forty Immortals*.

We give to represent Mr. Stockton, an extract from his novel of "Ardis Claverden", containing one of those clever conversations so characteristic of the author, and success in which marks a high order of dramatic genius, in making characters express to the listener or reader their own individuality through familiar talk.

EXTRACT FROM "ARDIS CLAVERDEN."

Mr. and Mrs. Chiverly were artists.

* * * * *

The trouble with Harry Chiverly was that he

had nothing in himself which he could put into his work. He could copy what he could see, but if he could not see what he wanted to paint, he had no mental power which would bring that thing before him, or to transform what he saw into what it ought to be.

*　　　*　　　*　　　*　　　*

The trouble with Mrs. Chiverly was that she did not know how to paint. With her there was no lack of artistic imagination. Her brain was full of pictures, which, if they could have been transferred to the brain of her husband, who did know how to paint, would have brought fame and fortune. At one end of her brush was artistic talent, almost genius ; at the other was a pigment mixed with oil. But the one never ran down to the other. The handle of the brush was a non-conductor.

We pass on to a scene in the studio. An elderly man enters, a stranger, to examine pictures, and stops before Mr. Chiverly's recently finished canvass.

"Madam," said he, "can you tell me where the scene of this picture is laid? It reminds me somewhat of the North and somewhat of the South, and I am not sure that it does not contain suggestions of the East and the West."

"Yes," thought Ardis at her easel, "and of the North-east, and the Sou- sou'-west, and all the other points of the compass."

Mrs. Chiverly left her seat and approached the visitor. She was a little piqued at his remark.

"Some pictures have a meaning," she said, "which is not apparent to every one at first sight."

"You are correct, madam," said the visitor.

"This painting, for instance," continued Mrs. Chiverly, "represents the seven ages of trees." And then with as much readiness as Jacques detailed the seven ages of man to the duke, she pointed out in the trees of the picture the counterparts of these ages.

"Madam," said the visitor, "you delight me. I admit that I utterly failed to see the point of this picture ; but now that I am aware of its meaning I understand its apparent incongruities. Meaning despises locality."

"You are right," said Mrs. Chiverly, earnestly. "Meaning is above everything."

"Madam," said the gentleman, his eyes still fixed upon the canvass, "as a student of Shakespeare, as well as a collector, in a small way, of works of art, I desire to have this picture, provided its price is not beyond my means."

Mrs. Chiverly gazed at him in an uncertain way. She did not seem to take in the import of his remark.

From her easel Ardis now named the price which Mr. Chiverly had fixed upon for the picture.

He never finished a painting without stating very emphatically what he intended to ask for it.

"That is reasonable," said the gentleman, "and you may consider the picture mine." And he handed Mrs. Chiverly his card. Then, imbued with a new interest in the studio, he walked about looking at others of the pictures.

"This little study," said he, "seems to me as if it ought to have a significance, but I declare I am again at fault."

"Yes," said Mrs. Chiverly, "it ought to have a significance. In fact there is a significance connected with it. I could easily tell you what it is, but if you were afterwards to look at the picture you would see no such meaning in it."

"Perhaps this is one of your husband's earlier works" said the gentleman, "in which he was not able to express his inspirations."

"It is not one of my husband's works," said Mrs. Chiverly ; "it is mine."

* * * * *

The moment that the gentleman had departed Ardis flew to Mrs. Chiverly and threw her arms around her neck. "Now my dearest," she exclaimed, "you know your vocation in life. You must put meanings to Mr. Chiverly's pictures."

When the head of the house returned he was, of course, delighted to find that his painting had been sold.

"That is the way with us!" he cried, "we have spasms of prosperity. One of our works is bought, and up we go. Let us so live that while we are up we shall not remember that we have ever been down. And now my dear, if you will give me the card of that exceptional appreciator of high art, I will write his bill and receipt instantly, so that if he should again happen to come while I am out there may be nothing in the way of an immediate settlement."

Mrs. Chiverly stood by him as he sat at the desk. "You must call the picture," she said, "'The Seven Ages of Trees.'"

"Nonsense!" exclaimed Mr. Chiverly, turning suddenly and gazing with astonishment at his wife. "That will do for a bit of pleasantry, but the title of the picture is 'A Scene on the Upper Mississippi.' You do n't want to deceive the man, do you?"

"No, I do not," said Mrs. Chiverly, "and that is one reason why I did not give it your title. It is a capitally painted picture, and as a woodland 'Seven Ages' it is simply perfect. That was what it sold for; and for that and nothing else will the money be paid."

Mr. Chiverly looked at her for a moment longer, and then bursting into a laugh he returned to his desk. "You have touched me to the quick," he said. "Money has given title before and it shall do so now. There is the receipted bill!" he cried, pushing back his chair.

Francis Bret Harte.

Bret Harte, so far as we can discover, has written the only story of Revolutionary times in Morristown, and the only story of those times in New Jersey except Miss Holdich, who follows, and James Fenimore Cooper, whose "Water Witch" is located about the Highlands of New Jersey. By a passage from his story of "Thankful Blossom" we shall represent him at the close of this sketch.

Between 1873 and 1876 Bret Harte lived in Morristown, in several locations: in the picturesque old Revere place on the Mendham Road, the very home for a Novelist, now owned and occupied by Mr. Charles G. Foster; in the Whatnong House for one summer, near which are located old farms, which seem to us to have many features of the "Blossom Farm" and to which we shall refer; in the Logan Cottage on Western Avenue and in the house on Elm Street now owned and occupied by Mr. Joseph F. Randolph.

The steps by which Bret Harte climbed to the eminence that he now occupies, are full of romantic interest. Left early by his father, who was a Professor in an Albany Seminary and a man of culture, to struggle with little means, the boy, at fifteen, had only an ordinary education and went in 1854, with his mother, to California. He opened a school in Sonora, walking to that place from San Francisco. Fortune did not favor him either in this undertaking or in that of mining, to which, like all young Californians in that day, he resorted as a means to live. He then entered a printing office as compositor and began his literary career by composing his first articles in type while working at the case. Here he had editorial experiences which ended abruptly in consequence of the want of sympathy in the miners with his articles. He returned to San Francisco and became compositor in the office of *The Golden Era*. His three years experience among the miners served him in good stead and his clever sketches describing those vivid scenes, soon placed him in the regular corps of writers for the paper. *The Californian*, a literary weekly, then engaged Harte as associate manager and, in this short-lived paper appeared the "Condensed Novels" in which Dickens' "Christmas Stories", Charlotte Brontë's "Jane Eyre", Victor Hugo's "Les Misérables", and other prominent and familiar writings of distinguished authors are most cleverly taken off. These have amused and delighted the reading world since their first appearance. During the next six years, he filled the office of Secretary of the United States Branch Mint, and also wrote for California journals, many of his important poems, among them, "John Burns of Gettysburg", and "The Society upon the Stanislau", which attracted wide attention by their originality and peculiar flavor of the "Wild West". In July, 1868, Harte organized, and became the editor of, what is now a very successful journal, *The Overland Monthly*.

For this journal he wrote many of his most characteristic stories and poems and introduced into its pages, "The Luck of Roaring Camp"; "The Outcasts of Poker Flat", and others having that peculiar pseudo-dialect of Western mining life of which he was the pioneer writer. He had now taken a great step towards high and artistic work. At this point his reputation was established.

As for Revolutionary New Jersey poems, abundant as the material is for inspiration, Bret Harte's "Caldwell of Springfield" seems to be one of very few. At the luncheon of the Daughters of the American Revolution held in May of 1892, a prominent member of the Association recited "Parson Caldwell" and mentioned, that strange to say, it was as far as she had been able to ascertain, the only poem on Revolutionary times in New Jersey that had ever been written, though she had searched thoroughly. In addition to this, we find only, besides the two poems of Mr. Charles D. Platt, given in this volume, (and others of his referred to) one or two of the sort in a volume published years ago, privately, by Dr. Thomas Ward, of New York (a great uncle of Mrs. Luther Kountze). Very few copies of his poems were printed and all were given to his friends, not sold.

We must not forget the very beautiful poem of "Alice of Monmouth", by Edmund Clarence Stedman, and also, perhaps, might be included his spirited "Aaron Burr's Wooing". There was also an early writer, Philip Freneau, of Monmouth County, who lived in Colonial and Revolutionary times, and wrote some quaint and charming poems of that period.

If there are any others we would be glad to be informed.

In this book, " Plain Language From Truthful James", better known as "The Heathen Chinee", represents Mr. Harte among the poets, in our group of writers, for the reason that it is so widely known as a satire upon the popular prejudices against the Chinese, who were at that time pursued with hue and cry of being shiftless and weak-minded.

From 1868, Harte became a regular contributor to the *Atlantic Monthly* and he also entered the lecture field. It was during this period that he lived in Morristown. In 1878 he went to Crefeld, Germany, as United States Consul, and here began his life abroad. Two years later he went, as Consul, to Glasgow, Scotland, since which time he has remained abroad, engaged in literary pursuits.

The Contributor's Club, of the *Atlantic Monthly*, gives a curious little paper on "The Value of a Name", in which the writer insists that Bret Harte, Mark Twain, Dante Rossetti and others owe a part of their success, at least, to the phonic value of their names. He says that "much time and thought are spent in selecting a name for a play or novel, for it is known that success is largely dependent on it" and he therefore censures parents who are "so strangely careless and unscientific in giving names to their children."

Bret Harte's publications include besides "Condensed Novels", "Thankful Blossom", and others already mentioned, several volumes of Poems issued at different periods : among them are "Songs of the Sierras" and "Echoes of the Foot Hills". Then there are "Tales of the Argonauts and Other Stories"; "Drift from Two Shores"; "Twins of Table Mountain"; "Flip and Found at Blazing Star"; "On the Frontier"; "Snow Bound at Eagle's"; "Maruja, a Novel"; "The Queen of the Pirate Isle", for children ; "A Phyllis of the Sierras"; "A Waif of the Plains" and many others, besides his collected works in five volumes published in 1882.

Writing to Bret Harte in London, for certain information about the story of "Thankful Blossom", the author of this volume received the following reply :

15 Upper Hamilton Terrace, N. W., 31st May, '90.

Dear Madam :

In reply to your favor of the 14th inst., I fear I must begin by saying that the story of "Thankful Blossom", although inspired and suggested by my residence at Morristown at different periods was not *written* at that place, but in another part of New Jersey. The "Blossom Farm" was a study of two or three old farm houses in the vicinity, but was not an existing fact so far as I know. But the description of Washington's Head-Quarters was a study of the actual house, supplemented by such changes as were necessary for the epoch I described, and which I gathered from the State Records. The portraits of Washington and his military family at the Head-Quarters were drawn from Spark's "Life of Washington" and the best chronicles of the time. The episode of the Spanish Envoy is also historically substantiated, and the same may be said of the incidents of the disaffection of the "Connecticut Contingent."

Although the heroine, " Thankful Blossom", as a *character* is purely imaginary, the *name* is an actual one, and was borne by a (chronologically) remote maternal relation of mine, whose Bible with the written legend, "Thankful Blossom, her book", is still in possession of a member of the family.

The contour of scenery and the characteristics of climate have, I believe, changed but little since I knew them between 1873 and 1876 and "Thankful Blossom" gazed at them from the Baskingridge Road in 1779.

I remain, dear madam,

Yours very sincerely,

BRET HARTE.

Two of the farms from which Bret Harte *may* have drawn the inspiration for the surroundings of his story, may be seen on the Washington Valley road as you turn to the right from the road to Mendham. Turning again to the left,—before you come to the junction of the road which crosses at right angles to the Whatnong House, where Mr. Harte passed a summer,—you come upon the Carey Farm, the house built by the grandfather of the present occupants. There you see the stone wall, —crumbling now,— over which the bewitching Mistress Thankful talked and clasped hands with Captain Allen Brewster of the Connecticut Contingent. The elm-tree, upon whose bark was inscribed "the effigy of a heart, divers initials and the legend 'Thine Forever'", has been lately cut down and the trunk decorated with growing plants and flowers.

We see the black range of the Orange Hills over which the moon slowly lifted herself as the Captain waited for his love, "looking at him, blushing a little, as if the appointment were her own". We see also the faintly-lit field beyond,— the same field in which, further on in the story after Brewster's treachery, Major Van Zandt and Mistress Thankful picked the violets together and doing so, revealed their hearts' love to one another on that 3rd of May, 1780.

The orchard is there, still bearing apples, but the "porch" and the "mossy eaves" evidently belong to the next farm house, which we find exactly on the corner at the junction of the two roads. It is the old Beach farm. The original house has a brick addition, with the inscription among the bricks, "1812".

It is on the wooden part built earlier and evidently an ancient structure, that we see the "porch and eaves".

We select from "Thankful Blossom" the very fine pen portrait of Washington and his military family at the Headquarters.

THANKFUL BLOSSOM.

A Romance of the Jerseys,
1779.

CHAPTER III.

The rising wind, which had ridden much faster than Mistress Thankful, had increased to a gale by the time it reached Morristown. It swept through the leafless maples, and rattled the dry bones of the elms. It whistled through the quiet Presbyterian churchyard, as if trying to arouse the sleepers it had known in days gone by. It shook the blank, lustreless windows of the Assembly Rooms over the Freemason's Tavern, and wrought in their gusty curtains moving shadows of those amply petticoated dames and tightly hosed cavaliers who had swung in " Sir Roger," or jigged in " Money Musk," the night before.

But I fancy it was around the isolated "Ford Mansion," better known as the "Headquarters," that the wind wreaked its grotesque rage. It howled under its scant eaves, it sang under its bleak porch, it tweaked the peak of its front gable, it whistled through every chink and cranny of its square, solid, unpicturesque structure. Situated on a hillside that descended rapidly to the Whippany River, every summer zephyr that whispered through the porches of the Morristown farm houses charged as a stiff breeze upon the swinging half doors and windows of the "Ford Mansion"; every wintry wind became a gale that threatened its security. The sentinel who paced before its front porch knew from experience when to linger under its lee, and adjust his threadbare outer coat to the bitter North wind.

Within the house something of this cheerlessness prevailed. It had an ascetic gloom, which the scant fire-light of the reception room, and the dying embers on the dining room hearth, failed to dissipate. The central hall was broad, and furnished plainly with a few rush-bottomed chairs, on one of which half dozed a black body-servant of the commander-in-chief. Two officers in the dining-room, drawn close by the chimney corner, chatted in undertones, as if mindful that the door of the drawing-room was open, and their voices might break in upon its sacred privacy. The swinging light in the hall partly illuminated it, or rather glanced gloomily from the black polished furniture, the lustreless chairs, the quaint cabinet, the silent spinet, the skeleton-legged centre-table, and finally upon the motionless figure of a man seated by the fire.

It was a figure since so well known to the civilized world, since so celebrated in print and painting, as to need no description here. Its rare combination of gentle dignity with profound force, of a set resoluteness of purpose with a philosophical patience, have been so frequently delivered to a people not particularly remarkable for these qualities, that I fear it has too often provoked a spirit of playful aggression, in which the deeper underlying meaning was forgotten. So let me add that in manner, physical equipoise, and even in the mere details of dress, this figure indicated a certain aristocratic exclusiveness. It was the presentment of a king,—a king who by the irony of circumstances was just then waging war against all kingship ; a ruler of men, who just then was fighting for the right of these men to govern themselves, but whom by his own inherent right he dominated. From the crown of his powdered head to the silver buckle of his shoe he was so royal that it was not strange his brother George of England and Hanover—ruling by accident, otherwise impiously known as the "grace of God"—could find no better way of resisting his power than by calling him "Mr. Washington."

The sound of horses' hoofs, the formal challenge of sentry, the grave questioning of the officer of the guard, followed by footsteps upon the porch, did not apparently disturb his meditation. Nor did the opening of the outer door and a charge of cold air into the hall that invaded even the privacy of the reception room, and brightened the dying embers on the hearth, stir his calm pre-occupation. But an instant later there was the distinct rustle of a feminine skirt in the hall, a hurried whispering of men's voices, and then the sudden apparition of a smooth, fresh-faced young officer over the shoulder of the unconscious figure.

"I beg your pardon, general," said the officer doubtingly, "but"——

"You are not intruding, Colonel Hamilton," said the general quietly.

"There is a young lady without who wishes an audience of your Excellency. 'Tis Mistress Thankful Blossom,—the daughter of Abner Blossom, charged with treasonous practice and favoring the enemy, now in the guard-house at Morristown."

"Thankful Blossom?" repeated the general interrogatively.

"Your Excellency doubtless remembers a little provincial beauty and a famous toast of the countryside—the Cressida of our Morristown epic, who led our gallant Connecticut Captain astray"——

"You have the advantages, besides the better memory of a younger man, colonel," said Washington, with a playful smile that slightly reddened the cheek of his aide-de-camp. "Yet I think I *have* heard of this phenomenon. By all means, admit her—and her escort."

"She is alone, general," responded the subordinate.

"Then the more reason why we should be polite," returned Washington, for the first time altering his easy posture, rising to his feet, and lightly clasping his ruffled hands before him. "We must not keep her waiting. Give her access, my dear colonel, at once: and even as she came,—alone."

The aide-de-camp bowed and withdrew. In another moment the half opened door swung wide to Mistress Thankful Blossom.

She was so beautiful in her simple riding-dress, so quaint and original in that very beauty, and, above all, so teeming with a certain vital earnestness of purpose just positive and audacious enough to set off that beauty, that the grave gentleman before her did not content himself with the usual formal inclination of courtesy, but actually advanced, and, taking her cold little hand in his, graciously led her to the chair he had just vacated.

"Even if your name were not known to me, Mistress Thankful," said the commander-in-chief, looking down upon her with grave politeness, "nature has, methinks, spared you the necessity of any introduction to the courtesy of a gentleman. But how can I especially serve you?"

Miss Henrietta Howard Holdich.

It is a curious fact that although New Jersey was the theatre of some of the most stirring scenes of the Revolution, only two stories seem to have been written, founded on the events of those times, if we except the "Water Witch", by J. Fenimore Cooper, in which we find the location of Alderman Van Beverout's house, the villa of the "Lust in Rust" to be on the Atlantic Highlands, between the Shrewsbury river and the sea. This spot is pointed out to-day and was associated with the smugglers of that period. The other two stories are "Thankful Blossom", by Bret Harte, and "Hannah Arnett's Faith", a Centennial Story, by Miss Holdich, which latter, as a singular history attaches to it, we shall give at length.

Miss Holdich was born at Middletown, Conn., but left there too young to remember much about it and she lived in New York until 1878 when she came to Morristown. When she was not quite two years of age her mother discovered she could read and since she was seventeen, she has written for various well-known papers and periodicals, more children's stories than anything else, she tells us, but also a good many stories for *Harpers' Magazine* and *Bazar*,—also poems, by one of which she is represented in our group of poets.

"Hannah Arnett's Faith" is a true story of the author's great grandmother, familiar to all the family from infancy. In 1876 Miss Holdich published it, as a Centennial story, in *The New York Observer*. In 1890, a lady of Washington published it as her own in *The Washington Post*, (she asserts that she did not intend it as a plagiarism but used it merely as a historical incident). The story was recognized and letters written to, and published in, *The Post*, giving Miss Holdich's name, as the true author. However, this publication of the story led to a curious result, and gave the story a wide celebrity. In a published statement, Miss Mary Desha (one of the Vice Presidents of the D. A. R.) announces that "the Society of the Daughters of the American Revolution sprang from this story".

"On July 21st", Miss Desha says, after the publication of the story in *The Washington Post*, accompanied by an appeal for a woman's organization to commemorate events of the Revolution in which women had bravely borne their part,—"a letter from William O. McDowell of New Jersey, was published, in which he said that he was the great-grandson of Hannah Arnett and called on the women of America to form a society of their own, since they had been excluded from the Society of the Sons of the American Revolution at a meeting held in Louisville, Kentucky, April 30th, 1890".

Miss Holdich soon after this was urgently requested to become Regent of the Morristown Chapter of the Daughters of the American Revolution, which position she accepted and holds to-day.

HANNAH ARNETT'S FAITH.

A Centennial Story.

1776-1876.

The days were at their darkest and the hearts of our grandfathers were weighed down with doubt and despondency. Defeat had followed defeat for the American troops, until the army had become demoralized and discouragement had well-nigh become despair. Lord Cornwallis, after his victory at Fort Lee, had marched his army to Elizabethtown (Dec. 1776) where they were now encamped. On the 30th of November the brothers Howe had issued their celebrated proclamation, which offered protection to all who within sixty days should declare themselves peaceable British subjects and bind themselves neither to take up arms against their Sovereign, nor to encourage others to do so. It was to discuss the advisability of accepting this offered protection that a group of men had met in one of the large old houses of which Elizabethtown was, at that time, full.

We are apt to think of those old times as days of unmitigated loyalty and courage; of our ancestors as unfaltering heroes, swerving never in the darkest hours from the narrow and thorny path which conscience bade them tread. Yet human nature is human nature in all ages, and if at times the "old fashioned fire" burned low even in manly hearts, and profound discouragement palsied for a time the most ardent courage, what are we that we should wonder at or condemn them? Of this period Dr. Ashbel Green wrote:

"I heard a man of some shrewdness once say that when the British troops over-ran the State of New Jersey, in the closing part of the year 1776, the whole population could have been bought for eighteen-pence a head."

The debate was long and grave. Some were for accepting the offered terms at once; others hung back a little, but all had at length agreed that it was the only thing to be done. Hope, courage, loyalty, faith, honor—all seemed swept away upon the great flood of panic which had overspread the land. There was one listener, however, of whom the eager disputants were ignorant, one to whose heart their wise reasoning was very far from carrying conviction. Mrs. Arnett, the wife of the host, was in the next room, and the sound of the debate had reached her where she sat. She had listened in silence, until, carried away by her feelings, she could bear no more, and springing to her feet she pushed open the parlor door and confronted the assembled group.

Can you fancy the scene? A large low room, with the dark, heavily carved furniture of the period, dimly lighted by the tall wax candles and the wood fires which blazed in the huge fire place. Around the table, the group of men --pallid, gloomy, dejected, disheartened. In the doorway the figure of the woman, in the antique costume with which, in those latter days, we have become so familiar. Can you not fancy the proud poise of her head, the indignant light of her blue eyes, the crisp, clear tones of her voice, the majesty and defiance and scorn which clothed her as a garment?

The men all started up at her entrance; the sight of a ghost could hardly have caused more perturbation than did that of this little woman. Her husband advanced hastily. She had no business here; a woman should know her place and keep it. Questions of politics and political expediency were not for them;, but he would shield her as far as possible, and point out the impropriety of her conduct afterwards, when they should be alone. So he went quickly up to her with a warning whisper:

"Hannah! Hannah! this is no place for you. We do not want you here just now;" and would have taken her hand to lead her from the room.

She was a docile little woman, and obeyed his wishes in general without a word: but now it seemed as if she scarcely saw him, as with one hand she pushed him gently back and turned to the startled group.

"Have you made your decision, gentlemen?" she asked. "Have you chosen the part of men or of traitors?"

It was putting the question too broadly,—so like a woman, seeing only the bare, ugly facts, and quite forgetting the delicate drapery which was intended to veil them. It was an awkward position to put them in, and they stammered and bungled over their answer, as men in a false position will. The reply came at last, mingled with explanations and excuses and apologies.

"Quite hopeless; absurd for a starving, half-clothed, undisciplined army like ours to attempt to compete with a country like England's unlimited resources. Repulsed everywhere—ruined; throwing away life and fortune for a shadow;"—you know the old arguments with which men try to prop a staggering conscience.

Mrs. Arnett listened in silence until the last abject word was spoken. Then she inquired simply: "But what if we should live, after all?"

The men looked at each other, but no one spoke.

"Hannah! Hannah!" urged her husband. "Do you not see that these are no questions for you? We are discussing what is best for us, for you, for all. Women have no share in these topics. Go to your spinning-wheel and leave us to settle affairs. My good little wife, you are making yourself ridiculous. Do not expose yourself in this way before our friends."

His words passed her ear like the idle wind; not even the quiver of an eyelash showed that she heard them.

"Can you not tell me?" she said in the same strangely quiet voice. "If, after all, God does not let the right perish,—if America should win in the conflict, after you have thrown yourself upon British clemency, where will you be then?"

"Then?" spoke one hesitating voice. "Why, then, if it ever *could* be, we should be ruined. We must leave the country forever. But it is absurd to think of such a thing. The struggle is an utterly hopeless one. We have no men, no money, no arms, no food and England has everything."

"No," said Mrs. Arnett; "you have forgotten one thing which England has not and which we have—one thing which outweighs all England's treasures, and that is the Right. God is on our side, and every volley from our muskets is an echo of His voice. We are poor and weak and few; but God is fighting for us. We entered into this struggle with pure hearts and prayerful lips. We had counted the cost and were willing to pay the price, were it our heart's blood. And now—now, because for a time the day is going against us, you would give up all and sneak back, like cravens, to kiss the feet that have trampled upon us! And you call yourselves men—the sons of those who gave up home and fortune and fatherland to make for themselves and for dear liberty a resting-place in the wilderness? Oh, shame upon you, cowards!"

Her words had rushed out in a fiery flood, which her husband had vainly striven to check. I do not know how Mrs. Arnett looked, but I fancy her a little fair woman, with kindly blue eyes and delicate features,—a tender and loving little soul, whose scornful, blazing words must have seemed to her amazed hearers like the inspired fury of a pythoness. Are we not all prophets at times—prophets of good or evil, according to our bent, and with more power than we ourselves suspect to work out the fulfillment of our own prophecies? Who shall say how far this fragile woman aided to stay the wave of desolation which was spreading over the land?

"Gentlemen," said good Mr. Arnett uneasily, "I beg you to excuse this most unseemly interruption to our council. My wife is beside herself I think. You all know her and know that it is not her wont to meddle with politics, or to brawl and bluster. To-morrow she will see her folly, but now I pray your patience."

Already her words had begun to stir the slumbering manhood in the bosoms of those who heard her. Enthusiasm makes its own fitting times. No one replied; each felt too keenly his own pettiness, in the light cast upon them by this woman's brave words.

"Take your protection, if you will," she went on, after waiting in vain for a reply. "Proclaim yourselves traitors and cowards, false to your country and your God, but horrible will be the judgment you will bring upon your heads and the heads of those that love you. I tell you that England will never conquer. I know it and feel it in every fibre of my heart. Has God led us so far to desert us now? Will He, who led our fathers across the stormy winter sea, forsake their children who have put their trust in Him? For me, I stay with my country, and my hand shall never touch the hand, nor my heart cleave to the heart of him who shames her."

She flashed upon her husband a gaze which dazzled him like sudden lightning.

"Isaac, we have lived together for twenty years, and for all of them I have been a true and loving wife to you. But I am the child of God and of my country, and if you do this shameful thing, I will never again own you for my husband."

"My dear wife!" cried the husband aghast, "you do not know what you are saying. Leave me, for such a thing as this?"

"For such a thing as this?" she cried scornfully. "What greater cause could there be? I married a good man and true, a faithful friend and a loyal Christian gentleman, and it needs no divorce to sever me from a traitor and a coward. If you take your protection you lose your wife, and I—I lose my husband and my home!"

With the last words the thrilling voice broke suddenly with a pathetic fall and a film crept over the proud blue eyes. Perhaps this little touch of womanly weakness moved her hearers as deeply as her brave, scornful words. They were not all cowards at heart, only touched by the dread finger of panic, which, now and then, will paralyze the bravest. Some had struggled long against it and only half yielded at last. And some there were to whom old traditions had never quite lost their power, whose superstitious consciences had never become quite reconciled to the stigma of *Rebel*, though reason and judgment both told them that, borne for the cause for which they bore it, it was a title of nobility. The words of the little woman had gone straight to each heart, be its main-spring what it might. Gradually the drooping heads were raised and the eyes grew bright with manliness and resolution. Before they left the house that night, they had sworn a solemn oath to stand by the cause they had adopted and the land of their birth, through good or evil, and to spurn the offers of their tyrants and foes as the deadliest insults.

Some of the names of those who met in that secret council were known afterwards among those who fought their country's battles most nobly, who died upon the field of honor, or rejoiced with pure hearts when the day of triumph came at last. The name of the little woman figured on no heroic roll, but was she the less a heroine?

This story is a true one, and, in this Centennial year, when every crumb of information in regard to those old days of struggle and heroism is eagerly gathered up, it may not be without interest.

Mrs. Miriam Coles Harris.

Mrs. Harris was well known during her stay in Morristown and is remembered as a charming woman. "In Morristown", she writes, she found "restoration to health, many friends, and much enjoyment",—adding "I think I shall always love the place".

Mrs. Harris has been a voluminous writer of stories and novels. Her first work, "Rutledge", published without her name, excited immediate and wide attention and established her reputation. Since then, she has given to the world, among others, the following volumes : "Louie's Last Term at St. Mary's"; "The Sutherlands"; "Frank Warrington"; "St. Philip's"; "Round-hearts" (for children); "Richard Vandermarck"; "A Perfect Adonis"; "Missy"; "Happy-go-Lucky"; "Phoebe"; "A Rosary For Lent" and "Dear Feast of Lent".

The selection given to represent Mrs. Harris in Stedman and Hutchinson's "Library of American Literature" is a chapter from her novel, "Missy". An appropriate selection for this volume would be an extract from her chapter on "Marrowfat" (Morristown) in her novel, "Phoebe", published in 1884.

The two principal characters of the book, Barry and Phoebe, lately married, are described in Marrowfat, going to church on Sunday morning :

EXTRACT FROM "PHOEBE."

They were rather late ; that is, the bell had stopped ringing, and the pews were all filled, and the clergyman was just entering from the sacristy, when they reached the door. It was an old stone church, with many vines about it, greensward and fine trees. * * The organist was playing a low and unobtrusive strain ; the clergyman, having just entered, was on his knees, where unfortunately, the congregation had not followed him. They were all ready to criticise the young people who now walked down the silent aisle ; very far down, too, they were obliged to walk. It was the one moment in the week when they would be most conspicuous. *   *   Barry looked a greater swell than ever, and his wife was so much handsomer than anybody else in Marrowfat that it was simple nonsense to talk of ignoring the past. If one did not want to be walked over by these young persons they must be put down ; self preservation joined hands with virtuous indignation ; to cancel the past would be to sacrifice the future. Scarce a mother in Marrowfat but felt a bitter sense of injury as she thought of Barry. Not only had he set the worst possible example to her sons, but he had overlooked the charms of her daughters ; not only had he outraged public opinion, but he had disappointed private hopes. Society should hold him to a strict account ; Marrowfat was not to be trifled with when it came to matters of principle.

It was an old town, with ante-Revolutionary traditions ; there was no mushroom crop allowed to spring up about it. New people were permitted but only on approbation of the old. It was not the thing to be very rich in Marrowfat, it was only tolerated ; it was the thing to be a little cultivated, a little clever, very well born, and very loyal to Marrowfat. It was not exactly provincial ; it was too near the great city and too much mixed up with it to be that; but it was very local and it had its own traditions in an unusual degree. That people grew a little narrow and very much interested in the affairs of the town, after living there awhile, was not to be wondered at. It is always the result of suburban life, and one finds it difficult to judge, between having one's nature green like a lane, even if narrow, or hard and broad like a city pavement, out of which all the greenness has been trampled and all the narrowness thrown down.

The climate of the place was dry and pure; it was the fashion for the city doctors to send their patients there; and many who came to cough, remained to build. The scenery was lovely; you looked down pretty streets and saw blue hills beyond; the sidewalks were paved and the town was lit by gas, but the pavements led you past charming homes to bits of view that reminded you of Switzerland, and the inoffensive lamp-posts were hidden under great trees by day, and by night you only thought how glad you were to see them. The drives were endless, the roads good; there were livery-stables, hotels, skilled confectioners, shops of all kinds, a library, a pretty little theatre, churches of every shade of faith, schools of every degree of pretension; lectures in winter, concerts in summer, occasional plays all the year; two or three local journals, the morning papers from the city at your breakfast table; fast trains, telegraphs, telephones, all the modern amenities of life under your very hand; and yet it was the country, and there were peaceful hills and deep woods, and the nights were as still as Paradise. Can it be wondered at that, like St. Peter's at Rome, it had an atmosphere of its own, and defied the outer changes of the temperature?

Marrowfat certainly was a law unto itself. Why certain people were great people, in its view, it would be difficult to say. Why the telegraphs, and the telephones, and the fashionable invalids from the city and the rich people who bought and built in its neighborhood, did not change its standards of value one can only guess. But it had a stout moral sentiment of its own; it had resisted innovations and done what seemed it good for a long while; and when you have made a good moral sentiment the fashion, or the fact by long use, you have done a good thing. Marrowfat never tolerated married flirtations, looked askance on extremes in dress or entertainment, dealt severely with the faults of youth. All these things existed more or less within its borders, of course, but they were evil doings and not approved doings.

In a certain sense, Marrowfat was the most charitable town in the world; in another the most uncharitable. If you were to have any misfortune befall you, Marrowfat was the place to go to have it in ; if you lost your money, if you broke your back, if your children died, if your house burned down, Marrowfat swathed you in flowers, bathed you in sympathy, took you out to drive, came and read to you, if need were took up subscriptions for you. But if you did anything disgraceful or discreditable, it is safe to say you would better have done it in any other place.

Miss Maria McIntosh.

Miss McIntosh was born in the little village of Sunbury, Georgia, in 1804. She was educated by an old Oxford tutor who was teacher and pastor combined and she led the class of boys with whom she studied. After her mother's death, (her father had died in her infancy), she came to the north, wholly for the purpose of studying and improving herself.

Her first stories were for children. Then appeared two very successful tales for youth ; " Conquest and Self-Conquest," and " Praise and Principle". "To Seem and To Be"; "Charms and Counter-Charms", and their successors followed on during a period of twenty years. Several of her books were translated into both French and German and all were widely read abroad, but the joy in her work lay in the rich harvest for good which was constantly made known to her. In the year before her death, many letters came to her from women then married and heads of families, thanking her for first impulses to better things arising from her words.

Not long ago, Marion Harland, (Mrs. Terhune), wrote to a dear friend of this author, that she owed to Miss McIntosh the strongest influences of her young life and those which had determined its bent and development.

Miss McIntosh was intensely interested in the maintenance of Republican simplicity and purity of morals and wrote a strong address, which was widely circulated, to the "Women of America" which led to a correspondence with the then Duchess of Sutherland and other English women who were interested in the elevation of women and of the family life.

She died in Morristown, at the residence of her devoted niece and namesake, Mrs. James Farley Cox, and soothed by her loving ministrations,-- after a protracted illness, lasting over a year. Mrs. Cox tells us, "she loved Morristown and said amidst great pain, that her last year, was, despite all, the happiest of her life".

"Lofty and Lowly"; "Charms and Counter-Charms", and "To Seem and To Be", are all alike noble books. Miss McIntosh seems a woman of strong creative powers, with a delicacy of feeling and a fine touch of womanliness, united to a certain delicate perception of character. She did not write from what we now so grandly call *types*, or, for the sake of displaying a surgical dissection of character; but her books are groupings of individuals as real as those we meet in daily life. There are no strained situations, no fanciful make-ups, and no unnatural poses.

There are the lovely Alice Montrose with a strangely beautiful blending of delicate refinement and womanly strength, rising to meet every requirement of her varied life ; Mr. Gaston, the New England merchant ; Richard Grahame the hero of "Lofty and Lowly", with some telling contrasts in the way of villians and weaker characters. Beside this, Miss McIntosh has a strong sympathy for nature and all through her stories she stops, as it were to show us the flowering fields and summer skies and as she draws us to her, we feel the beatings of her own warm human heart going out as it does to the young and inexperienced.

Again, Miss McIntosh gives in her stories faithful representations of life both north and south, before the war, forty years ago. These pictures are of peculiar value as few books preserve pictorial records of that condition of life now passed away forever. She had a power in massing details and binding them by a thread of common interest and common action. She seemed in her writings, like one who had been spiritually "lifted higher" and like all such spirits she could not but draw others after her. Her books in past years have had wide and lasting influence and it is a pity they could not now be substituted for much of the miserable literature which only pleases a passing hour or teaches false views of life.

Mrs. Maria McIntosh Cox.

Mrs. Cox, long a resident of Morristown, was named for the dear aunt to whom the preceding sketch relates, and, as is often the case with namesakes for some unexplained reason, the mantle of Miss McIntosh's genius fell upon her.

From girlhood, Mrs. Cox has written for various papers and magazines. Some years ago, the Appletons published a little volume of hers for very young children, called "A year with Maggie and

Emma", which was afterwards translated into French.

"Raymond Kershaw", published in 1888, is a volume of larger size. To this we shall refer later. In March, 1890, *The Youth's Companion* published a short story founded on an adventure of the author's father with Lafitte, the famous pirate. It was entitled "A Brave Middy", and won a prize of $500, in a contest of similar tales.

In the current numbers of *Wide Awake* from December to June 1891–'92 appeared a story of ten chapters called "Jack Brereton's Three Months' Service", which, in August, 1892, was brought out in book form by D. Lothrop & Co., Boston. The idea most prominent in this story, the "motif", is the reflex action of a soldier's enlistment on his deserted family. "I chanced", says the author, "to thoroughly see and know what sudden *three months'* calls entailed on the volunteer and those who fought the battle out at home, and I enjoyed telling what is, in spirit and in most details, a true story, though not as connected with such people as the story describes".

"Brave Ben Broughton", written by request for the McClure Syndicate, and a Folk Lore story are the latest from the pen of Mrs. Cox.

"Raymond Kershaw; a Story of Deserved Success", was published by Roberts Brothers in 1888. The story is a touching one commencing in pathos

and ending in heroism ; a lesson to every boy and
girl who, plunged suddenly and unexpectedly into
difficulty, have to face the hard realities of life.
There is an extremely fine passage in this book.
Winthrop, the author of "John Brent", could not
have done it better. It is the description of a mad-
dened bull, "Meadow King", which Paul Potter
might have painted. It needs no comment. Spirited and full of life, every actor in the scene performs
his or her part with a truthfulness which is wonderful. Many a more voluminous writer than Mrs. Cox
has done far less superior work than this truly great
scene exhibits in its dramatic attitudes.

EXTRACT FROM "RAYMOND KERSHAW."

After country fashion, every farmer for miles
around came to look at "Kershaw's new bull".
Without mistake they saw a royal animal. Without a spot to mar his jet-black coat, through which
the great veins were visible like netted cords, his
small, strong, sinewy legs, all muscle and bone,
carried his heavy body as lightly as if he were a
horse, and his flanks and shoulders, when James
pushed up his supple skin with his hand, felt as if
he wore a velvet coat over an iron frame ; his neck,
not too short for grace, was still very heavy and
muscular, with wrinkles like necklaces encircling

it, and his fiery eyes glowed, far apart, under his tight-curled poll, from which those mischievous horns, sharp, long and slightly out-curving, stood in beautiful harmony with the whole outline; and his great lashing tail, with its tasselated end, completed his perfections.

All went well for a fortnight, after which, on a hot Sunday morning all drove off to church leaving Mrs. Kershaw and Mary at home together.

(Mrs. Kershaw, the sweet and tenderly-loved invalid mother, was half-lying in her chair and Mary sat, Bible in hand, on the first step of the piazza near her, when)

Suddenly a roar struck upon their ears with horror; and, filled with one of those blind accesses of rage to which his race is so strangely subject, tearing, bellowing along, up the hillside came Meadow King. As he halted for a breath behind the fence, he was like one's night-dreams of such a creature,—an ideal of pure brute force and wrath. His head tossed high, he gave a prolonged bellow, and leaped the high bars without an effort.

Mary rose without a word, and laying her Bible on Mrs. Kershaw's lap, stood white as the dead to watch him; destroying the delicate things in his way, he ran madly towards the sheds. Mary gave silent thanks that he had not taken to the road. The high gates of the cow-yards stood wide open, and through them he rushed.

"Miss Kershaw, I've got to shut them gates!" said Mary.

"Oh, do n't think of it, Mary!" said Mrs. Kershaw, her hands clasped and trembling. "Are you not afraid?"

"Skeered!" said Mary,—"I'm skeered out of my life; *but them gates has got to be shut!*"

Down in the yard the voice kept up its dreadful din. Mary rushed down the steps like a flash, and as suddenly back again. "Miss Kershaw, would you mind just kissing me *once?*" A quick warm touch on her pale lips, and she was gone; it was all in the space of a long breath.   *   *   Her way was down a slight inclination and her swift, light feet carried her with incredible speed. One terrified glance at the open gate showed her the enemy lashing himself at the farther end of the enclosure, with the scattered dust and leaves rising about him as he pawed the ground. The gates were heavy and wide apart; the right-hand leaf swung shut, and then, darting across the opening, she pushed the left forward and clasped it, and springing up drew down the heavy cross-bar, and the gates were shut!

*   *   "He's in, Miss Kershaw," said Mary, "but the worst is to come! How under the sun can they ketch him? Can you keep still if I go up the road and watch for 'em? They're most sure to drive in by the farm-yard gate if they come Chester way, and if they come upon him unbeknownst, Heaven help 'em!"

"Go Mary, *go*; do n't think about me at all," said Mrs. Kershaw.   *   *   *

"Not until you are in your chair, and promise to stay there, ma'am," said Mary. "Young Doctor's got trouble enough on his hands without your bein' hurt. If you hear Meadow King tearing the gates down, and me a-screechin' my life out, do n't you stir!"

(Mary goes to warn them and stops their entrance. James the farmer takes command. Raymond carries an axe and Bob a stick. They open the gates Mary had closed. The brute rushes forward. At this moment James with a rope he had carried, undertakes to lasso the bull but misses and falls back, facing the foe but pinioned in the angle of a beam and the side-wall; one of the mad King's horns imbedded in the beam, the other projecting in terrible proximity, while the unspeakably angry, brutal face of the beast is only a few inches from his chest.

At this moment, Ray seized his axe.) His hat had fallen off and his face was stern and ghastly white as he watched like a lion his gigantic prey; until coming with long powerful steps close enough to strike, he gave an agonizing look of dread at James, and then brought down one tremendous crashing blow, straight, strong and true, between those cruel horns, and the Meadow King sank like a loosened rock upon the floor, pulling his head loose by his own weight.

David Young.

"Why, as to that, said the engineer,
Ghosts ain't things we are apt to fear,
Spirits don't fool with levers much,
And throttle-valves don't take to such ;
    And as for Jim,—
    What happened to him
Was one-half fact and t'other half whim!"
                  —*Bret Harte.*

David Young is principally known as the reviser and publisher of "The Morristown Ghost" in 1826, but he was also the compiler of the well-known "Farmer's Almanac", published first in 1834, and he wrote a poem of thirty-four pages in two parts, entitled "The Contrast".

The original volume of "The Morristown Ghost" was published in 1792, by whom, it is not certainly known. It gave the names of the "Society of eight", their places of meeting, and all the proceedings of the Society. The copies were bought up and destroyed, says tradition, by the son of one of its members, one lone volume not being obtainable, but this cannot be distinctly traced at present. There was published in 1876, by the Messrs. L. A. and B. H. Vogt, a fac-simile copy of the original history of "The Morristown Ghost" without the names of the original members, "with an appendix compiled from the county records". The following is the title page:

"The Morristown Ghost; an Account of the Beginning, Transactions and Discovery of Ransford Rogers, who seduced many by pretended Hobgoblins and Apparitions and thereby extorted Money from their pockets. In the County of Morris and State of New Jersey, in the Year 1788. Printed for every purchaser—1792".

In the copy of 1826, the title page is as follows:

"The Wonderful History of the Morristown Ghost; thoroughly and carefully revised. By David Young, Newark. Published by Benjamin Olds, for the author. I. C. Totten, Printer, 1826."

The author tells us in his preface he has "very scrupulously followed the sense of the original." He continues: "The truth of this history will not, I presume, be called in question by the inhabitants of Morris and the adjacent counties. The facts are still fresh in the memories of many among us; and some survive still who bore an active part in the scenes herein recorded." He continues: "For the further satisfaction of the distant reader, on this point, I would inform him that I am myself a native of the County of Morris; that I was seven years and seven months old when Rogers first emigrated to this county; and that I well remember hearing people talk of these affairs during their progress. Every reader may rest assured that if the truth of this narrative had been doubtful, I should have taken no pains to rescue it from oblivion."

There seems to have been also another intermediate publication. From an ancient copy of this curious story, found in an old, discolored volume in our Morristown library, in which are compiled papers on various subjects, (among them a "Review on Spiritual Manifestations"), we copy the title page:

"The Morristown Ghost, or Yankee Trick, being a True, Interesting and Strange Narrative. This circumstance has excited considerable laughter and no small degree of surprize. Printed for purchasers, 1814."

The man who conducted the plot was Ransford Rogers, of Connecticut. He was a plausible man who had the power of inspiring confidence, and though somewhat illiterate, was ambitious to be thought learned and pretended, it is said, to possess deep knowledge of "chymistry" and the power to dispel good and evil spirits.

It will be remembered that Washington Irving remarks, in his description of the family portrait gallery, of Bracebridge Hall at twilight, when he almost hears the rustling of the brocade dresses of the ladies of the manor as they step out from their frames,—"There is an element of superstition in the human mind". It seems there had long been a conviction prevailing that large sums of money had been buried during the Revolutionary War by tories and others in Schooley's Mountain, near by. There also seemed to be something of the New England belief in witchcraft throughout the community. Says the Preface of the early volume ; "It is obvious to all who are acquainted with the county of Morris, that the capricious notions of witchcraft have engaged the attention of many of its inhabitants for a number of years and the existence of witches is adopted by the generality of the people." And we read on page 213 of the "Combined Registers of the First Presbyterian Church," a record as follows : "Dr. John Johnes' servant Pompey, d. 17 July, 1833, aet. 81 ; frightened to death by ghosts."

To obtain the treasure of Schooley's Mountain, then, was the occasion of the occurrences related in this story. Two gentlemen who had long been in search of mines, taking a tour through the country in 1788, "providentially," says David Young.

fell in with Rogers at Smith's Clove, and discovered him to be the man they were in search of, and one who could "reveal the secret things of darkness," for they, too, were "covetous of the supposed treasure of Schooley's Mountain."

A society was organized by Ransford which at first numbered "about eight" but afterwards was increased to about forty. His first object was to convince them of the existence of the hidden treasure lying dormant in the earth at Schooley's Mountain. It seems repeated efforts had before been made to obtain the treasure, but all had proved abortive, for whenever they attempted to break the ground, it was said, "there would many hobgoblins and apparitions appear which in a short time obliged them to evacuate the place".

Rogers called a meeting of the eight and "communicated to them the solemnity of the business and the intricacy of the undertaking and the fact that there had been several persons murdered and buried with the money in order to retain it in the earth. He likewise informed them that those spirits must be raised and conversed with before the money could be obtained. He declared he could by his art and power raise these apparitions and that the whole company might hear him converse with them and satisfy themselves there was no deception. This was received with belief and admiration by the whole company without ever investigating whether it was probable or possible. This meeting therefore terminated with great assurance, they all being confident of the abilities, knowledge and powers of Rogers". To confirm the illusion of his supernatural power, Rogers had made chemical compositions of various kinds, of which, "some, by being buried in the earth for many hours, would break and cause great explosions which appeared dismal in the night and would cause great timidity. The company were all anxious to proceed and much elevated with such uncommon curiosities". A night was therefore appointed for the whole company to convene. The scene which the author proceeds to describe is worthy of Washington Irving in his "Legends of Sleepy Hollow", (see page 25 Young's edition, 1826). The night was dark and the circle "illumined only by candles caused a ghastly, melancholy, direful gloom through the woods". The company marched round and round in (concentric) circles as directed, "with great decorum" until suddenly shocked by "a most impetuous explosion from the earth a short distance from them". Flames rose to a considerable height, "illuminating the circumambient atmosphere and presenting to the eye many dreadful objects, from the supposed haunted grove, which were again instantaneously involved in obscurity". Ghosts made their appearance and hideous groans were heard. These were invisible to the rest of the company but conversed with Rogers in their hearing and told of the vast treasures in their possession which they would not resign except under certain conditions, one of which was "every man must deliver to the spirits twelve pounds in money". The procession continued 'till three o'clock in the morning, and "the whole company looked up to Rogers for protection from the raging spirits. This was in the month of November 1788". It will be noticed that the money required had to be advanced in "nothing but silver or gold" for which the paper money circulated in New Jersey could only be exchanged at twenty-five per cent. discount. Yet there was a sort of emulation among them, "who should be the first in delivering the money to the spirits."

A frequent place of meeting for this company was what is now known as the Hathaway house on Flagler street, the first house on the left after entering Flagler street from Speedwell avenue. A little distance back of this house may be seen the stump of a tree beneath which tree, it is said, the money was left for the spirits. Another field used for the midnight marches is behind the Aber house on the Piersonville Road, and still another on the road between Piersonville and Rogers' school house, the location of which is known. Other localities are also known, by old residents, of the events recorded in this story. Mt. Kemble avenue has often been the actual scene of ghostly flittings to and fro as well as of the famous imaginary ride to the Headquarters of "Thankful Blossom". Rogers was in the habit of wrapping himself up in a sheet, going to the house of a certain gentleman in the night, and calling him up by rapping at the doors and windows, and conversing in such sleek disguise that the gentleman thought he was a spirit; ending his conversation also with the words: "I am the spirit of a just man, and am sent to give you information how to proceed, and to put the conducting of it into your hands; I will be ever with you, and give you directions when you go amiss; therefore fear not, but go to Rogers and inform him of your interview with me. Fear not I am ever with you".

It must be remembered that this company, at the first, was composed of the best and most highly honored citizens of Morristown, also that toward the last, "the numbers increased daily of aged, abstemious, (at first material spirits were freely used at the nightly meetings) honest, judicious, simple church members."

What led finally to the discovery of the plot, was, that it was ordained, "a paper of sacred powder, said to be some of the dust of the bodies of the spirits, was to be kept by every member, and to be preserved inviolate. One of the aged members, having occasion to leave home for a short time on some emergency, through forgetfulness left his paper in one of his pockets at home. His wife happened to find it, and out of curiosity, broke it open; but, preceiving the contents, she feared to touch it, lest peradventure it should have some connection with witchcraft. She went immediately to Rev. Mr. ———, the pious clergyman of the congregation for his advice on the subject; who, not knowing its composition, was unwilling to touch it, lest it might have some operation upon him, and knew not what advice to give her. Her husband returning declared she had ruined him forever by breaking open that paper, which increased her anxiety to know its contents. Upon her promising not to divulge anything, he then related to her the whole of their proceedings, whereupon she declared they were serving the devil and it was her duty notwithstanding her promise to put an end to such proceedings. Great disturbance was thereby caused in the company."

It was at the house of one of the members, which is now standing, that Rogers was discovered in the following manner, as the story is told. Rogers, taking his sheet with him, rode, on a certain evening to this house, for the purpose of conversing with the gentleman, as a spirit. Having drank too freely he committed several blunders in his conversation, and was not so careful as usual about the ghostly costume. The good wife, whose suspicions had been aroused, managed to peep and listen dur-

.ing the interview, and after the ghost had left the house she remarked to her husband, says tradition: "My dear, do spirits wear shoe buckles? Those were very like Ransford Rogers' buckles". Rogers' foot-tracks were followed to the fence where his horse was tied, and the tracks of his horse to the house where he lived and hence to another house where he was found. He was apprehended and committed to prison, where he asserted his innocence so persistently that "in a few days he was bailed out", says our author, "by a gentleman, whom I shall call by the name of Compassion." A second time he was apprehended, when "he acknowledged his faults and confessed" the whole matter. He, however, "absconded, and under the auspices of Fortune saved himself by flight from the malice of a host."

So ends the, perhaps, most famous historic ghost story of modern times.

Mrs. Nathaniel Conklin.

(JENNIE M. DRINKWATER.)

Mrs. Conklin has been a voluminous writer of novels and stories, published by Robert Carter & Brothers and by the Presbyterian Board. Before her marriage she was widely known as Miss Jennie M. Drinkwater, and her latest book, "Dorothy's Islands," published in Boston, August, 1892, bears that name of authorship. She has written for many papers and magazines, besides the books she has published, and of these there are twenty and more. Among them are "Tessa Wadsworth's Discipline", a love story of high order and well told; "Rue's Helps", for boys and girls, and "Electa", in which we find a certain quality of naturalness in the people, and the scenes described,—a literary quality which is prominent in Mrs. Conklin's works. "They introduce the reader", says a critic, "to agreeable people, provide an atmosphere which is tonic and healthful and enlist interest in every page." Then there are "The Story of Hannah Marigold"; "Wildwood"; "The Fairfax Girls"; "From Flax to Linen" and "David Strong's Errand", besides others, and the last one published to which we have referred, and from which we shall quote.

Several years ago, Mrs. Conklin being out of health, had her attention called to the special needs of invalids for sympathy from the active world about them, and organized a society, now worldwide and well-known, called the "Shut-In Society". It is an organization of invalids throughout the country, and now extending beyond it, who cheer each other with correspondence, send letters to prisoners in jails and sufferers in hospitals, and do other good work. Nine-tenths of its membership never see each other, but they help make each other's lives to be as cheery as possible in affliction. The amount of comfort and consolation carried by this organization to many a bed-ridden or helpless invalid, is beyond description, and the good that goes out also from those quiet chambers of sickness to the souls who seek them, mostly by *letter*, is greater than would be easily imagined. Mrs. Conklin was president of the Society for four years from its organization in 1885, and it now numbers several thousand members.

We quote from "Dorothy's Islands", Mrs. Conklin's latest book.

Dorothy was a child taken from a New York orphan asylum and adopted by a lighthouse keeper and his wife. She grows up supposing them to be her own father and mother, but the mother and child are antagonistic, and it is impossible for them to attract one another. This peculiarity of nature is very well given in the first chapter.

EXTRACT FROM "DOROTHY'S ISLANDS."

"When I grow up," said Dorothy "I am going to find an island all green and beautiful in winter as well as in summer. All around it the sand will be as golden as sunshine, and the houses—the happy houses—will be hidden away in green things, and flowers of yellow and scarlet and white. And then, father, after I find it, I will come and get you, and we will sing, and learn poems, and do lovely things all day long."

"You are going to do wonderful things when you grow up," replied the amused, tender voice overhead.

"Don't all grown-up people do wonderful things?" questioned child Dorothy.

"I never did," answered the voice, not now either tender or amused.

"No, you never *did*," broke in a woman's voice with harsh force.

"I think father does *beautiful* things," said Dorothy in her warm voice. "He brought the sea-bird home to me, and we loved it so, but you threw it off with its wounded wing."

"Let nature take care of her own things," responded the voice that had nothing of love in its quality.

"I'm nature's thing," Dorothy laughed; "father said so to-day. He said I was made out of nature and poetry."

"It's he who puts the poetry in you; some day I'll send those poetry books adrift, and then you will both find something practical in your finger ends."

The child looked at the chubby ends of her brown fingers. Her nine-year-old hands, under her mother's sharp teaching, had learned to do many practical things. The only "practical thing" she loathed—and that was her own name for it—was mending Cousin Jack's pea-jacket.

One room in the lighthouse was packed with boxes containing her father's books. The "poetry box" was the only one that had been opened since their stay on the island.

"It was one of your father's beautiful things to strand us on this desert island. I told him I wouldn't come."

"But you *did*," said the child.

"It's the last time he will have his own way," remarked the woman, with the heavy frown that marred her handsome face.

"Oh, don't say that!" cried Dorothy distressed. "I never like your way."

"You have got to like my way some day, miss,

or it will be the worse for one of us. . Don't hang any longer around your father; poetry enough has oozed out of him to spoil you already; go and pick those beans over, and put them in soak for to-morrow—a quart, mind you, and pick them over clean."

* * * * * *

She liked to pick beans when her father sat near reading aloud to her. He had promised to read to-night "How the water comes down from Lodore," but she knew her mother's mood too well to hope for such a pleasure to-night.

When her mother was cross, she wasn't willing for anybody to have anything.

But she couldn't take away what she had learned of it; the child hugged herself with the thought repeating gleefully :—

"Then first came one daughter,
 And then came another,
To second and third
 The request of their brother,
And to hear how the water
 Comes down at Lodore,
With its rush and its roar—"

"Dorothy, stop!" commanded her mother. "That muttering makes me wild. It sounds like a lunatic."

Dorothy's mouth shut itself tight ; the flash of defiance from the big brown eyes her mother missed; her father's observant eyes noted it. There was always a sigh in his heart for Dorothy, for her naughtiness, and for the misery she was growing up to. The misery was as inevitable as the growing up. Once in his agony he had prayed the good Father to take the child before her heart was rent, or his own.

After the gleeful music ceased the chubby fingers moved wearily, the brown head drooped; there were tears as well as sleep in the eyes that seemed made to hold nothing but sunshine.

(Dorothy is in bed for the night.)

"Will you keep the door open so I can hear voices?" pleaded Dorothy.

"Why child, what ails you?" said the mother.

"The wind ails me; and it is so black, black, black out over the water. When I find my island there shall be sunshine on the sea."

"But night *has* to come."

"Perhaps there will be stars there," said hopeful Dorothy.

"You may learn a Bible verse to-morrow,— 'There shall be no night there.'"

"'I'll say it now: 'There shall be no night there.' Where *is* 'there'?"

But her mother had left her to her new Bible verse and the candle-light; and Dorothy went to sleep, hoping "there" did not mean heaven, for then what *would* she do when she was sleepy?

Mrs. Catharine L. Burnham.

A valuable contributor to the literature for children and young people, is Mrs. Burnham. Her volume of "Bible Stories in Words of One Syllable", has been of great use and influence and has no doubt led to the writing of other historical narratives in the same manner.

Count Tolstoi gives a most interesting account of his own experience in the use of the Bible in teaching children. He says "I tried reading the Bible to them", speaking of the children in his peasant's school, "and it took complete possession of them. They grew to love the book, love study and love me. For the purpose of opening a new world to a pupil and of making him love knowledge before he has knowledge, there is no book like the Bible."

Mrs. Burnham has also written a number of children's story-books which have been warmly received and still continue to please and benefit the young. Among them are "Ernest"; "The Story of Maggie" and the three volumes of the "Can and Can't Series"; "I Can"; "I Can't", and "I'll Try". "Ernest" is quite a wonderful little book and has done much good among a large class of children. Mr. A. D. F. Randolph, the New York publisher, who took it through several editions, gave it high praise to a friend just before the last edition, about three years ago, and Rev. Dr. Tyng the elder, late of St. George's Church, New York, gave it also very high praise.

We do not always fully realize that a peculiar talent is required for this department in literature. In talking, some years ago, with a young man who has now become an important editor in New York, he said : " It is my greatest ambition to be a good and interesting author of children's books ; not only because it requires the best writing and the best thought, but because no literature has a more extended influence and involves higher responsibilities."

In addition to these volumes, Mrs. Burnham has for many years, been an occasional contributor to the *Churchman, Christian Union* and other important papers.

The following extract is selected :

EXTRACT FROM "I'LL TRY."

CHAPTER VIII.

Society.

"Our Daisy is a singular girl," said Mrs. Bell to her husband the evening after Mrs. Lane's party, as they sat alone over the library fire, after all the young people had retired, and fell to talking about their children, as parents will.

"Is she? I think most parents would be glad to have a daughter as 'singular.'"

"Yes, I knew you would say that; and I appreciate her as highly as you do; but nevertheless, sometimes I am puzzled to know what to do with her. If she gets an idea into that quiet little head of hers, it is hard to modify it."

"Well, what is it now?"

"It's just this. I don't believe she will ever be willing to go out anywhere, or even have company at home. I proposed to her to-day that we should have a little company next week, and she looked absolutely pained, and said, 'O, mamma, if we could get along without it, I should be so glad—unless you wish it very much. Or, perhaps, I could stay up stairs.' I was quite provoked for the moment, and said, 'No, indeed, you couldn't. I should insist on your entertaining our friends.' And then she was so sorry she had offended me. She is so good and conscientious, that I can't bear to thwart her; and yet I am sure it will not be good for her to shut herself up entirely."

"Oh, well dear," said Mr. Bell, who had the most utter confidence in his wife's ability to train her children, as he might well have, "she will get over it in time. Let her go out a little and she will soon learn to like it."

"No, I am afraid not. Everything she does is done on principle, and unless I can make society a matter of principle, I am afraid she will never enter into it at all, her diffidence makes it a positive pain to her to meet strangers."

"Well, get a principle into it, then, somehow," said Mr. Bell. "You can manage it; you understand all these matters. I am sure Daisy is just like you in requiring a principle for everything."

"She is not a bit like me," said Mrs. Bell; but she could not help smiling nevertheless, and the conversation turned to something else. But the mother, who was in real difficulty about this matter, carried her perplexities where she always did, to the throne of grace, and there obtained light to show her how to act. She knew that nothing in her children's lives was unimportant in the eyes of the Heavenly Father, and prayed for wisdom to guide her young daughter aright at this important time of her life.

The next time that Daisy brought her work basket to her mother's room, for a "good quiet sit-down," as she expressed it, Mrs. Bell resolved to open the subject that was on her mind; but the young girl anticipated her design by saying, "Now, mamma, before we begin the second volume of our Macauley (how tempting it looks and what lovely readings we will have!) I want to ask you something."

"Well, dear?"

"I know I troubled you yesterday when you spoke about having company, dear mamma. I was so sorry afterwards; but if you knew how I dread it, I don't think you would blame me. I have been thinking about it a great deal since, and now I want to ask you a question and get one of your real good answers—a *settling* answer, mamma. Do you think it is *my duty* to go into company? Now begin, please, and tell me all about it;" and Daisy took up her work and assumed the attitude of a listener, as though she had referred her question to an oracle, and was waiting for a response.

The mother smiled a happy and gratified smile before she answered. It was very pleasant to her to see how her sweet daughter deferred to her opinion; and kissing the fair cheek she said: "I can't answer you in one word, darling. What do you mean by 'going into company?' Of course you know that I have no desire to see you absorbed in a round of parties, or even going often to companies."

"Oh, I know that, mamma; I mean quiet parties, such as you and papa go to; reading and talking parties, and big sewing societies and musicals."

"You mean going anywhere out of your own family?"

"Yes'm, that is just it. I am so happy at home. I have plenty to do, and all I want to enjoy. With you and papa and Nelly and our pet Lucy, and the boys coming home Sundays, what could one wish for more? I am perfectly happy, mamma."

"And would you never care to make acquaintances, then—to make and receive calls?"

"Oh, no 'm. I dislike calls of all things, except, of course, to go and see Mrs. Lane, for she asked me to come and see her, mamma, and to go over to Fanny's to play duets, and to a few other places."

"You are a singular girl, Daisy."

"I know I am," said Daisy, earnestly, dropping her work, "and that's the very reason why I think it's just as well for me to stay at home. Now, last night, I'm sure there wasn't a girl there thought of such a thing as being frightened, except me; but I didn't really enjoy the last part very much; it was so disagreeable being among so many strangers; and even during the reading, I wished myself back in our old composition room, where I could hear Mrs. Lane without being dressed up, and being surrounded by girls dressed even more than I was."

"And would you like, then, always to live retired at home?"

"Indeed I should, mamma! and I can't see why I may not. We are told not to love the world," said Daisy in a lower tone. "Why is it not better to keep out of it entirely?"

"I will tell you, darling, why it is not," said

Mrs. Bell, seriously. "Because our Master did not do so, and we cannot follow His example perfectly, if we do."

"Was it not the poor and sick that He visited, mamma, chiefly?"

"Yes, dear, and so it should be with us; but He visited, too, the rich and the high. He seems to have gone wherever His presence was desired, to make that presence felt by all classes of people, and we ought to imitate Him in this as in all other things."

"Do you think we can do that?"

"Yes, I think we can in some measure. At any rate, I am sure we ought to try. Suppose, Daisy, that every one adopted your rule — that every house was a castle, and no one in it cared for anybody outside. What a selfish world this would be! Our Christian love would be limited to our own family."

"But I would visit the poor, mamma."

"Yes, and that is by far the most important. But, dear, you have gifts of mind and heart and education that enable you to do good in other ways than in ministering to the poor and the ignorant. There are other hearts to reach, over whom you can have even greater influence, because they sympathize more entirely with you. You can show forth the love of Christ, and set a Christian example in your own sphere, darling, where you were born and brought up, and it would be wrong for my daughter to hide the talents God has given her under a bushel, and not to care for anyone or anything outside of these four walls."

"Daisy had left her seat and taken her favorite place at her mother's feet, and now looking up into her face, she said, earnestly, "You are right, mamma, as you always are. But poor me! I would rather face an army, it seems to me, than a roomful of people. I know what you are going to say—all the more my duty—and I shall try with all my might."

"My darling, in every roomful of people there are some whom you can cheer and please; and even Christ pleased not Himself. Think of that, and it will give you strength to overcome your timidity. You can serve your Master in some way, be sure of it. And you can learn much from others. You would not develop all round, but would be a one-sided character, if you had only books and your own family for companions."

"Mamma, let us have the company. I am ashamed that I have been so cowardly. You shall see how hard I will try."

Hon. John Whitehead.

Our grave and reverend scholar and historian, taking his place later among *Historians*, has surprised and delighted us all by appearing suddenly in a new character, writing a very lively, graphic, and, of course, instructive story for boys; "A Fishing Trip to Barnegat", which we find in the *St. Nicholas* for August, 1892. The following is an extract:

FROM "A FISHING TRIP TO BARNEGAT."

"Now this fish of yours, Jack," said the uncle, "is not only called the toad-fish and the oyster-fish, but, sometimes, the grunting toad-fish. There are species of it found all over the world, but this is the regular American toad-fish.

"This fish of mine is called the weakfish. Notice its beautiful colors, brownish blue on its back, with irregular brown spots, the sides silvery, and the belly white. It grows from one to three feet long and is a very sharp biter. When one takes the hook, there is no difficulty in knowing when to pull in. Why it is called the weakfish, I do not know, unless because when it has been out of the water its flesh softens and soon becomes unfit for food. When eaten soon after it is caught, it is very good."

Just as Uncle John finished his little lecture, an exclamation from Will, who had baited with a piece of the crab, and dropped his line into the water, attracted their attention. Not quite so impetuous as Jack, he landed his prize more carefully, and stood looking at it with wonder, hardly knowing what to say. At last he called out:

"Well, what have I caught?"

It was a beautiful fish, though entirely different from Uncle John's. It had a small head and the funniest little tail that ever was seen. Its back was of a bright, brown color, but its belly was almost pure white: it was quite round and flat, with a rough skin.

"Turn him over on his back, and rub him gently," said the captain. "Do it softly, and watch him."

Will complied and gently rubbed him. Immediately the fish began swelling and as Will continued the rubbing it grew larger and larger until Will feared that the fish would burst its little body.

"Well," he said, "I never saw anything like that, Captain! Do tell me what this is."

"This we call, here in Barnegat, the balloon-fish. It is elsewhere called the puffer, swell-fish, and globe-fish. One kind is called the sea-porcupine, because of its being covered with short, sharp spines. It is of no value for food."

Jack thought his time had come to catch another prodigy, and when his hook had been re-baited by the skipper, he dropped his line into the water, and was soon rewarded by another bite. Using more caution this time, he landed his fish securely on deck instead of over the sail, and exclaimed :

"Wonders will never cease ! I do n't know what I 've got now, but I suppose that Captain John can tell !"

Mrs. John King Duer.

Mrs. Duer, whose family as well as herself has long been associated with Morristown, has published, in Morristown, in 1880, a short story entitled " The Robbers of the Woods, by Grandmother". It is a pretty, fascinating tale for children, in which the winsome innocence of two loving boys charm away all the cruelty of the ' Robbers of the Woods". It is only thirty minutes reading and yet the story leaves after it an impression of the tender beauty of childhood.

The following extract is expressive both of the

touching pathos and of a certain nicety of description which belongs pre-eminently to Mrs. Duer.

FROM "THE ROBBERS OF THE WOODS."

The sun was up and the room quite light when Carl opened his eyes at the touch of a hand on his shoulder. "It is daylight now my little man and we must be getting you on your way home ere long, but first come and get some breakfast." The boys were soon dressed, and after saying a short prayer in which they thanked God for his goodness in making the robbers so kind to them, they opened the door and found themselves again in the hall and with a substantial meal before them. Having eaten enough and all being ready, the man who found them in the woods now came near, and putting his large brown hand gently on Carl's arm, he said, "My boys, before I can open that door you must let me tie a cloth over your eyes, and consent to let it be there till we tell you to take it off. No harm shall come to you, for I myself am going to take you through the woods and not leave you till I put you on the road that leads to your mother's door." When Eddie first heard that his eyes were to be blindfolded, he began to cry and clung tightly to his brother, fearing to look about him " lest one of the robbers should be there to cut my poor little head off," as he whispered to Carl. But when Carl said, "Eddie, you must be good and believe what these men say. They are not going to harm us and we are going straight home to mother. See I will put the bandage on your eyes myself, and will sit close to you and hold your hand all the time." He then tied a clean handkerchief, which the man gave him, close over Eddie's eyes and allowed the man to do the same to him. They then were led out of the hall.

They heard the heavy door close after them, and felt the cool, morning air blow over their faces, then the boys knew they were outside the stone wall. Soon they were lifted up, and put in a wagon, and a man's voice close to them said: "Boys, I am going to put your little cart in the wagon too, so that you may get it home safely." When all was ready, the wagon began to move away, and as they drove off, they heard the voices of the robbers calling after them, "good-bye, brave boys, we wish you good luck."

Little Eddie sat quite still beside Carl; as they drove away he held tight fast to his brother, and neither of them spoke a word.

They were astonished at all they had seen and heard, while they were in the robbers' castle, and now they were once more in the free and open woods, they could not do as they pleased, but sat with their eyes bound up, not knowing where they were going. Carl did not doubt the words of the men who told him that no harm should come to him, but at times he had to comfort and assure poor little Eddie, for he sat trembling with fear. After they had driven several miles, and the man who was with them had answered their questions as to how far they were from home now, the wagon stopped and the man got out saying, "Now boys, you are on the road that leads direct to your home and I am going to leave you very soon, but before I go you must promise me not to untie the bandage from your eyes, till you hear a long whistle, which will blow from my horn, after leaving you; you will then undo the bandage, and find something beside you to take to your mother." Saying this, the man took the boys from the wagon, and setting them carefully down, he lifted their cart out also and shaking hands with the still astonished boys, and wishing them good-bye, he sprang into the wagon and they heard him drive rapidly along the road.

They sat for some time very quiet, until the loud, long whistle from a distant horn told them the time of their captivity was at an end, and hastily tearing off the bandage from their eyes they looked eagerly around on all sides. Not a vestige of the wagon could be seen. It had been turned just at the spot where they had been left, and whether it went back the same way, or took another road, they never knew. But what was their surprise, when they turned to look for their own little cart, to see beside it a pile of wood cut just so as to fit in, and on top of the pile a package containing many pieces of money in bright shining gold. This was the present they were told to "take back to their mother." Carl's heart gave a great bound of joy, for he knew how sorely his dear mother needed help, and he knew now that these men were her friends, and would never harm them.

They had scarcely recovered from their surprise, and had just begun to load the little cart with the well-cut wood, when sounds of voices were heard, and the boys could distinctly hear their own names called. They knew it was the neighbors who were out searching for them, and soon saw them coming out in the open space where they stood.

* * * * * *

The neighbors were heartily glad to find the boys safe and well, and surprised at the wonderful things they had to tell of all that had befallen them.

Madame de Meisner.

Many Morristonians will remember well Miss Sophie Radford, first as a little girl, living in the old Doughty House on Mt. Kemble avenue, then owned and occupied by her grandfather, Mr. Joseph Lovell, who purchased it of the Doughty estate and lived in it for a long period of time. Afterwards, Miss Radford is recalled as a charming girl and a belle in Washington Society, whence her father, Rear Admiral Radford, U. S. N., went from here, and where she met and married the handsome and elegant Secretary of the Russian Legation, M. de Meisner. Their marriage was performed first in the Episcopal church and afterwards with the ceremony of the Greek church, at her father's house, it being a law of Russia, with regard to every officer of the Empire, that the marriage ceremony of the Greek church shall be always used, a law like "that of the Medes and Persians, that altereth not".

Both M. and Mme. de Meisner were in Morristown a few years ago and met many friends. It is since then, that they went to Russia and there, after a delightful reception and experience, Mme. de Meisner was inspired with the idea of writing "The Terrace of Mon Désir".

It was published in the fall of 1886, by Cuppies,

Upham & Co., of Boston. A curious fact about this book is that it was Mme. de Meisner's first appearance in the field of literature and she had never before contributed even the briefest article to the press.

"The Terrace of Mon Désir" is a pretty love story, gracefully written. The opening scenes are laid in Peterhoff, near St. Petersburg, and where is the summer residence of the Czar. The author thus finds an opportunity of describing a charming social life among the higher classes, with which, though an American girl, but married to a Russian, she seems to be and is perfectly at home, having it is evident taken kindly to the new and interesting situations of her adopted country. The characters are delightfully and simply natural and the combinations are vivacious and sparkling, by which quality American women are distinguished, and in which characteristic foreigners find an indescribable charm.

Mme. de Meisner herself has a bright animation in conversation. Some authors talk well only on paper, but to this observation the author of "The Terrace of Mon Désir" is a marked exception, as all those who know her graceful, easy flow of language will recognize.

The continuity of the story forbids an extract.

Miss Isabel Stone.

Miss Stone who has long lived and moved in our society, has written, beside the poem already given, many bright papers and stories for children which have been published in various magazines and journals, among them *The Observer; Life; Little Ones in the Nursery*, edited by Oliver Optic ; *The Press*, of Philadelphia ; *The Troy Press* and *The Christian Weekly*. These stories and other writings were published under an assumed name.

In 1885, she published a very clever booklet entitled Who Was Old Mother Hubbard ? A Modern Sermon from the *Portsmouth* (Eng.) *Monitor* and a Refutation by an M. M. C., New York ; G. P. Putnam Sons.

This booklet had a very large sale and went through several editions. The story of this publication is interesting. "The Modern Sermon" appeared anonymously, first in one of our prominent magazines. It was written in England and traced to its origin. This was read at a meeting of the Mediæval Club, (a literary club of some celebrity in Morristown), at the house of Mr. John Wood, one of its members. Miss Stone was at once inspired to write the "Refutation"; which was read at her own house by Mr. John Wood, arrayed in characteristic costume for the occasion. (For the benefit of those who may not know him, we may add that Mr. John Wood is one of Morristown's best readers and amateur actors.)

We give the "Refutation" which is a clever dissection of the subject. As "A Modern Sermon" illustrates the method upon which some Parsons Construct their Discourses", so "A Refutation" appears " in the Combative, Lucid and Argumentative Style of Some Others".

REFUTATION.

MY DEAR HEARERS: It is my purpose this evening to give to you the result of many hours of thought and consultation of various authors regarding the subject to which our attention has been lately called.

While I hesitate to engage in the controversial spirit of the day, I feel it my duty to expound to you the truth and to unmask any heresy that may be gaining ground.

The discourse to which I allude was upon the text,—

"Old Mother Hubbard went to the cupboard,
 To get her poor dog a bone ;
But when she got there the cupboard was bare,
 And so the poor dog got none."

I propose to prove to you this evening that all its arguments were founded on false premises; that the *whole picture* drawn of the subject of our text—viz., old Mother Hubbard—was diametrically the reverse of the reality; in short, to give *a complete refutation of the text* to all those who listened to those first erroneous statements.

Firstly, Old Mother Hubbard was *not* a widow.

I am at a loss to understand why our learned brother should so have drawn upon his imagination as to represent her as such, when, as I shall endeavor to set before you *conclusively* this evening, it is *distinctly* stated in the text that she was the wife of an *ogre!*

My friends, in those days *men* and *husbands* were designated by the term "poor dog;" and, indeed, the lightest scholar knows that the term has descended to the present day and is often appropriated by a man himself under certain existing circumstances.

Now, that this "poor dog" of a husband was an ogre is abundantly proved by the fact that Mother Hubbard provided for him bones.

Yes! bones! my friends; but—*they—were—human*—bones!

Deep research has convinced me of this fact. I find that in those days ogres did not catch and kill their own meat, as is commonly supposed. They were but human, my friends, and, like the rest of humanity, preferred rather to purchase labor than perform it. They, therefore, employed their own individual butchers; but, with rare wisdom, they chose some carnivorous animal to supply their table.

In proof of this, we come, *Secondly*, to the word cupboard, as mentioned in the text,—

"Old Mother Hubbard went to the cupboard,
To get her poor dog a bone."

This word cupboard is in our present version misspelt, owing to some fault in copying from the original, and thus is rendered c-u-p-b-o-a-r-d; but the word properly should be spelt c-u-b-b-e-d. This is a compound word, derived from cub—a young bear—and bed, or deposit, as we speak of the bed of a river.

This was a *bone* deposit—a place where the ogre's food was deposited by the cub.

A young cub was a less expensive butcher than a bear, as nowadays labor is cheaper from the young aspirant than from the assured professional. Therefore they were the usual employees.

But this ogre, though evidently in the habit of employing a cub in this department, had now become dissatisfied and procured the more satisfactory service of an old bear; for, if you will carefully examine the text, you will see that the meaning is *obvious*, for, as though to insure all its readers from misunderstanding, you will see that it is *distinctly* stated that—

"The cub-bed was *bear*."

Now we come *Thirdly* to the word "none."

"And so the poor dog got none."

This word in the original stands for two things —first, n-o-n-e, meaning nothing, which was the heretical sense deducted by my opponent, and the other and correct sense being n-u-n — a woman with black veil, generally of tender years; and Mother Hubbard, who intended to supply her lord's table with one small bone, found that instead the bear had secured the bones of a *whole nun!*

Fourthly and lastly, it is clear from the words "poor dog," that the ogre was poor, but *not* Mother Hubbard.

No, my hearers, *evidently* she was *rich*, evidently *she* held the purse-strings, and the ogre had stealthily supplied his table with a luxury, and his house with a steward, for which he individually was incapable of providing the means.

This is *clearly* the fact from the words of the text, for you will notice that it was *when* she got there—not *before*, but *when* she got there, that she found the change that had been made in the household arrangements.

And then, doubtless, ensued a scene such as some "poor dogs" nowadays understand only too well!

And now, my friends, we come to the moral. It is *not* to beware of widows as my opponent tried to prove, but for you, my hearers, on one hand, to beware of marrying a poor but extravagant dog, and you, on the other, to beware of marrying a rich but penurious wife.

Augustus Wood.

Charles P. Sherman.

Miss Helen M. Graham.

It is scarcely necessary to state the fact that Mr. Augustus Wood is a native of Morristown, belonging as he does to a very old and well-known family, or that he is the author of a little volume entitled "Cupid on Crutches". This is a summer story of life at Narragansett Pier and makes one of a group of light novels which we will give in succession

"A BACHELOR'S WEDDING TRIP."

BY "HIMSELF."

"Himself" we recognize as Mr. Charles Sherman, then a bachelor, who cleverly dedicates the book in these words : "To the Unmarried : as Instance of the Bliss which may be Theirs, and to the Married, as Reminiscent of THE trip, These Threaded Sketches are Fraternally Dedicated by the Author".

The third of the group is

GUY HERNDON
OR
"A TALE OF GETTYSBURG."

BY "ELAYNE."

Elayne, we know, is Miss Helen M. Graham, one of Morristown's Society girls who spends much of her time in New York.

This "Tale of Gettysburg" is the first venture of Miss Graham into the field of literature. Her choice of subject indicates that she is in touch with the growing realization among our novelists of how wide and fruitful a field is presented to them in the events of our civil war. The few graphic pictures already given by them of the social and other conditions of those stirring times, will be more and more valued by the present generation, and by those to come, as the years go on.

Other Novelists and Story Writers.

Among the poets, we have already mentioned as writers also of stories, many of them for children and young people,—

Mrs. M. Virginia Donaghe McClurg,
Miss Emma F. R. Campbell,
Miss Hannah More Johnson,
And *Mr. William T. Meredith,*
the last being the author of a summer novel, "Not of Her Father's Race".

Rev. James M. Freeman, D. D.,
who, in addition to his editorial work and more serious writing, has published more than thirty small juvenile works, written under the name of "Robin Ranger", and which are all very great favorites with children, and

Mrs. Julia McNair Wright,
who, besides her many volumes on many subjects, has written novels, among them, "A Wife Hard Won," published by Lippincott, and a large number of stories for young people, found in many Sunday School libraries, as well as stories on the subject of Temperance, which are found in the collected libraries of Temperance societies.

TRANSLATORS.

Mrs. Adelaide S. Buckley.

Mrs. Buckley, who has already been numbered among our *Poets*, has translated a German story called "Sought and Found" from the original work of Golo Raimund, which has passed to its second edition. The translator says, in her four line preface, "This romance was translated because of its rare simplicity and beauty, and is published that those who have not seen it in the original may enjoy it also."

One never takes up these charming little German stories without exclaiming, no other country-people ever write in the same sweet, simple way! The reason is evident to those who have lived among

Germans and experienced their unaffected hospitality. There is a peculiar simplicity of home life even among the nobility. A friend says: "I so well remember now, a lovely morning visit, in particular, to a little, gentle German lady in her beautiful drawing-room which contained the treasures of centuries. No one, I am sure, could have helped being struck by her gentle simplicity and unaffected courtesy. She came in dressed in the plainest of black dresses, a white apron tied around her waist, and on her head the simplest of morning caps. But her sweet German language,— how beautiful it seemed, as in the low, musical voice which bespoke her breeding, she talked of her own German poets; of Walther von der Vogelweide and the great Goethe and Schiller, of Auerbach and Richter and modern story writers." Afterwards, in speaking of the charm and beauty of such simplicity, the friend added, "Yes, and she belongs to one of the oldest noble, hereditary families of Germany, and carries the sixteen quarterings upon the family shield, which, to those who understand German heraldry, means the longest unmixed German descent. We could not help contrasting such quiet manners with many of the artificial assumptions and the aggressive boldness found that winter in Dresden." Therefore we always hail with pleasure translations of these stories of German life among all classes. Though to translate requires no creative power, translating is in some respects more difficult than creating, for the reason that to translate demands a quick comprehension and intuitive discernment of the spirit of a foreign language, of the conception of the writer and of the national life which the language embodies. And we must remember that it is in the power of interpretation that woman especially excels.

This little story is essentially well rendered, with the animation and vivacity of the original, and it has great merit in preserving its German spirit, that sentiment which is so marked and so unlike any other people.

What Dr. Johnson said of translation had a ring of truth as had all his mighty utterances, namely : " Philosophy and science may be translated perfectly and history, so far as it does not reach oratory, but poetry can never be translated without losing its most essential qualities." It would seem then that to know the poetry of a people one must read it in the original language, which every one surely cannot do. Mrs. Buckley however, recognizing this subtle quality of the poetry of a language, has left the little verses of the story untouched, wisely giving the translation at the bottom of the page. A very lovely translation it is however and after a short passage from the book, "Sought and Found", we shall give another poetic translation of the poem " Im Arm der Liebe", by Georg Scheurlin.

The following is a short passage from the story:

EXTRACT FROM "SOUGHT AND FOUND."

TRANSLATED FROM THE GERMAN OF GGLO RAIMUND.

Upon the table lay Veronica's picture, which in the meantime had been sent. The flowers, painted by her hand, appeared to him like a friendly greeting. He took it up and regarded it a long time; then, followed a sudden inspiration, he wrote upon the back:

(Here follows the German verse, the translation below:)

> Thy merry jest is gentle as the May,
> Thy tender heart a lily of the dell;
> Fragrant as the rose thy inmost soul,
> Thy wondrous song a sweet-toned bell.

As in sport he subscribed his name; and then, as this homage, which had so long existed in his heart, suddenly expressed in words, stood before him, black upon white it was to him as if another had opened his eyes and he must guard the newly discovered secret. He placed the picture in a portfolio, in order to lock it in his writing-desk, and his eye fell upon the journal which had so singularly come into his hands. He laid the portfolio beside it. Did they not belong together? Did not the mysterious author resemble Veronica?

Like a revelation it flashed over him and so powerfully affected his imagination that the blood mounted hotly to his temples, and, in spite of the severe cold, he threw open the window that he might have more air.

"If it were she!" thought he; restlessly striding up and down, and yet exultant that he had now found a trace which could be followed.

THE ARM OF LOVE.

TRANSLATED FROM THE GERMAN OF GEORG SCHEURLIN.

A young wife sits by a cradle nest,
Her fair boy smiling on her breast ;
In the quiet room draws on the night,
And she rocks and sings by the soft lamplight ;
On mother bosom the rest is deep ;
In the arm of love—so fall asleep.

In the cool vale, 'neath sunny sky,
We sit alone, my own and I ;
A song of joy wells in my breast,
Ah, heart to heart, how sweet the rest !
The brooklets ripple, the breezes sweep ;
In the arm of love—so fall asleep.

From the churchyard tolls the solemn bell,
For the pilgrim has finished his journey well ;
Here lays he down the staff, long pressed ;
In the bosom of earth, how calm the rest !

Above the casket the earth they heap;
In the arm of love—so fall asleep.

Miss Margaret P. Garrard.

It must be a poet who shall translate a poet and so naturally we find Miss Garrard as well as Mrs. Buckley, already in our group of "Poets".

The difficulty of reproducing well, in metrical forms, thoughts from the poetry of another language, is so great, that we give with pride the translation of Miss Garrard of one of Goethe's sweet wild-wood songs, in which he excelled.

THE BROOK.

TRANSLATED FROM THE GERMAN OF GOETHE.

Little brook, where wild flowers drink,
  Rushing past me, swift and clear—
Thoughtful stand I on the brink—
  "Where's thy home ? Whence com'st thou here ?"

I come from out the rock's dark gloom,
  My way lies o'er the flower-strewn plain;
And in my bosom there is room
  To mirror heaven's sweet face again.

Pain, sorrow, trouble have I none;
  I wander onward, blithe and free—
He who has called me from the stone
  Will to the end my guardian be.

Other Translators.

Hon. John Whitehead has translated considerably from the French and German, having used these translations in several of his writings, but individually they have not been published. He aided in translating the "History of the War of the Rebellion in North Western Virginia", which was written in German by Major F. J. Mangold, of the Prussian Army. The book was a monograph published by Major Mangold in Germany, but never published here. This translation was largely used by Judge Whitehead in his published articles on "The Fitz John Porter Case."

Miss Karch, a German lady long a resident of

Morristown, was also a translator, but it has not been possible to procure the details of her work. It is nine years since Miss Karch returned to Heilbronn, Germany, where she is now living. For the fifteen years preceding her return, she had been a resident of Morristown as a teacher of the German and French languages. Says a friend: "She was a conscientious, accomplished and true woman, intensely loyal as a true German, self-sacrificing, patient and kindly generous in bestowing her softening and refining influences, upon those who needed them."

LEXICOGRAPHER.

Charlton T. Lewis, LL. D.

The great work of Dr. Lewis is his Latin Dictionary, published in 1879, as "Lewis and Short's Revision of Andrew's Freund". This is recognized as the most useful and convenient modern Latin-English Lexicon.

Quite recently Dr. Lewis has brought out a Latin Dictionary for *schools*, which is not an abridgement of the larger work, but an original work on a definite plan of its own. "It has the prestige", says a critic, "of having been accepted in advance by the Clarendon Press of Oxford, and adopted among their publications in place of a similar lexicon projected and begun by themselves. Thus it may be said to be published in England under the official patronage of the University of Oxford".

Dr. Lewis also published in 1886 "A History of Germany From the Earliest Times".

He ranks among the first Greek scholars of the country, having been for many years a member of the well-known Greek Club of New York, of which the late Rev. Howard Crosby D. D. was pioneer and president.

He also ranks high as a Shakesperian scholar and critic, and as a poet. From his poem of "Telemachus", some lines are transcribed among the poetical selections of this book.

Dr. Lewis has made a profound study of the subject of prison reform and has been, and is, an active worker in that direction, in the New York Prison Association, being on the Executive Board of that Association.

In Stedman and Hutchinson's "Library of American Literature", Dr. Lewis is represented by a paper on the " Influence of Civilization on Duration of Life".

HISTORIANS
AND
ESSAYISTS.

William Cherry.

ANCIENT CHRONICLER.

William Cherry is a veritable "Old Mortality", judging from a unique volume found in the Morristown Library. This ancient sexton of the First Presbyterian Church, was a true wanderer among graves. It is said by those who remember, or who had it from their fathers, that the old house adjoining the Lyceum Building is the one in which Mr. Cherry lived and no doubt reflected on the uncertainty of life, while he compiled his melancholy record.

The following is the title of the old volume published by him and printed by Jacob Mann in the year 1806:

"Bill of Mortality : Being a Register of all the Deaths, which have occurred in the Presbyterian and Baptist Congregations of Morristown, New Jersey ; For Thirty-Eight Years Past, Containing (with but few exceptions) the Cause of every Disease. This Register, for the First Twenty-Two Years, was kept by the Rev. Dr. Johnes, since which Time, by *William Cherry*, the Present Sexton of the Presbyterian Church at Morris-Town".

"Time brushes off our lives with sweeping wings."— *Hervey*.

Some of the causes of disease given are as follows :

"Decay of Nature"; " Teething"; " Old Age"; "A Swelling"; " Mortification"; "Sudden"; "Phrenzy"; ."Casual"; " Poisoned by Night-Shade Berries"; " Lingering Decay", &c. We find no mention of " Heart Failure".

This curious and valuable volume needs no further comment.

Rev. Joseph F. Tuttle, D. D.

To the Rev. Joseph F. Tuttle, D. D. we are indebted for the invaluable chronicles of events, of the life of the people, and of Washington and his army in Morristown during the Revolutionary period. Apparently, all this interesting story, in its details, would have been lost to us, except for his indefatigable zeal in collecting from the lips of living men and women, the eye-witnesses of what he relates, or from their immediate descendants, the story he gives us with such pictorial charm and beauty, warm from his own imaginary dwelling in the period of which he writes.

For the following sketch of this author we are indebted to the historian who follows, the Hon. Edmund D. Halsey.

Rev. Joseph F. Tuttle, D. D., son of Rev. Jacob and Elizabeth Ward Tuttle, was born at Bloomfield, N. J., March 12th, 1818. Fitted for college principally at Newark Academy, he graduated at Marietta College with first honors of his class in 1841. He entered Lane Seminary and was licensed to preach in 1844. In 1847 he was called to pastorate of church at Rockaway, N. J., as associate to his aged father-in-law, Rev. Dr. Barnabas King. He left Rockaway to accept the Presidency of Wabash College in 1862, and, after thirty years in that position, resigned in 1892.

During his fifteen years in this county he was a most voluminous and acceptable writer for the press — writing for the *Observer*, *Evangelist*, *Tribune* and other papers. But he is principally remembered more for his work as a local historian. He wrote, "The Early History of Morris County"; "Biographical Sketch of Gen. Winds"; "Washington in Morris County"; "History of the Presbyterian Church at Rockaway"; "Life of William Tuttle"; "Revolutionary Fragments", (a series of articles published in *The Newark Sentinel of Freedom*); "Early History of Presbyterianism in Morris County", and other shorter articles. At the time his Revolutionary articles were published there were still men living who had personal knowledge of the events of that era and he gathered an immense amount of material which but for him would have been lost.

The following from the pen of Dr. Tuttle appeared in *The Newark Daily Advertiser* of April, 1883:

A FINE RELIC AND A FINE POEM.

Thirty years ago and more my surplus energy was devoted to the innocent delights of hunting up places, people, facts and traditions associated with the American Revolution as preserved in Morris County. Some very charming rides were taken to Pompton, Mendham, Baskingridge, Spring Valley, Kimball Mountain, Singack, and other places. My rides made me certain that Morris County is both rich in beautiful scenery and historic associations. The results of these rides appeared in a series of "Revolutionary Fragments" printed in the *Advertiser*, as also in some elaborate papers before the Historical Society.

One day I visited the Ford Mansion, and met that polished and elegant gentleman, the late Henry A. Ford, Esq., then its proprietor. He was the son of Judge Gabriel H. Ford, grand-son of Colonel Jacob Ford, Jr., whose widow was the hostess of Washington, the Winter of 1779-80, great-grandson of Colonel Jacob Ford, Sr., who built the "Ford Mansion," and great-great-grandson of John Ford, of Hunterdon County, whose wife was Elizabeth who was brought to Philadelphia from Axford, England, when she was a child a year old. Her father was drowned by falling from the plank on which he was walking from the ship to the shore. Philadelphia then had but one house in it. Mrs. Ford's second husband was Lindsley, and " the widow Elizabeth Lindsley died at the house of her son, Col. Jacob Ford, Sr., April 21, 1772, aged ninety-one years and one month," and so the courtly master of the " Ford Mansion," when I called to visit it, was of the fifth generation from the child-emigrant, whose father was drowned in the Delaware, in 1682.

The pleasure of the visit was greatly enhanced by the attentions of Miss Louisa, daughter of the gentleman named. She afterward became the wife of Judge Ogden of Paterson. The father and daughter with delightful courtesy took me over the famous house and associated in my memory the rooms and halls, and even the antique furniture with the family's most illustrious guest. I was especially interested in the old mirror that had hung in Washington's bed-room. Miss Ford produced a poem on that mirror, written, I think, by an aunt, and at my request she read it. She was a charming reader and promised me a copy.

Under date of Paterson, October 31st, 1856, Mrs. Ogden was kind enough to send me the promised copy with a note apologizing for the delay and adding : "I think, however, you will find the poetry has not spoiled by keeping." I have not ceased to be thankful that my first visit to the Ford Mansion was so pleasantly associated with the attentions of the father and daughter, both of whom have since died.

The mirror is a fine relic still to be seen with other elegant old furniture, belonging to the Ford family, at the "Washington Quarters" at Morristown, and I am sure all will regard the poem which pleased me so much thirty years ago as "one that has not spoiled by keeping."

ON AN OLD MIRROR USED BY WASHINGTON AT HIS HEADQUARTERS IN MORRISTOWN.

Old Mirror! speak and tell us whence
Thou comest, and then, who brought thee thence.
Did dear old England give thee birth ?
Or merry France, the land of mirth ?
In vain another should we seek
At all like thee—thou thing antique.
Of the old mansion thou seem'st part ;
Indeed, to me, its very heart ;
For in thy face, though dimmed with age,
I read my country's brightest page.
Five generations, all have passed,
And yet, old Mirror, thou dost last ;
The young, the old, the good, the bad,
The gay, the gifted and the sad
Are gone ; their hopes, their sighs, their fears
Are buried deep with smiles and tears.
Then speak ; old Mirror ! thou hast seen
Full many a noble form, I ween ;
Full many a soldier, tall and brave,
Now lying in a nameless grave ;
Full many a fairy form and bright
Hath flitted by when hearts were light ;
Full many a bride—whose short life seemed
Too happy to be even dreamed ;
Full many a lord and titled dame,
Bearing full many an honored name ;

And tell us, Mirror, how they dressed—
Those stately dames, when in their best ?
If robes and sacques the damsels wore,
And sweeping skirts in days of yore ?
But tell us, too, for we *must* hear
Of *him* whom all the world revere.
Thou sawest him when the times so dark
Had made upon his brow their mark ;
Those fearful times, those dreary days,
When all seemed but a tangled maze ;
His noble army, worn with toils,
Giving their life blood to the soils.
Disease and famine brooding o'er,
His country's foe e'en at his door ;
But ever saw him noble, brave,
Seeking her freedom or his grave.
His was the heart that never quailed ;
His was the arm that never failed !
Old Mirror ! thou hast seen what we
Would barter all most dear to see ;
The great, the good, the *noblest* one ;
Our own *immortal Washington* !
Well may we gaze—for now in thee
Relics of the great past we see,
Well may we gaze—for ne'er again,
Old Mirror, shall we see such men ;
And when we too have lived our day,
Like those before us passed away,
Still, valued Mirror, may'st thou last
To tell our children of the past ;
Still thy dimmed face, thy tarnished frame
Thy honored house and time proclaim ;
And ne'er may sacrilegious hand,
While Freedom claims this as her land

One stone or pebble rashly throw
To lay thee, honored Mirror, low.

Y. F.

Hon. Edmund D. Halsey.

Mr. Halsey, historian, biographer, as well as lawyer, has published our most valuable "History of Morris County", and is considered an authority upon that subject, his accuracy being unquestioned. By his sterling integrity and superior intellectual ability, he has, in the practice of his profession, gained the entire confidence of the community in which, as a lawyer, he has passed the greater part of his life.

Included in his literary work are "Personal Sketches" of Governor Mahlon Dickerson, Colonel Joseph Jackson, and others ; "The Revolutionary Army in Morris County in 1779-'80"; and a brief sketch of the Washington Headquarters entitled "History of the Washington Association of New Jersey", published in Morristown in 1891.

Mr. Halsey also assisted Mr. William O. Wheeler in the publication of a book of unique interest and of unusual value, especially to genealogists and antiquarians, the title of which reads "Inscriptions on Tombstones and Monuments in the Burying Grounds of the First Presbyterian Church and St. John's Church at Elizabeth, New Jersey".

Mr. Halsey is a prominent member of the "Historical Society of New Jersey", as well as of the "Washington Association of New Jersey".

We quote from his "History of the Washington Association" the following "brief history of the title of the property".

FROM "HISTORY OF THE WASHINGTON ASSOCIATION OF NEW JERSEY."

Colonel Jacob Ford, Senior - prominent as a merchant, iron manufacturer, and land owner, who was president Judge of the County Court from the formation of the County in 1749 until his death in 1777, and who presided over the meeting, June 27, 1774, which appointed the first "Committee of Correspondence" - conveyed the tract of 200 acres surrounding the house to his son, Jacob Ford, junior, March 24, 1762. In 1768 he conveyed to him the Mount Hope mines and meadows where the son built the stone mansion still standing. In 1773 Jacob Ford, junior, rented this Mount Hope property for fifty years to John Jacob Faesch and David Wrisbery, and these men proceeded to build the furnace afterward useful to the patriot army in supplying it with cannon and cannon-balls.

Colonel Jacob Ford, junior, after making this lease returned to Morristown, and, probably with his father's aid, began at once the erection of these Headquarters, and had just completed the building when the war broke out. He was made Colonel of the Eastern Battalion of the Morris County Militia and was detailed to cover Washington's retreat across New Jersey in the "mud rounds" of 1776—a service accomplished with honor and success. In this or in similar service, Colonel Ford contracted pneumonia, of which he died January 10, 1777, and was buried with military honors by order of Washington. He left a widow, Theodosia Ford, and five young children. She was the daughter of Rev. Timothy Johnes, whose pastorate of the First church extended from 1742 to 1794, and who is said to have administered the Communion to Washington. This lady in 1779-80 offered to Washington the hospitality of her house, and here was his Headquarters from about December 1, 1779 to June 1780. In 1805, Judge Gabriel H. Ford, one of the sons of Colonel Jacob, purchased his brothers' and sister's interest in the property and made it his home until his death in 1849. By his will dated January 27, 1848, Gabriel H. Ford, devised this, his homestead to his son, Henry A. Ford, who continued to occupy it until his death, which occurred April 22, 1872. From the heirs of Henry A. Ford title was derived to the four gentlemen who organized the Association, namely: Governor Theodore F. Randolph, Hon. George A. Halsey, General N. N. Halsted, and William Van Vleck Lidgerwood, Esq.

Hon. John Whitehead.

BIOGRAPHER AND HISTORIAN.

Of Mr. Whitehead's new departure into the field of romance, we have already spoken and a portion of his story "A Fishing Trip to Barnegat", is given to represent him among "Novelists and Story Writers".

His literary work of many years covers a variety of departments in literature.

In the *Northern Monthly Magazine* which began some years ago, as a periodical of high order we find running through several numbers a "History of the English Language", contributed by Mr. Whitehead, in which he starts from a true and philosophic premise. It is this: "It would be difficult to separate any one creation from the whole universe and pronounce that it is not subject to law." The reader discovers that these magazine articles contain the germs of all that has been written in many exhaustive works on the philosophy and growth of language.

For a number of years, Mr. Whitehead was editor of *The Record*, a small sheet opened by the First Presbyterian Church of Morristown, the value of which historically increases with each year. For this, he wrote largely, sketches of prominent men of Revolutionary times and of others connected with the congregation of the church.

Some important papers were contributed by him to the local press, including "A Review of Fitz John Porter's Case", in the Morristown *Banner*, also "Sketches of Morris County Lawyers". A series of "Sketches" was also published in the *Newark Sunday Call*, entitled "Newark Aforetime", referring to Newark and Newark people, fifty years ago.

Many of Mr. Whitehead's speeches and addresses have been published, among them, those given at the Centennial Celebration of the First Presbyterian Church of Morristown; at the Centennial Celebration of the Presbyterian Church at Springfield, N. J.; two or three addresses before the Society of the Sons of the American Revolution, and an address delivered two or three years ago before the Washington Association of N. J. Of the latter Association, Mr. Whitehead is an honored member as well as of the Historical Society of New Jersey.

In the course of his study and writing, we have already mentioned among "Translators," Mr. Whitehead has made several valuable translations from German and French authors.

We must not overlook one principal labor which is far more herculean than we, who are so greatly benefited by it, perhaps fully comprehend, namely, the Catalogue, in two volumes, of the Library, in which Morristown justly takes so much pride.

Mr. Whitehead is now engaged on a "History of Morris County", to form one chapter in a new illustrated "History of New Jersey," to be published by Colonel U. S. Sharp. He has also in preparation the "History of the First Presbyterian Church" of Morristown, in which will appear the interesting proceedings of the Centennial exercises, recently held there.

A series of fine articles on "The Supreme Court of New Jersey" are now appearing in *The Green Bay* of Boston. This *Green Bay* is a magazine published in the interests of the legal fraternity, as from its significant name we see, and this magazine is the nearest approach so far made by

Americans towards the traditional appendage of the English barrister, everywhere seen over the border in Canada, by which, it is well known, he is always accompanied when he goes to court and while he remains there in attendance. This bag contains his briefs, papers and other impedimenta connected with trials. It is not surprising, but it is touching, to find Boston holding on to this last hope of accomplishing that for which so many frantic efforts have been made in this country, only to meet with failure.

The last article in this magazine, of the series on "The Supreme Court of New Jersey", is delightful in expression and in form; it has a fine large type, is illustrated with well-executed portraits of the judges, in group and singly, and is altogether most attractive and interesting.

Bayard Tuckerman.

Mr. Tuckerman, who resided for some time in Morristown, and whose ancestry is associated with artistic and literary taste and genius, is the author of "The Life of General Lafayette", published in 1889, during his residence in Morristown, and, a copy of which was presented by the author, in person, to the Morristown Library. Before this, he published a "History of English Prose Fiction", in 1882, and after it, in 1889 again, he edited "The Diary of Philip Hone". This author is now engaged on another book, to be published in the spring in the "Makers of America" series, with the title of "Peter Stuyvesant".

"The Diary of Philip Hone" is a charming book, especially to those familiar with old New York. The editorship of any life requires a talent for selection and a gift for combining and drawing together much desultory matter, but when we consider that the two volumes, into which Mr. Tuckerman compressed his material were less than one-fourth the original diary, which fills twenty-eight quarto manuscript volumes, the herculean task is at once apparent. A critic in one of the popular journals says of it : "As a rule the diary needs little interpretation and it may be welcomed as an agreeable, gossipy contribution to civic annals, and as a pleasant record of a citizen of some distinction, parts and usefulness in his generation".

In the "Life of General Lafayette", Mr. Tuckerman has evinced his superior love of industrious, conscientious study. The book is acknowledged to be essentially truthful and exceptionally just above anything ever written of Lafayette. It has been truly said of Mr. Tuckerman that "he tells the story of Lafayette's life in such a way that the interest increases as it proceeds" and that "he shows his skill as a biographer in this as in making both the narrative itself and his own criticism of the subject heighten our sympathy". He has not allowed himself to be turned from the actual statement of fact by that peculiar sentiment of the romantic side of Lafayette's career which has more or less colored the opinions of so many other biographers. Mr. Tuckerman himself says that "Lafayette's name has suffered more from the admiration of his friends than from the detraction of his enemies."

FROM THE "LIFE OF GENERAL LAFAYETTE."

The visit to America was supplemented in the following summer of 1785 by a journey through Germany and Austria.

* * *

Many distinguished officers were met. At one camp, as he (Lafayette) wrote to Washington, he found Lord Cornwallis, Colonels England, Abercrombie, and Musgrave; "on our side" Colonel Smith, Generals Duportail and Gouvion; "and we often remarked, Smith and I, that if we had been unfortunate in our struggle, we would have cut a poor figure there." Again ;

Writing from Valley Forge to the Comte de

Broglie, he gave a sad picture of the poverty and sufferings of the army. "Everything here", he said, "combines to inspire disgust. At the smallest sign from you I shall return home". But the misery of Valley Forge never abated one jot of Lafayette's enthusiasm. The privations which he saw and shared only made him put his hand the more often into his own pocket, and redouble his efforts to obtain aid from the treasury of France.

*   *   *

To Lafayette, the happiest portion of this voyage to America was the time passed in the company of Washington. Hastening from New York immediately on his arrival, he allowed himself to be delayed only at Philadelphia. "There is no rest for me," he wrote thence to Washington, "until I go to Mt. Vernon. I long for the pleasure to embrace you, my dear general; in a few days I shall be at Mt. Vernon, and I do already feel delighted with so charming a prospect." Two weeks of a proud pleasure were then passed in the society of the man who was always to remain his beau ideal. To walk about the beautiful grounds of Mt. Vernon with its honored master, discussing his agricultural plans; to sit with him in his library, and listen to his hopes regarding the nation for which he had done so much, were honors which Lafayette fully appreciated. He has left on record the feelings of admiration with which he saw the man

HISTORIANS AND ESSAYISTS.

who had so long led a great people in a great struggle retire to private life, with no thought other than satisfaction at duty performed. And it was a legitimate source of pride to himself that he had enlisted under his standard before fortune had smiled upon it, and had worked with all his heart to crown it with victory. The two men thoroughly knew each other.

The words of Lafayette will be found, in this volume, in the paper on "George Washington."

*   *   *

He (Washington) responded to Lafayette's demonstrative regard by a sincere paternal affection. Later in the summer, Layafette met Washington again, and visited in his company some of the scenes of the late war. When the time for parting had come, Washington accompanied his guest as far as Annapolis in his carriage. There the two friends separated, not to meet again.

On his return to Mt. Vernon, Washington added to his words of farewell, a letter in which occur the following passages ; " In the moment of our separation, upon the road as I travelled, and every hour since, I have felt all that love, respect, and attachment for you, with which length of years, close connection and your merits have inspired me. I often asked myself, as our carriages separated, whether that was the last sight I ever should have of you, and though I wished to say no, my fears answered yes. I called to mind the days of my youth, and found they had long since fled, to return no more; that I was now descending the hill I had been fifty-two years climbing, and that, though I was blest with a good constitution, I was of a short-lived family, and might soon expect to be entombed in the mansion of my fathers. These thoughts darkened the shades and gave a gloom to the picture, and consequently to my prospect of seeing you again. But I will not repine; I have had my day. * * * * It is unnecessary, I persuade myself, to repeat to you, my dear Marquis, the sincerity of my regards and friendship; nor have I words which could express my affection for you, were I to attempt it. My fervent prayers are offered for your safe and pleasant passage, happy meeting with Madame de Lafayette and family, and the completion of every wish of your heart." To these words Lafayette replied from on board the "Nymphe," on the eve of his departure for France: "Adieu, adieu, my dear general. It is with inexpressible pain that I feel I am going to be severed from you by the Atlantic. Everything that admiration, respect, gratitude, friendship, and filial love can inspire is combined in my affectionate heart to devote me most tenderly to you. In your friendship I find a delight which words cannot express. Adieu, my dear general. It is not without emotion that I write this word, although I know I shall soon visit you again. Be attentive to your health. Let me hear from you every month. Adieu, adieu."

Loyall Farragut.

BIOGRAPHER.

With Morristown is associated the beautiful memoir of our great Admiral, in honor of whom one of the streets of our city is named. In the old house now removed from its original position to the end of Farragut Place, this honored commander once visited for several days, walking over the ground now occupied by the houses of many families, delighted as a boy with everything in nature; noticing and observing the smallest detail of what was going on around him and interesting himself equally in the humblest individual who crossed his path and in the most distinguished visitor who asked to be presented.

The "Life of David Glasgow Farragut" was written according to the admiral's expressed wish, by his only son, Loyall Farragut, who for a short time had, in Morristown, his summer home, and who presented to the Morristown Library a copy of his book.

The Farraguts came from the island of Minorca, where the name is now extinct. In the volume referred to, we find these words : "George Farragut, father of the admiral was sent to school at Barcelona, but was seized with the spirit of adventure, and emigrated to America at an early age. He arrived in 1776, promptly sided with the colonists, and served gallantly in the struggle for independence, as also in the war of 1812. It is said that he saved the life of Colonel Washington in the battle of Cowpens.

In reading this volume one is transported to the times and scenes described, and everywhere is felt the grandeur, beauty and simplicity of character of this truly great and lovable man. In the touching letter to his devoted wife, on the eve of the great battle, is seen, as an example to all men of future generations, the realization of a man's fidelity to the woman of his choice, even in the moment of greatest extremity, and the possibility of the tenderest heart existing side by side with the daring courage of one of the bravest men the world has ever seen.

Wonderfully stirring are the descriptions given of the river fight on the Mississippi and of the battle of Mobile Bay, after which Admiral Farragut received from Secretary Welles the following congratulatory letter :

"In the success which has attended your operations, you have illustrated the efficiency and irresistible power of a naval force led by a bold and vigorous mind and the insufficiency of any batteries to prevent the passage of a fleet thus led and commanded. You have, first on the Mississippi and recently in the bay of Mobile, demonstrated what had previously been doubted,—the ability of naval vessels, properly manned and commanded, to set at defiance the best constructed and most heavily armed fortifications. In these successive victories, you have encountered great risks, but the results have vindicated the wisdom of your policy and the daring valor of our officers and seamen "

Josiah Collins Pumpelly.

Mr. Pumpelly, long a resident of Morristown, claims our attention as a writer, rather than an author, as he has not been a publisher of books, beyond a collection of three Addresses in pamphlet form entitled "Our French Allies in the Revolution and Other Addresses".

Several sketches entitled "Reminiscences of Colonial Days", and others of the same character, all involve considerable research and add to our literary possessions in connection with historic Morristown. His "Address on Washington", delivered before the Washington Association of New Jersey, at the Morristown Headquarters, February 22, 1888, was published by the Association, and has long been for sale there. Of this, the writer says, "I rejoice that even in this slight way, I can be of service to an Association whose faithful care of this home of Washington in the trying winter of 1779 and '80 deserves the lasting gratitude of every loyal Jerseyman." In closing this address, Mr. Pumpelly said, quoting from our favorite historian, Rev. Dr. Tuttle, "each old parish in our County had its heroes, and each old church was a shrine at which brave men and women bowed in God's fear, consecrating their all to their country." Mr. Pumpelly adds: "So instead of referring our children to Greek and Roman patriots, we have but to call up for them the names of our own men and women, who have here amid the hills of Morris, wrought out for us this heritage, so much grander, so much nobler than they themselves ever dreamed." This address is now bound in a larger pamphlet with "Our French Allies", to which we have referred and which was read before the New Jersey Historical Society, at Trenton, January 22d, 1889 and "Fort Stanwix and Battle of Oriskany", an address delivered before the Society of the Sons of the Revolution, in New York City, Dec. 3, 1888.

There was an important paper read by Mr. Pumpelly before the New Jersey Society of the Sons of the Revolution, on June 10th, 1889, and by them adopted in their meeting of that date, and afterwards published, on "The Birthplace of our Immortal Washington and the Grave of his Illustrious Mother, shall they not be Sacredly Preserved?"

Another address followed on "Joseph Warren" before the Massachusetts Society of the Sons of the American Revolution, on April 18th, 1890, on the occasion of the 114th Anniversary of the Battle of Lexington. He was then President of the New Jersey Society of the Sons of the American Revolution.

A paper was read by request on "Mahlon Dickerson, Industrial Pioneer and old time Patriot," on January 27, 1891, before the New Jersey Historical Society.

Mr. Pumpelly has also given much time and literary effort in philanthropic and sanitary directions. Many articles have appeared from time to time from his pen in behalf of reforms in the treatment of our dependent, delinquent, and defective classes, all tending to social economic improvement and, at one time, assisting materially the advance of the State Charities Aid Association of New Jersey of which he was for several years an active member.

His attention is now being turned to the story of the Huguenots in this country. He is just completing a quite exhaustive paper upon the Huguenots in New Jersey, which is to be given by request before the Genealogical Society of New York, in January 1893, after which the subject is to be prepared by him for use in a school text-book.

In *The New York Genealogical and Biographical Record*, of April 1892, is "A Short Sketch of the Character and Life of John Paul Jones", written in a most interesting and delightful manner and given before the New York Genealogical and Biographical Society, January 8, 1892. We quote from

WHAT DOES THE CAUSE OF HUMAN FREEDOM OWE TO THE HUGUENOT?

In looking back over the milestones which mark in history the relapse and advance, the failure and the successes, of the principles of civilization, we note that at a certain period it was the Teutonic Nations which broke loose from Rome and the Latin Nations who adhered to the Pope. Also, that in France, opposition to Rome was early and considerable. Thus the Waldenses, Albigenses, and Lefevre and his colleagues were Huguenots and lovers of human freedom before the name itself was known

—Calvinists before Calvin, Lutherans before Luther, Wiclyfites before Wiclyf.

That great movement for the liberty of conscience and personal freedom, civil and religious, was not in France an importation, for God had deposited the first principles of the work in a few brave hearts of Picardy and Dauphiny before it had begun in any other country of the globe. Not to Switzerland nor to Germany belongs the honor of having been first in the work, but to France and the Huguenot.

It was the voice of Lefevre, of Etaples, France, a man of great nobility of soul as well as genius of mind, which was to give the signal of the rising of this morning star of liberty. He it was who taught Farel, the great French reformer and "master-builder" with Luther.

Hannah More Johnson.

Miss Johnson's poem, "The Christmas Tree", has taken its place in our Poet's corner. She is also mentioned among *Novelists and Story-Writers* for her well-known stories of "Lost Willie"; "Ella

Dutton"; "Snow Drifts"; "Signal Lights", and "First the Blade" published by A. D. F. Randolph and by the Presbyterian Board. But perhaps her most important work is "Mexico, Past and Present", an excellent and charmingly written history of Mexico, a book of interest and importance, with sixty three maps and illustrations, treating not only the history, but the present condition and prospects of that country. This work is found in many libraries, and places Miss Johnson among our *Historians*.

Miss Johnson is the daughter of Mr. Jacob Johnson and niece of our townsman, Mr. J. Henry Johnson, who was the last preceptor of the old Morris Academy. Though long a resident of Morristown, she now makes her home in Philadelphia where she is editor of a Missionary Publication.

"I first thought of myself as a writer", says Miss Johnson, "when I saw my name for the first time in print and nearly fainted with fright. I have never recovered from that shock and not until I had had more than one collision with publishers have I consented to give my name to articles."

Last September (1892) "Bible Lights in Mission Paths" was published. "The long interval between my first and my last book," says the author, "was filled with what seems to me the true work of my life." And it is curious how this work of life came to her quite unsought and unexpectedly. Let us hear it in her own words. "About twelve years ago," she tells us, "a relative became proprietor of a small religious weekly in Philadelphia, *The Presbyterian Journal*. I had the entire charge of the missionary department. Shortly afterward, the Presbyterian Alliance met in our city and the Woman's Foreign Missionary Society, (of which I was and still am a Director), held in connection with that great convocation in the Academy of Music, an all-day meeting in one of the churches. Presbyterian women were there from every quarter of the world beside others from sister churches. At noon as I sat, talking over the programme for the afternoon with Mrs. A——, she said regretfully, 'I am afraid that we shall not be able to get these women to speak loud enough to be heard all over this great church. It would be delightful if we could have a full report.' 'I think I could get one up, Mrs. A——,' said I. 'I have been taking notes of the speeches all the morning and this afternoon we are to have written reports and papers.' 'I can get them all for you,' she said quickly. That night I went home laden with documents, three-fourths of them from the Old World. The *Journal* publishers offered to send out an extra and send it to any address I gave. Within a week, this extra was mailed to every mission station throughout the world, which had been in any way represented at this woman's meeting or mentioned in its reports. Ever since that busy, busy week with French, English, Scotch, German, Italian, Belgian and Irish women, I have been a constant reporter of Missionary meetings. This led to a series of articles for Monthly Concerts, proposed for the use of pastors and other leaders of missionary meetings. Twelve articles a year for about four years, each one of which had cost months of research and study, I had time for nothing else. It was weary work. All roads led to Rome and I could n't pick up a book or a daily that did n't give me an item or a suggestion. The nameless writer was generally supposed to be some Doctor of Divinity shelved with a sore throat or other ministerial disability. I remember one time when a carefully prepared article (of mine) on Siam appeared in *The Gospel of all Lands*, credited to *The London Missionary News*. It had been taken from the magazine in which it was first published, profusely illustrated and sent out as an English production."

Besides this Miss Johnson has furnished monthly articles for various papers and occasional poems for magazines. Thus we see her very busy life has been fruitful of unusual results.

Mrs. Julia McNair Wright.

Mrs. Wright has already been mentioned among *Novelists and Story-Writers*. For the following graphic sketch, we are indebted to one of our writers, Mrs. Julia R. Cutler.

"One of the authors whose sojourn in our 'beautiful little town', as she calls it, was of a comparatively brief period, from 1881-'83, but whose writings, as showing deep research in many fields of thought, both scientific and historical, entitle her to more than a brief mention, is Mrs. Julia McNair Wright.

"Her husband, the Rev. Dr. William J. Wright, is President of and, Professor of Metaphysics, in a Western College. Much of Mrs. Wright's time is spent in visiting different large cities, at home and abroad, where she can have access to libraries and gain information on various subjects connected with her books.

"While in Morristown, she wrote, at the request of the Presbyterian Board of Publication, her book on "The Alaskans" and also a short work on the religious life, called "Mr. Standfast's Journey", besides preparing for the press a book entitled "Bricks from Babel", which she had previously written while visiting London and the British museum. The Rev. Joseph Cook fully endorses this book, and calls it 'a most admirable compendium of ethnography.' A set of religious biographies were, also, about this time, published in Arabic.

"These works written and prepared for the press while she was occupying her quiet cottage home on Morris Plains, would alone have entitled her to a prominent place among the authors of whom Morristown has reason to be proud. But these are but a small portion of her literary labors. Judging from the number of books which appear over her signature, she must indeed be gifted with the 'pen of a ready writer.'

"Among the more prominent works are ' The Early Church in Britain'; 'The Complete Home', of which over one hundred thousand copies have been sold; 'Saints and Sinners of the Bible'; 'Almost a Nun'; 'The Priest and Nun'; 'A Wife Hard Won', a novel published by Lippincott; ' The Making of Rasmus'; ' Rasmus a Made Man'; and ' Rag Fair and May Fair'. The last deals with social questions in England, and is being re-published in London, as indeed a number of her other books have been, as well as translated into the French language.

"Mrs. Wright's latest work, completed during a recent visit to the British museum, is a Series of Readers on Natural Science, called 'Nature Readers, Seaside and Wayside', which are having a large run in this country, in England and in Canada and which are a new invention in school books. They have been more warmly received than any books for our schools, for the past twenty-five years.

"Very few persons have the talent of dealing with so many subjects and doing it so well. Even the Temperance cause owes much to Mrs. Wright, as its earnest advocate, and many of her thrilling stories on this subject have touched the hearts and inspired the actions of those who have read them. Nor has she, amid her multitude of duties, forgotten the young, as the large number of volumes on the shelves of our Sabbath School libraries, bearing her name can testify.

"May the pen Mrs. Wright has so wisely and deftly used, in the cause of education and humanity, long continue through her skillful hand, to trace its characters upon the hearts and minds of those with whom it comes in contact!"

Mrs. Edwina L. Keasbey.

Though Mrs. Keasbey has published a most attractive and useful book, full of practical thoughts idealized, yet we place her and Mrs. Stockton in this grouping for the reason that a large part of her writing was of this character, on the whole. Much of it was graphically descriptive of scenes in foreign lands and at home, usually accompanied with reflections which indicate the *Essay* character. Like others of our writers, there is a variety in her writing and choice of subjects which makes it somewhat difficult to place her with exactness.

Most of Mrs. Keasbey's writing was originally done for *The Hospital Review*, a paper edited by her, during eleven years, for the St. Barnabas Hospital, which was founded largely through her efforts and influence and was a work to which she devoted her life. For this was written a series of papers entitled "A Lame Woman's Tramp through some Alpine Passes", and "Bits of English Scenery Sketched by a Lame Hand", among which is a fine and vivid picture of the first sight of Durham Cathedral. So, for this *Hospital Review* were originally written the papers now collected and bound in one of the prettiest little volumes one could desire, convenient in size, artistic in design and with clear, large type and broad margins. This is entitled "The Culture of the Cradle".

In the education of children, Mrs. Keasbey has found the key and basis of all true and reasonable training, in the development of the child's individuality. The object of this book is to suggest the meaning and purpose of true culture and to show how it must begin with the cradle and, says the author, "to give some suggestions and leaves from experience that may be of use to those who are striving to begin, in the right way, the education of their children." The book, published in 1886, has had a large sale and the entire proceeds have been devoted to the Hospital of St. Barnabas, which the author so much loved.

Mrs. Keasbey was the eldest daughter of the Hon. J. W. Miller, and she inherited well her intense love of good works from her honored mother, who was so long identified with Morristown's philanthropic and charitable work. She was born in the old Macculloch mansion on Macculloch Avenue and lived there till her marriage in 1854, after which her literary qualities and rare executive abilities went to adorn the city of Newark where she will be tenderly remembered, and where her works live after her.

FROM "THE CULTURE OF THE CRADLE."

As I sit by my window on this beautiful spring day, preparing my article upon "The Nurture of Infants," a pair of little birds are building their nest in the vine that grows about my piazza, so I take my text from them.

How busy they are, how absorbed in their

work! The whole world contains for them no other point of interest, but only this little crotch in the vine which they have chosen to build their cradle in for their future little ones. We may be quite sure that it is the best spot in the whole vine, not too shady or too sunny, just happily out of the reach of cruel cat or mischievous boys, and then the cradle will be so perfect, strong enough to resist the winds that shake the vine, and covered enough to withstand the spring rains, and warm enough to shelter the little ones as they crack the shell; and so comfortable with its soft padding of cotton and down to cherish and protect the little tender bodies when they come into this cold world.

I think it is nearly finished to-day, for the little mother has settled herself down into it and nestled herself in it and picked off her own soft down, and stuffed it in with the cotton that she had lined the nest with. She looks so satisfied and content, as if she would say, "it is quite ready now for my little darlings."

With this little mother there is no word of complaint or selfish murmur though she is going to sit in that nest for many a long day and dark night, through storm and sunshine, until the little ones come forth from their eggs to gladden her heart and repay her care and work of preparation.

Can we mothers have a better teacher or a wiser example than this little bird, whose lessons in motherhood have come to her direct from her Creator?

Mrs. Marian E. Stockton.

As to Mrs. Stockton's charming pen, we must reluctantly refrain from noticing her many essays and writings in various directions, principally prepared at the request of literary societies and other organizations,—always read by some one else, owing to the writer's great dislike for coming into public notice, and always published, and sent about, by the Society or group of people for whom they were written. The title of this book compels us, however, to mention this gifted woman's name, and we give below an extract from one delightful paper, written as usual by request for an important occasion, read by a distinguished literary woman, and as usual published.

FROM "HOME AND SOCIETY."

It may help to a proper understanding of the line of thought followed in this paper if I state in the beginning that it is, chiefly, an attempt to get a definite answer to the question so often asked: What is Society? It is an effort to arrive at a conclusion which the majority of American women may be willing to accept. Otherwise we shall find ourselves so beset with perplexities that we shall not be able to get anything out of our subject. For most persons have very vague ideas regarding society, and would find it difficult to express them. I have tried to get at the ideas of a few persons who might be supposed to know, with but small result. One says: "It is a limited company of persons of wealth and leisure who give up their time chiefly to entertainments and pleasure." This view of the subject suggests the familiar advertisements of a certain soap, reversing the sign ; for taking out the pure article—*i. e.*, the persons composing this society—we would have 99 44-100 of the people of the United States with no society at all. *So very little* of the pure article will, I think, scarcely suffice to float this definition.

Another says: "It is a collection of the best people in a city or neighborhood who give a tone to the place." This is better, but calls forth other questions. Whom do you mean by the "best people"? What is "tone"? What sort of "tone" do they give? New York, New Orleans, and Poker Flat would give widely different answers to these questions.

Another defines it as "a number, large or small, of cultured people." This conveys a charming idea to the mind, but it is too limited, for we are considering to-day society in its broadest as well as its best aspects; and, surely, we would none of us be willing to deny to good-hearted, honest, decent people, the pleasure of forming a society of their own kind, and enjoying it in a rational—if uncultured— fashion. We want to-day to get hold of a comprehensive idea of society.

Last summer, at a fashionable resort, I heard some New York ladies speaking, with admiration, of another lady in the hotel, and one exclaimed: " What a pity she is not in Society !" To this they all agreed, and another kindly asked: " Can't we do something to help her to know people?" As I knew this lady, and was aware of the fact that, when she returned to the city at the beginning of every season, she sent out cards to six hundred people, I was much surprised; for, if visiting and being visited by six hundred people is not being "in society", I do not know what is. Therefore, I could only infer that she was not in their special coterie.

A very intelligent woman once told me frankly, that she could not imagine anything that could be called society outside the City of New York.

Again I was told, some time ago, by a literary lady who was then residing in this city (but who is not here now): " Literary people are not recognized in New York society." I use her own words and they puzzled me. Soon after, there chanced to fall in my way a description of New York life by a Frenchman who had been entertained by all sorts of people. He stated that the most charming society in this city is the literary society, and he proceeded to paint it in glowing colors. Between the literary lady on one side and Max O'Rell on the other, I gave up that conundrum.

These few examples of misconceptions and wrong-headedness in regard to what society really is will suffice to show how necessary it is to get a clear and comprehensive definition for it. To get this we must disentangle ourselves from all these figments, go back, and enter through the gate which naturally leads into society.

TRAVELS
AND
PERSONAL REMINISCENCES.

Marquis de Chastellux.

The Marquis de Chastellux, counted in France a clever historian, is considered by us as a traveler, for he was one of the earliest French travelers in North America and, on his return to France, published a book entitled "Travels in North America in the years 1780, 1781 and 1782, by the Marquis de Chastellux, one of the Forty Members of the French Academy, and Major General in the French Army, serving under the Count de Rochambeau." This book was published in 1787 in London. In it we find the most graphic descriptions of the soldiers and officers of the Revolution, of West Point in its character of a military outpost; of the road between it and Morristown; of the beauty and grandeur of the Hudson River, as it burst for the first time upon his vision; of several interviews, visits and dinners with Washington and Lafayette, always giving his impressions in a unique and original way and with a sprinkle of humor which keeps a continuous smile upon the lips of the reader as he progresses in this remarkable narrative. It is really most difficult to choose from this fascinating book, for the short space we can allow.

In speaking of his arrival here he refers to the *Arnold Tavern*, which may still be seen, removed from its original location but restored with great care, (though enlarged), and is now standing on Mt. Kemble Avenue, the old "Baskingridge Road" of the Revolution. He says:

"I intended stopping at Morris Town only to bait my horses, for it was only half past two, but on entering the inn of Mr. Arnold, I saw a dining room adorned with looking glasses and handsome mahogany furniture and a table spread for twelve persons. I learnt that all this preparation was for me and what affected me more nearly was to see a dinner corresponding with the appearances, ready to serve up. I was indebted for this to the goodness of General Washington and the precautions of Colonel Moyland who had sent before to acquaint them with my arrival. It would have been very ungenerous to have accepted this dinner at the expenses of Mr. Arnold who is an honest man and a good Whig and who has not a particle in common with Benedict Arnold; it would have been still more awkward to have paid for the banquet without eating it. I therefore instantly determined to dine and sleep in this comfortable inn. The Vicomte de Noailles, the Comte de Damas, &c., were expected to make up the dozen."

Chastellux apparently came as a passing traveler and seems to have been induced to prolong his stay and during that time gives us very graphic and interesting glimpses, to which we have referred, of the General and his officers, dinners at which he was present, reviews of troops, the army itself and its condition, with passing reflections about the country and the manners and customs of the time. Among the latter remarks, he observes: "Here, as in England, by *gentleman* is understood a person possessing a considerable *freehold*, or land of his own." Of the officers, he says:

"I must observe on this occasion the General Officers of the American Army have a very military and a very becoming carriage; that even all the officers, whose characters were brought into public view, unite much politeness to a great deal of capacity; that the headquarters of this army, in short, neither present the image of want nor inexperience. When one sees the battalion of the General's Guards encamped within the precincts of his house ; nine waggons, destined to carry his baggage, ranged in his court.; a great number of grooms taking care of very fine horses belonging to the General Officers and their Aides de Camp ; when one observes the perfect order that reigns within these precincts, where the guards are exactly stationed, and where the drums beat an alarm, and a particular retreat, one is tempted to apply to the Americans what Pyrrhus said of the Romans : *Truly these people have nothing barbarous in their discipline.*"

Of his coming to Morristown, he says : "I pursued my journey, sometimes through fine woods at others through well cultivated lands and villages inhabited by Dutch families. One of these villages, which forms a little township bears the beautiful name of *Troy.* Here the country is more open and continues so to *Morris-Town.* This town celebrated by the winter quarters of 1779, is about three and twenty miles from Peakness, the name of the headquarters from whence I came : It is situated on a height, at the foot of which runs the rivulet called Vipenny River ; the houses are handsome and well built, there are about sixty or eighty round the meeting-house."

The Marquis tells of his reception at the Camp of Lafayette and, in giving us his picture, he gives us also what is of value to us in this day,--a

Frenchman's impression of Lafayette in America:

"Whilst they were making this slight repast, I went to see the Camp of the *Marquis*, it is thus they call M. de La Fayette: the English language being fond of abridgments and titles uncommon in America."

Here, our eye is attracted to a note of the Translator, (an Englishman residing in America,)—who says, with much more besides: "It is impossible to paint the esteem and affection with which this French nobleman is regarded in America. It is to be surpassed only by the love of their illustrious chief."

"The rain appearing to cease," continues the Marquis, "or inclined to cease for a moment, we availed ourselves of the opportunity to follow his Excellency to the Camp of the Marquis; we found all his troops in order of battle, on the heights on the left, and himself at their head; expressing by his air and countenance, that he was happier in receiving me there, than at his estate in Auvergne. The confidence and attachment of the troops, are for him invaluable possessions, well acquired riches, of which no body can deprive him; but what, in my opinion, is still more flattering for a young man of his age, is the influence, the consideration he has acquired amongst the political, as well as the military order; I do not fear contradictions when I say that private letters from him have frequently produced more effect on some states than the strongest exhortations of the Congress. On seeing him one is at a loss which most to admire, that so young a man as he should have given such eminent proofs of talents, or that a man so tried, should give hopes of so long a career of glory."

His impression of the Hudson at West Point, will interest us all :

"I continued my journey in the woods, in a road hemmed in on both sides by very steep hills which seemed admirably adapted for the dwelling of bears, and where, in fact, they often make their appearance in Winter We availed ourselves at length of a less difficult part of these mountains to turn to the westward and approach the river but which is still invisible. Descending them slowly, at the turning of the road, my eyes were struck with the most magnificent picture I had ever beheld. It was a view of the North River, running in a deep channel, formed by the mountains, through which, in former ages it had forced its passage. The fort of West Point and the formidable batteries which defend it fix the attention on the Western bank, but on lifting your eyes, you behold on every side lofty summits, thick set with redoubts and batteries."

One more passage we must give in this day of Morristown's horsemanship ; in this year of '92 when all young Morristown is jumping fences and ditches in pursuit of the fox or the fox's representative. It is Chastellux's reference to Washington's horsemanship :

"The weather being fair, on the 26th I got on horseback, after breakfasting with the General. He was so attentive as to give me the horse he rode on the day of my arrival, which I had greatly commended ; I found him as good as he is handsome ; but above all perfectly well broke, and well trained, having a good mouth, easy in hand, and stopping short in a gallop without bearing the bit. I mention these minute particulars, because it is the General himself who breaks all his own horses ; and he is a very excellent and bold horseman, leaping the highest fences, and going extremely quick, without standing upon his stirrups, bearing on the bridle, or letting his horse run wild ; circumstances which our young men look upon as so essential a part of English horsemanship, that they would rather break a leg or an arm than renounce them."

John L. Stephens.

Over fifty years ago, a traveler in Central America, Mr. John L. Stephens, records a curious and interesting allusion to Morristown, which we give below, from one of his two volumes of "Incidents of Travel in Central America and Yucatan"; 12th Edition; published in 1856. He says:

"In the midst of the war rumours, the next day, which was Sunday, was one of the most quiet I passed in Central America. It was at the hacienda of Dr. Drivon, about a league from Zonzonate. This was one of the finest haciendas in the country. The doctor had imported a large sugar mill, which was not yet set up, and was preparing to manufacture sugar upon a larger scale than any other planter in the country. He was from the island of St. Lucie and, before settling in this out-of-the-way place, had travelled extensively in Europe and the West India Islands and knew America from Halifax to Cape Horn, but surprised me by saying that he looked forward to a cottage in Morristown, New Jersey, as the consummation of his wishes."

Hon. Charles S. Washburn.

Mr. Washburn, who lived for several years in Morristown, was the brother of our late Minister to France. His most popular work is "The History of Paraguay," in two volumes, written while he was Commissioner and Minister Resident of the United States at Asuncion from 1861 to 1868. The writer may truly add on his title page, "Reminiscences of Diplomacy under Difficulties." As is well known, Mr. Washburn was minister to Paraguay under Lopez, one of the three most noted tyrants of South America, whose character is admirably brought out in this history of the country. His description of Lopez is most graphic. The work is so exhaustive that we get up from it with a feeling, "We know Paraguay". Besides this "History of Paraguay", Mr. Washburn has also written "Gomery of Montgomery", in two volumes and "Political Evolution from Poverty to Competence".

At the close of the first volume, we find a masterly summing up of the singular character of Lopez, in these words :

"Previous to the death of Lopez, history furnishes no example of a tyrant so despicable and cruel that at his fall he left no friend among his own people ; no apologist or defender, no follower or participant of his infamies, to utter one word in palliation of his crimes ; no one to regret his death, or who cherished the least spark of love for his person or his memory ; no one to utter a prayer for the repose of his soul. In this respect, Lopez had surpassed all tyrants who ever lived. No sooner was he dead, than all alike, the officer high in command, the subaltern who applied the torture, the soldier who passively obeyed, the mother who bore him, and the sisters who once loved him, all joined in denouncing him as an unparalleled monster ; and of the whole Paraguayan nation there is perhaps not one of the survivors who does not curse his name, and ascribe to his folly, selfishness, ambition and cruelty all the evils that his unhappy country has suffered. Not a family remains which does not charge him with having destroyed the larger part of its members and reduced the survivors to misery and want. Of all those who were within reach of his death-dealing hand during the last years of his power, there are but two persons living to say a word in mitigation of the judgment pronounced against him by his countrymen and country-women."

General Joseph Warren Revere.

The late General Revere, one of Morristown's old and well-known residents, wrote, at the close of his military and naval career, a graphic and interesting book of travels entitled "Keel and Saddle; a Retrospect of Forty Years of Military and Naval Service"; published in 1872 by James R. Osgood of Boston. Another book appeared later, called "A Tour of Duty in California."

General Revere tells us in "Keel and Saddle" that he entered the United States Navy at the age of fourteen years as a midshipman and, after a short term spent at the Naval School at the New York Navy Yard, he sailed on his first cruise to the Pacific Ocean on board the frigate "Guerrière", "bearing the pennant of Com. Charles C. B. Thompson, in the summer of the year 1828." For three years he served in the Pacific Squadron. After cruising in many waters and experiencing the various vicissitudes of naval life, in 1832 he passed his examination for lieutenant and sailed in the frigate "Constitution" for France.

During this Mediterranean cruise, when he made his first visit to Rome, he saw Madame Letitia, mother of the first Napoleon, by whom he was received with a small party of American officers. We shall give this scene as he describes it.

In this book, "Keel and Saddle", (page 140) occurs a very fine description of a great oceanic disturbance known to mariners in Southern seas as a "comber", or great wave. Suddenly encountered, it causes the destruction of many vessels.

Of Madame Letitia, in 1832 he writes as follows:

"Madame Mère or Madame Letitia, as she was usually called, being requested to grant an interview to a small party of American officers, of which I was one, graciously assented, and fixed a day for the reception at the palace she occupied.

"Repairing thither at the hour appointed, after a short detention in a spacious ante-chamber, we were ushered into one of those lofty saloons common to Italian palaces, handsomely, not gorgeously furnished, and opening by spacious windows into a beautiful garden. There, with her back towards the subdued light from the windows, we saw an elderly lady reclining on a sofa, in a graceful attitude of repose. She was attended by three ladies, who all remained standing during our visit. In the recess of one of the windows, on a tall pedestal of antique marble, stood a magnificent bust of the emperor; while upon the walls of the saloon, in elegant frames, were hung the portraits of her children, all of whom had been kings and queens of royal rank though not of royal lineage. Madame Letitia received us with perfect courtesy, without rising from her reclining position; motioning us gracefully to seats with a polite gesture of a hand and arm still of noble contour and dazzling whiteness. It was easy to see where the emperor got his small white hands, of which he was so vain, as we are told ; while the classic regularity of his well-known features was clearly traceable in the lineaments of the lady before us. Her head was covered with a cap of lace; and her somewhat haughty but expressive face, beaming with intelligence, was framed in clustering curls *à l'antique*. Her eyes were brilliant, large and piercing. (I think they could hardly have been more so in her youth); and the lines of her mouth and chin gave an expression of firmness, courage and determination to a fine physiognomy perfectly in character with the historical antecedents and attributes of Letitia Ramolini. Of the rest of her dress, we saw but little ; her bust being covered by a lace handkerchief crossed over the bosom, and her dark silk robe partially concealed by a superb cashmere shawl thrown over the lower part of her person. She opened the conversation by making some complimentary remark about our country ; asking after her son Joseph, who resided then at Bordentown, N. J.; and seemed pleased at receiving news of him from one of our party, who had seen him not long before. She asked this officer whether the King (*le roi d'Espagne*) still resembled the portrait in her possession which was a very fine one ; and upon our asking permission to examine the bust of the emperor, the greatest of her sons, told us that it was considered a fine work of art, it being, indeed, from the chisel of Canova ; adding, I fancied with a little sigh of melancholy, 'Il resemble beaucoup a l'empereur.' After some further commonplaces, she signified in the most delicate and dignified manner, more by looks than by words, addressed to the ladies of our party, referring to her rather weak state of health, that the interview should terminate ; and, having made our obeisance, we left her."

Henry Day.

In 1874, an interesting volume of travels appeared, entitled "A Lawyer Abroad. What to See and How to See : by Henry Day, of the Bar of New York."

Mr. Day's house " On the Hill", with its superb view, is occupied only in summer ; but year after year, with the birds and the spring sunshine, he returns to us from his home in New York, so he is thoroughly associated with Morristown. His book, unlike a large majority of "Travels" is not merely a "Tourist's Guide" or a series of descriptive sketches hung together by commonplace reflections, and interlarded with meaningless drawing-room or roadside dialogue.

Evidently, it is written with a high purpose and it is rich in valuable information concerning men and things, as if the writer himself were in living touch with the best interests of humanity whether found in the cities of Egypt, among the learned and polished minds of Edinburgh or in the Wynds of Glasgow, of which he so graphically says :

"They are now long filthy, airless lanes, packed with buildings on each side and each building packed with human beings ; and, geographically as well as morally they receive the drainage of all the surrounding city of Glasgow."

Here it was in the old Tron Church that Dr. Chalmers did his finest preaching and his most effective practical work. Mr. Day has an evident loving sympathy with the great Scotch preacher, quite apart from the intellectual qualities of his gigantic mind. In these few condensed pages, Mr. Day has given us a more compact idea of Dr. Chalmer's work than may be found in many elaborated chapters of his life.

The chapter upon "The Lawyers and Judges of England" is one of exceptional interest to those in the profession, as well as to those out of it, and this is one unique quality of the book—that we have given to us the impressions of a traveler from a lawyer's standpoint, not only in England, but in Ireland, Scotland, France, Germany, Holland, Switzerland, Greece, Turkey, Egypt and the Holy Land. And, not only from a lawyer's standpoint does he see the world, but evidently from the standpoint of a man of high general culture whose spiritual and religious sentiments and principles enlighten and illuminate his understanding.

In the chapter on "The Early Life of Great Men", speaking of Edinburgh, he says:

"Everything gives you the feeling that you are among the most learned and polished minds of the present and past generations. It is not business or wealth that has given to Edinburgh its prominence. It is learning; it is its great men."

One of Mr. Day's finest descriptions is found in his chapter on the Nile.

In 1877 this author published, through Putnams' Sons, a book having the title "From the Pyrenees to the Pillars of Hercules", giving sketches of scenery, art and life in Spain.

Mr. Day has also written a good deal for a few years past for publication in the *New York Evangelist* on the great questions now agitating the

Presbyterian church, namely, the revision of its creed called "The Confession of Faith" and also on the Briggs case and the Union Theological Seminary case. Mr. Day wisely says; "this newspaper writing can hardly be called authorship although the articles are more important than the books."

THEOLOGIANS.

Rev. Timothy Johnes, D. D.

Of the historic characters of Morristown, none are more prominent than the Rev. Dr. Johnes, who began his pastorate in the old Meeting House of Morristown which was probably reared before his coming. His labors began August 13th, 1742. He was ordained and installed February 9th, 1743, and continued pastor through the scenes of the Revolution till his death in 1791. He was the friend of Washington and supported him effectually in many of the measures he adopted in which his strong influence with the community was of great weight and value.

It was the daughter of Rev. Dr. Johnes, Theodosia, who married Col. Jacob Ford, jr., who lived at what is now known as the Washington Headquarters and offered the hospitality of her mansion to Washington during his second winter at Morristown. He also offered the Presbyterian church building for hospital use during the terrible scourge of small-pox,—himself acting as chief nurse to the soldiers,—and, with his congregation, worshipped for many months in the open air, on a spot still shown behind his house, on Morris' street, which is standing to-day, and now owned and occupied by Mrs. Eugene Ayers. It was on this spot, in a natural basin which the congregation occupied as being somewhat sheltered from the bitter winds of winter, and which may still be seen, that good Pastor Johnes administered the Communion to Washington. "This was the only time," says Rev. Dr. Green, in his "Morristown" in the "History of Morris County", after his entrance upon his public career, that Washington is certainly known to have partaken of the Lord's Supper. In *The Record* for June and August, 1880, we find a full account of this historic incident. As the Communion time drew near, Washington sought good Pastor Johnes, we are told, and inquired of him, if membership of the Presbyterian church was required "As a term of admission to the ordinance." To this the doctor replied, "ours is not the Presbyterian table, but the Lord's table, and we hence give the Lord's invitation to all his followers of whatever name." "On the following Sabbath," says Dr. Green, "in the cold air, the General was present with the congregation, assembled in the orchard in the rear of the parsonage", on the spot before referred to, "and joined with them in the solemn service of Communion."

In the family of good Pastor Johnes, a granddaughter of whom, Mrs. O. L. Kirtland, is with us still, the last of a large number of brothers and sisters, it has been known for generations that they originated in Wales. We have from Mrs. Kirtland's grand-daughter the following interesting record :

"Rev. Timothy Johnes came to Morristown, N. J., from Southampton about 1742. His great-great-grand-father, Richard Johnes, of Somerset, Eng., descended from a younger branch of the Johnes of Dolancotlie in Caemarthenshire, Wales, came over and settled in Charleston, Mass., in 1630, was made constable, and had 'Mr.' before his name, an honor in those days. He went to live at Southampton, L. I., in 1644, and he and his decendants held important positions there for nearly two hundred years. Burke's *Landed Gentry* states that the Johnes were descended from Urien Reged, one of King Arthur's Knights, and who built the Castle Caer Caenin, and traced descent back to Godebog, King of Britain. But accurate record must begin at a later date, when William Johnes, in the reign of

Elizabeth, was Commander on the 'Crane' and killed in a battle against the Spanish Armada."

Rev. Timothy Johnes, D. D., was the great-great-grandson of the first Johnes who arrived in this country. Rev. Timothy graduated at Yale in 1737; was born in 1717 and died in 1794. He received many ordination calls while at Southampton, Long Island, and was perplexed as to which one to accept, so "he referred the matter, says the great-great-grand-daughter before referred to," to Providence, deciding to accept the next one made. He had not risen from his knees more than twenty minutes, when two old men came to his house and asked him to become pastor of a small congregation that had collected at Morristown, then called by the Indian tongue Rockciticus. When nearly here, after traveling long in the forest, he inquired of his guides: "Where is Rockciticus?" "Here and there and every where," was the reply, and so it was, scattered through the woods.

Of Dr. Johnes' children,—Theodosia, as we have stated, was the hostess of Washington at the Ford mansion, her home, and now the Washington Headquarters. Anna, the eldest daughter, married Joseph Lewis and is the ancestress of one of our distinguished authors, the Rev. Theodore Ledyard Cuyler, D. D. The daughter of this Anna Lewis, married Charles Morrell and they occupied the house of Mr. Wm. L. King on Morris St., and there entertained Lafayette as their guest in the winter of '79 and '80. Their daughter, Louisa married Ledyard Cuyler and they had a son, Theodore Ledyard Cuyler, well-known to us and to all the world. Mary Anna, a grand daughter, married Mr. Williams, of Newburg, and others of the family followed there. They pronounce the name *John*-es, giving up the long *o* (Jones), of the old Doctor's sounding of the name. A grandson, Frank, went west and had a large family who are more or less distinguished in Decatur, Illinois. They omit the *e* in the name and call themselves Johns. It is only in Morristown that the family retain the original spelling of Johnes and pronunciation of *Jones*.

The son of the old Doctor, William, remained in the old house, and there brought up a large family of whom the above two, named, were members, also Mrs. Kirtland, who is still with us, with her daughter and grand-children, and Mrs. Alfred Canfield, who long lived among us but has passed away.

One of the old Doctor's sons was named, as we might expect, George Washington and was the grandfather of Mrs. Theodore Little, and built the old house on the hill near our beautiful Evergreen Cemetery. This house was built soon after Washington's occupation of Morristown, and the large place including the ancient house has lately been sold and will soon be laid out in streets and lots, as the demand comes from the increasing population of our city. Fortunate are we to have so many of the old land-marks left to us!

Mrs. Woodruff, the step-mother, honored and beloved, of Mrs. Whelpley Dodge, was also a daughter of old Doctor Johnes.

Another son of the old Doctor was Dr. John B. Johnes, who built the house with columns opposite the old place, still standing, and there he lived and died, high in his profession, greatly honored and beloved. His daughter Margaret, was the step-mother of another of our distinguished men and writers, the Rev. Arthur Mitchell, D. D.

And so we find this ancient family from Wales, the land of the poetic Celts, and many of whom are yet living in that corner of the world from which these came, still sending on their influence and maintaining their high standard of principle and honor, which characterized good Pastor Johnes, during the fifty-four years of his ministry in Morristown.

Rev. James Richards, D. D.

The Rev. Dr. Richards, who was settled as the third pastor over the First Church of Morristown, May 1st, 1795, was a theological author, many of whose sermons and other writings are published, and later, he was professor of theology in the Auburn theological seminary. Dr. Richards, like Dr. Johnes, was of Welsh descent. His salary was $440, in quarterly payments, the use of the parsonage, and firewood. To supplement this income, resort was had to a "wood-frolick", which was, we are told, a great event in the parish and to which the men brought the minister's years' supply of fuel and for which the ladies prepared a supper. The "spinning visit" was another feature of his pastorate, on which occasion were brought various amounts of "linen thread, yard and cloth". The thread brought, being not always of the same texture and size, it was often a puzzle indeed to the weaver to "make the cloth and finish it alike". At last the meagreness of this pastor's salary proved so great a perplexity, especially as his expenses were increasing with his growing family, that he gave up the problem, and went to Newark, N. J., accepting a call from the First Presbyterian

Church there, from which, after fifteen years, he went as professor of theology to the Auburn Seminary, where he remained until his death in 1843.

Rev. Albert Barnes.

Fifth in order of these early divines of the Morristown's First Church, is the Rev. Albert Barnes. He occupied this pastorate from 1825 to June 1830. It was here that he preached, in 1829, that remarkable sermon, "The Way of Salvation", which was the entering wedge that prepared the way for the unfortunate division among the Presbyterians into the two schools Old and New, which division and the names attached to each side, it may gladly be said, came to an end by a happy union of the two branches, a few years ago.

The Rev. Albert Barnes was also a pioneer of the Temperance movement in Morristown and his eloquence and influence in this cause resulted in the closing of several distilleries. From Morristown he was called to Philadelphia, where he passed through his severest trials. It is needless to mention that he was a voluminous writer and that he has made a world-wide reputation by his valuable "Notes on the Gospels", so well-known to all Biblical scholars. Rev. Mr. Henderson of London says: "I consider Barnes 'Notes on the New Testament' to be one of the most valuable boons bestowed in these latter days upon the Church of Christ." And the Rev. David King of Glasgow says: "The primary design of the Rev. Albert Barnes' books is to furnish Sunday School teachers with plain and simple explanations of common difficulties."

We are impressed with the rare modesty of so eminent a writer and distinguished divine when he read that the Rev. Albert Barnes several times refused the title of "D. D.", from conscientious motives.

Among the celebrated sermons and addresses published by this author was one very powerful sermon on "The Sovereignty of God", and also an "Address delivered July 4th, 1827," at the Presbyterian church, Morristown. In the "Advertisement" or preface, to the former, the author says in pungent words: "It was written during the haste of a weekly preparation for the Sabbath and is not supposed to contain anything new on the subject. * * * The only wonder is that it (the very plain doctrine of the Bible) should ever have been called in question or disputed—or that in a world where man's life and peace and hopes, all depend on the truth that GOD REIGNS, such a doctrine *should have ever needed any demonstration.*

The condition of Morristown when Mr. Barnes came into the pastorate, in respect of intemperance was almost beyond the power of imagination, serious, as the evil seems to us at the present day. He found "drinking customs in vogue and distilleries dotted all over the parish." Fearlessly he set himself to stem this evil, which indeed he did succeed in arresting to a large extent. His "Essays on Temperance" are marvellous productions, as full of fire and energy and the power of conviction to-day as when first issued from the press, and these addresses were so powerful in their effect on the community that "soon," says our historian, Rev. Dr. Green, "seventeen (of the 19) distilleries were closed and not long after his departure, the fires of the other two went out."

In the course of one of his arguments, he says: "There are many, flitting in pleasure at an imagined rather than a real distance, who may be saved from entering the place of the wretched dying, and of the horrid dead. Here I wish to take my stand. I wish to tell the mode in which men become abandoned. In the language of a far better moralist and reprover than I am (Dr. Lyman Beecher), I wish to lay down a chart of this way to destruction, and to rear a monument of warning upon every spot where a wayfaring man has been ensnared and destroyed.

I commence with the position that no man probably ever became designedly a drunkard. I mean that no man ever sat down coolly and looked at the redness of eyes, the haggardness of aspect, the weakness of limbs, the nausea of stomach, the profaneness and obscenity and babbling of a drunkard and deliberately desired all these. I shall be slow to believe that it is in human nature to wish to plunge into all this wretchedness. Why is it then that men become drunkards? I answer it is because the vice steals on them silently. It fastens on them unawares, and they find themselves wallowing in all this corruption, before they think of danger."

The power and beauty of Mr. Barnes' most celebrated sermon on "The Way of Salvation", impresses the reader, from page to page. Towards the close, he says:

FROM "THE PLAN OF SALVATION."

The scheme of salvation, I regard, as offered to the *world*, as free as the light of heaven, or the rains that burst on the mountains, or the full swelling of broad rivers and streams, or the heavings of the deep. And though millions do not receive it—though in regard to them the benefits of the plan are lost, and to them, in a certain sense, the plan may be said to be in vain, yet I see in this the hand of the same God that pours the rays of noonday on barren sands and genial showers on desert rocks, and gives life, bubbling springs and flowers, where no man is in *our* eyes, yet not to *His, in vain*. So is the offer of eternal life, to every man here, to every man everywhere, sincere and full—an offer that though it may produce no emotions in the sinner's bosom *here*, would send a thrill of joy through all the panting bosoms of the suffering damned."

Rev. Samuel Whelpley.

Rev. Mr. Whelpley became Principal of the Morristown Academy in 1797 and remained until 1805. He came from New England and was originally a Baptist, but in Morristown he gave up the plan which he had cherished of becoming a Baptist minister and united with the Presbyterian church. In 1803, he gave his reasons for this change of views, publicly, in a "Discourse delivered in the First Church" and published. His "Historical Compend" is one of his important works. It contains, "A brief survey of the great line of history from the earliest time to the present day, together with a general view of the world with respect to Civilization, Religion and Government, and a brief dissertation on the importance of historical knowledge." This was issued in two volumes "By Samuel Whelpley, A. M., Principal of Morris Academy" and was printed by Henry P. Russell and dedicated to Rev. Samuel Miller, D. D.

This author was not, by-the-way, the father of Chief Justice Whelpley, of Morristown, who also is noticed in this book, but was the cousin of his father, Dr. William A. Whelpley, a practicing physician here.

"Lectures on Ancient History, together with an allegory of Genius and Taste" was another of Mr. Whelpley's books. Among his works, perhaps the most celebrated was, and is, "The Triangle", a theological work which is "A Series of numbers upon Three Theological Points, enforced from Various Pulpits in the City of New York." This was published in 1817, and a new edition in 1832. In this work, says Hon. Edmund D. Halsey "the leaders and views of what was long afterward known as the Old School Theology were keenly criticised and ridiculed. The book caused a great sensation in its day and did not a little toward hastening the division in the Presbyterian Church into Old and New School. This book was published without his name, by "Investigator". In it the author says :

FROM "THE TRIANGLE."

"You shall hear it inculcated from Sabbath to Sabbath in many of our churches, and swallowed down, as a sweet morsel, by many a gaping mouth, that a man ought to feel himself actually guilty of a sin committed six thousand years before he was born; nay, that prior to all consideration of his own moral conduct, *he ought to feel himself deserving of eternal damnation for the first sin of Adam.* * * * No such doctrine is taught in the Scriptures, or can impose itself on any rational mind, which is not trammeled by education, dazzled by interest, warped by predjudice and bewildered by theory. This is one corner of the triangle above mentioned.

This doctrine perpetually urged, and the subsequent strain of teaching usually attached to it, will not fail to drive the incautious mind to secret and practical, or open infidelity. An attempt to force such monstrous absurdities on the human understanding, will be followed by the worst effects. A man who finds himself condemned for that of which he is not guilty will feel little regret for his real transgressions.

I shall not apply these remarks to the purpose I had in view, till I have considered some other points of a similar character;—or, if I may resort to the metaphor alluded to, till I have pointed out the other two angles of the triangle.

Stevens Johnes Lewis.

Mr. Lewis was a grandson of Rev. Dr. Timothy Johnes and great uncle of the Rev. Theodore L. Cuyler, D. D. He was a theologian whose writings made a ripple in the orthodox stream of thought, and was disciplined in the First church for his doctrines. He published two pamphlets in justification of his peculiar views. The first was on "The Moral Creation the peculiar work of Christ. A very different thing from that of the Physical Creation which is the exclusive work of God", printed in Morristown by L. B. Hull, in 1838. Also there was one entitled "Showing the manner in which they do things in the Presbyterian church in the Nineteenth Century". "For the rulers had agreed already that if any man did confess that Jesus was Christ ('was Christ, not God Almighty'), he should be put out of the synagogue." "Morristown, N. J., Printed for the author, 1837."

Rev. Rufus Smith Green, D. D.

The Rev. Dr. Green, so much esteemed by the people of all denominations in Morristown, has a claim to honorable mention among our authors, having written largely and to good purpose.

His "History of Morristown," a division of the book entitled the "History of Morris County", published by Munsell & Co., New York, in 1882, is a valuable contribution to our literature, combining in delightful form, a large amount of information from many sources, which has cost the writer much labor. As a book of reference it is in constant demand in the "Morristown Library" now, and one of the books which is not allowed long to remain out, for that reason. This fact carries its own weight without further comment.

Dr. Green succeeded the Rev. John Abbott French in June, 1877, to the pastorate of the First Presbyterian Church of Morristown, and remained until 1881, when he accepted the charge of the Lafayette St. Presbyterian Church of Buffalo, N. Y., and removed to that city.

After his graduation at Hamilton College, N. Y., in 1867, Dr. Green went abroad and was a student in the Berlin University during 1869 and '70. During this period he gained complete command of the German language, which has been vastly helpful to him in his writing as well as, in many instances, in his pastoral work. He was graduated from the Auburn Theological Seminary in 1873. He then accepted a charge at Westfield, N. Y., and in 1877 came to Morristown. During his Morristown pastorate, he began the publication of *The Record*, a monthly periodical devoted to historical matter connected with the First Church in particular, but also with Morristown generally and Morris County as well,—the First Church, in its history, striking it roots deep, and radiating in many directions. This was continued for the years 1880 and 1881, 24 numbers. Rev. Wm. Durant, Dr. Green's successor in the pastorate of the First Church, resumed the work in January 1883, and continued its publication until January 1886. It is an invaluable contribution to the early history of the town and county.

Another of Dr. Green's publications is "Both Sides, or Jonathan and Absalom", published in 1888 by the Presbyterian Board of Publication, Philadelphia. This is a volume of sermons to young men, the aim of which can be seen from the preface which we quote entire :

"It would be difficult to find two characters better fitted than those of Jonathan and Absalom to give young men right views of life—the one, in its nobleness and beauty, an inspiration ; the other, in its vanity and wicked self-seeking, an awful warning. The two present both sides of the picture, and from opposite points of view teach the same lessons never more important than at the present time. It has been the author's purpose to enforce these lessons rather than to write a biography. May they guide many a reader to the choice of the right side!"

In writing of the friendship of Jonathan and David the author says :

"The praises of Friendship have been sung by poets of all ages,—orator's have made it a theme for their eloquence,—philosophers have written treatises upon it,—historians have described its all too rare manifestations. No stories from the far off Past are more charming than those which tell of Damon and Pythias,—of Orestes and Pylades -of Nisus and Euryalus—but better and more inspiring than philosophic treatise or historic description, more beautiful even than song of poet, is the Friendship of which the text speaks,—the love of Jonathan for David. It is one of the world's ideal pictures, all the more prized, because it is not only ideal but real. It was the Divine love which made the earthly friendship so pure and beautiful."

For *Our Church at Work*, a monthly periodical of many years' standing connected with the Lafayette Street church, of Buffalo, Dr. Green has largely written.

An important pamphlet on "The Revised New Testament" was published in 1881, by the *Banner* Printing Office, of Morristown, and, in addition to these, fugitive sermons, and numerous articles for newspapers and periodicals have passed from his pen to print.

When Dr. Green left Morristown, this was the tribute given him at the final service in the old church where hundreds of people were turned away for want of room. These were the words of the speaker on that occasion : "Dr. Green came to a united people ; he has at all times presided over a united people and he leaves a united people."

Rev. William Durant.

Rev. Wm. Durant followed the Rev. Dr. Green in his ministry in the First Presbyterian Church in Morristown, May 11th, 1883, remaining in this charge until May, 1887, when he resigned, to accept the call of the Boundary Avenue Church, Baltimore, Md. He took up also, with Hon. John Whitehead as editor, at first, the onerous though very interesting work of *The Record*, which labor both he and

Rev. Dr. Green as well as Mr. Whitehead, gave "as a free will offering to the church and the community".

Rev. Mr. Durant was born in Albany, N. Y., and prepared for college at the Albany Academy. He then travelled a year in Europe, studied theology at Princeton and was graduated from that college in 1872. The same year he took charge of the First Presbyterian Church in Milwaukee, for the summer only, after which he traveled through the west, and was then ordained to the ministry, in Albany, and installed pastor of the Sixth Presbyterian Church of that city, from which, in 1883, he came to Morristown, as we have said.

While in Albany he edited "Church Polity", a selection of articles contributed by the Rev. Charles Hodge, D. D., to the *Princeton Review;* Scribner's Sons, publishers. Afterwards, in Morristown, he published a "History of the First Presbyterian Church, Morristown," with genealogical data for 13,000 names on its registers; a part of this only has been published. "A Letter from One in Heaven; An Allegory", is a booklet of singular interest as the title would suggest. One or two short stories of his have been published among numerous contributions to religious papers on subjects of ecclesiology and practical religion, also a score or more of sermons in pamphlet form.

He is at present preparing, for publication, a

"Durant Genealogy", to include all now in this country of the name and descent. This was begun in the fall of 1886.

In the opening number of *The Record* for January 1883, after the suspension of the publication for two years, we print the following paper of "Congratulations" from Rev. Wm. Durant, which as it concerns the spirit of Morristown, we give in full :

"CONGRATULATIONS", ON THE REVIVAL OF "THE RECORD".

The season is propitious. *The Record* awakes from a long nap—not as long as Rip VanWinkle's—to greet its readers with a Happy New Year.

But where is the suggestion of those garments all tattered and torn ? We mistake. It is not Rip VanWinkle, but the Sleeping Beauty who comes to us, by fairy enchantment, decked in the latest fashion. Sleep has given her new attractions.

Happy we who may receive her visits with the changing moons, and scan her treasures new and old. Her bright look shows a quick glance to catch flashes of present interest. And there is depth, too, a far offness about her glance. Its gleam of the present is the shimmer that lies on the surface of a deep well of memory. What stories she can tell us of the past ! Though so youthful her appearance, she romped with our grandmothers and made lint for the hospital and blankets for the camps, that winter Washington was here, when his bare-foot soldiers shivered in the snows on Mount Kemble or lay dying by scores in the old First Church. Yes, she was a girl of comely parts, albeit of temper to enjoy a tiff with her good mother of Hanover, when our city was a frontier settlement, full only of log cabins and primitive hardships in the struggle against wild nature.

For a maiden still, and one who has seen so many summers, marvelous is her cheery, youthful look. Ponce de Leon made the mistake of his life when he sought his enchanted fountain in Florida instead of where Morristown was to be. It is not on the Green, for the aqueduct folks now hold the title.

From lips still ruddy with youth, is it not delicious to hear the gossip of olden time! And our maiden knows it all, for she was present at all the baptisms, danced at all the weddings, thrilled with heavenly joy when our ancestors confessed the Son of Man before the high pulpit, and stood with tears in her eyes when one after another they were laid in the graves behind. Their names are still on her tongues' end, and it is with loving recollection that she tells of the long lists like the one she brings this month.

But her gossip is not all of names. What she

will tell of events and progress, of the unwritten history that has given character to families, to State or Nation, there is no need of predicting, we have only to welcome her at our fireside and listen while she speaks.

Rev. J. Macnaughtan, D. D.

Dr. Macnaughtan, present pastor of the First Presbyterian Church and successor of Rev. Wm. Durant, a profound scholar and thinker and most interesting writer, has not entered largely into the world of letters as an author or a publisher of his writings. Some papers of his, and some articles have, however, been published from time to time and a sermon now and then, notably, within two years, one on "Revision : Its Spirit and Aims", and the Centennial Sermon that was delivered on Sunday, October 11th, 1891, on the memorable occasion of the Centennial of the erection of the present First Church building. This sermon was published in the *Banner*, of Morristown, and is to appear again, with all the interesting addresses and sketches, given on that day and on the following days of the celebration,—in the book which Mr. Whitehead is preparing on "The History of the First Presbyterian Church".

Dr. Macnaughtan's pastorate will always be associated with this time of historic retrospection and also with the passing away of the old building and the introduction of the new. Of this old building, endeared to many of Morristown's people, this book will probably be the last to make mention while it stands. An old-time resident touchingly says of the coming event : "There have been great changes within my remembrance (in Morristown). I was born in 1813 and have always lived where I do now. My memory goes back to the time when there were only two churches in the town ; the First Presbyterian and the Baptist. The latter is now being removed for other purposes, and our old church, that has stood through its 100 years, will soon be removed, to make place for a new one. I was in hopes it would remain during my days, but the younger generation wants something new, more in the present style."

FROM THE "CENTENNIAL SERMON."

Ask now of the days that are past.
—*Deuteronomy 4 : 32.*

One hundred years ago on the 20th of last September (1891), a very stirring and animated scene could have been witnessed on this spot where we are so quietly assembled this morning for our Sabbath worship. On the morning of that day, some 200 men were assembled here, with the implements of their calling, and the task of erecting this now venerable structure was begun. The willing hands of trained mechanics and others, under the direction of Major Joseph Lindsley and Gilbert Allen, both elders of the church, lifted aloft these timbers, and the work of creating this sanctuary was begun. When one inspects the timbers forming the frame of this structure, great masses of hewn oak, and enough of it to build two structures of the size of this edifice, as such buildings are now erected, one sees how necessary it was that so great a force of men should be on hand. One can well believe that the animation of the scene was only equalled by the excited emotions of the people, in whose behalf the building was being erected. The task begun was a gigantic one for that time. The plans contemplated the erection of a structure which, "for strength, solidity and symmetry of proportion."

should "not be excelled by any wooden building of that day in New Jersey." But it was not alone the generosity of the plan of the structure that made it a gigantic enterprise, but the material circumstances of the people who had undertaken the work. The men of a hundred years ago were rich for the most part only in faith and self-sacrifice. But looking at this house as it stands to-day, and remembering the generations who under this roof have been reproved, guided, comforted, and pointed to the supreme ends of being, who shall say that they who are rich only in faith and self-sacrifice are poor? Out of their material poverty our fathers builded this house through which for a century God has been sending to our homes and into our lives the rich messages of his grace and salvation—where from week to week our souls have been fronted with the invisible and eternal, and where by psalm and hymn, and the solemn words of God's grand Book, and the faithful preaching of a long line of devoted and consecrated men, we have been reminded of the seriousness and awfulness of life, of the sublime meanings of existence, and the grand ends which it is capable of conserving; where multitudes have confessed a Saviour found, and have consecrated their souls to their new found Lord; where doubts have been dispelled, where sorrow has been assuaged, where grief has found its antidote and the burdened heart has found relief; where thought has been lifted to new heights of outlook, and the heart has been enriched with conceptions of God and duty that have given a new grandeur to existence, where the low horizons of time have been lifted and pushed outward, till the soul has felt the thrill of a present eternity. Our heritage has indeed been great in the possession of this old white Meeting-House.

(Several points Dr. Macnaughtan makes as follows):

In scanning the life that has been lived here during the last hundred years, I find it, first of all, to have been *a consistent life*. It is a life that has been true to the great principles of religious truth for which the name of Presbyterian stands. * * I find, in the second place, that the life that has been lived here has been *an evangelistic life*. * * In the third place, it has been an *expansive life*. *

* * * Here has been nourished the mother hive from which has gone forth, to the several churches in the neighborhood, the men and women who have made these churches what they are to-day. * * * In the fourth place, it has been *a beneficent life*. The voices that have rung out from this place have but one accent—Righteousness.

Rev. C. DeWitt Bridgman.

The Baptist Church is the second of our Morristown churches in point of age. It was formed August 11, 1752. It was the Rev. Reune Runyon who was its pastor during those terrible days of the Revolution, when the scourge of small pox prevailed. All honor to him, for a "brave man and true", as says our historian, "loyal to his country as well as faithful to his God." He, with good Parson Johnes, upheld the arm of Washington and both offered, for their congregations, their church buildings, to shelter the poor, suffering soldiers, in their conflict with the dread disease. This constancy is all the more creditable when we consider that two of his immediate predecessors had already fallen victims to the disease, each, after a very short pastorate.

Rev. C. DeWitt Bridgman claims our attention as a writer. A friend writing of the Rev. Mr. Bridgman, at the present time, says: "The Baptist Church at Morristown was the first pastorate of the Rev. C. DeWitt Bridgman and I think was filled to the entire satisfaction of his friends and admirers who were and *are* many. His brilliant oratory and rare gifts as an eloquent, scholarly and polished speaker are well-known. A life-long friend of my family, I dwell on the lovable and loyal characteristics which have made him dear to us."

In a letter received by the author of this book, from the Rev. Mr. Bridgman, we find a little retrospect which is interesting. " I went to Morristown," he says, "immediately after graduating from the Baptist Theological Seminary, in Rochester, in 1857. The Baptist Church had a membership of about 130, all but five or six of them living outside the village. The House of Worship was small and uncomfortable, but at once was modernized and enlarged, and the congregation soon after grew to the measure of its capacity. As I was then but 22 years old, the success was in some measure due, I must believe, to the sympathy which the young men of the village had for one with their ardor. However that may be, the church, for the first time, seemed to be recognized as in touch with the life of the village, and it was the opening of a new chapter in the history of the church."

Rev. Mr. Bridgman made the oration at the 4th of July county celebration, soon after his arrival, in the First Presbyterian church. For two and a half years, he remained in this charge when he removed to Jamaica Plain, Mass. Subsequently he was pastor for fifteen years, of Emmanuel Baptist church, Albany, then for thirteen years of the Madison Avenue church in New York, when he entered the Episcopal church and became rector of "Holy Trinity," on Lenox avenue and 122nd St., New York, a position which he still occupies.

Articles from this writer's pen have appeared from time to time during this long career, in the religious press, besides occasional sermons of power and impressiveness.

In the letter above referred to, Mr. Bridgman says he remembers very pleasantly many acquaintances among those not connected with his church as well as those in its membership and "it will be a great pleasure," he adds, "to recall the old faces and the old days, over the pages of your book, when it shall have been issued."

Rev. G. D. Brewerton, who is already among our *Poets*, followed the Rev. Mr. Bridgman, in 1861, for a short pastorate.

Rev. J. T. Crane, D. D.

The Methodist Episcopal church was the third in order among our local churches and was organized in 1826. Among the many pastors of this church, the Rev. Dr. Crane demands our notice as an author. It was he who laid the corner-stone, while pastor in 1866, of the third church building, a superb structure, which is mostly the generous gift of the Hon. George T. Cobb, who gave to it $100,000.

We find in our Morristown library, an interesting and valuable volume entitled "Arts of Intoxication ; the Aim and the Results." By Rev. J. T. Crane, D. D., author of "Popular Amusements", "The Right Way", &c. This author was a voluminous writer, and recognized as one of the ablest in the Conference. This book was published in 1870 and in it the author says :

"The great problem of the times is, 'What shall be done to stay the ravages of intoxication?' The evil pervades every grade of civilization as well as all depths of barbarism, the degree of its prevalence in any locality being determined apparently more by the facilities for indulgence than by climate, race or religion.

"In heathen China the opium vice is working death. On the eastern slopes of the Andes, the poor remnants of once powerful nations are enslaved by the coca-leaf, and the thorn-apple, and thus are fixed in their fallen estate. In Europe and America the nations who claim to be the leaders of human progress are fearfully addicted to narcotic indulgences which not only impose crushing burdens upon them, wasting the products of their industry and increasing every element of evil among them, but render even their friendship dangerous to the savage tribes among whom their commerce reaches. Italy, France, Germany, England and the United States are laboring beneath a mountain weight of crime, poverty, suffering and wrong of every description, and no nation on either continent is fully awake to the peril of the hour. Questions of infinitely less moment create political crises, make wars, and overthrow dynasties." Then, Dr. Crane proceeds to show that the "Art of Intoxication" is not a device of modern times, and quotes from the Odyssey, in illustration; he discusses the mystery of it and notices the mutual dependence of the body and spirit upon one another He tells the story of the coca-leaf, thorn-apple and the betel-nut, also of tobacco and treats of the tobacco habit and the question generally ; of the hemp intoxicant and the opium habit and, finally, of alcohol,—its production, its delusions, its real effect, the hereditary effect, the wrong of indulgence, the folly of beginning, the strength of the enemy, the damage done and remedial measures. It is the most picturesque and attractive little book on the subject that we have seen."

Rev. Henry Anson Buttz, D. D., LL. D.

Rev. Dr. Buttz, President of Drew Theological Seminary, ministered in the Methodist Episcopal Church in Morristown from 1868 to 1870. While preaching in Morristown he was elected Adjunct Professor of Greek in Drew Theological Seminary, filling the George T. Cobb professorship. This chair he occupied until December 7, 1880, when he was unanimously elected to succeed Bishop Hurst. He received the degree of A. M. in 1861 from Princeton College and in 1864 from Wesleyan University, and that of D. D. from Princeton in 1875.

Dr. Buttz is without doubt one of the most distinguished men of the Methodist Episcopal Church. His preaching, always without notes, is impressive and of the style usually designated as expository. His contributions to English literature have been to a large extent, fugitive articles on many subjects in various church periodicals, but his greatest published work is probably a Greek text book, "The Epistle to the Romans", which is regarded by scholars as one of the most accurate and critical guides to the study of that letter of St. Paul. It is announced by him that all the New Testament Epistles are to be published on the same plan. "The entire work, when completed," says a writer in the Mt. Tabor *Record*, "will be a valuable contribution to Biblical literature, and an enduring monument to the genius and research of the author."

Rev. Jonathan K. Burr, D. D.

Rev. Dr. Burr, one of the most distinguished divines of the Methodist Episcopal church, was stationed at Morristown in 1870-2. He was born in Middletown, Conn., on Sept. 21st, 1825; was graduated at Wesleyan University in 1845; studied in Union Theological Seminary in New York city in 1846; in 1847 he entered the ministry, occupying some of the most important pulpits within the Newark Conference of the M. E. Church. He was also professor of Hebrew and Exegetical Theology in Drew Theological Seminary, while pastor of Central church, Newark, N. J. He was author of the Commentary on the Book of Job, in the Whedon series, and a member of the Committee of Revision of the New Testament. He received the degree of D. D. from Wesleyan in 1872; also, in that year, he was delegate to the General Conference of the M. E. church. For many years he was a trustee of the Wesleyan University and also of Hackettstown Seminary.

He wrote the articles upon Incarnation and Krishna in McClintock and Strong's Biblical Cyclopædia and also made occasional contributions to the religious journals. In 1879 his health failed and he was obliged to retire from the ministry. His death followed on April 24th, 1882.

From his "Commentary on the Book of Job" we take the following paragraph out of an Excursus on the passage, "I know that my Redeemer liveth," &c.:

FROM "COMMENTARY ON THE BOOK OF JOB."

In the earlier ages truth was given in fragments. It was isolated, succinct, compressed, not unlike the utterances of oracles. The reader will be reminded of the gospel given in the garden, the prediction by Enoch of a judgment to come, the promise of Shiloh and the prophecies through the Gentile Balaam. They, who thus became agents for the transmission of divine truth, may have failed to comprehend it in all its bearings, but the truth is on that account none the less rich and comprehensive. In the living God who shall stand upon the dust, Job may not have seen Christ in the fulness of the atonement ; nor in the view of God "from the flesh", have grasped the glories of the resurrection morn: but the essential features of these two cardinal doctrines of Scripture are these, identical with those we now see in greater completeness; even as the outlines of a landscape, however incompletely sketched, are still one with those of the rich and perfected picture.

Rev. J. E. Adams.

Rev. Mr. Adams, the present pastor of the Morristown Methodist Episcopal Church, entered upon this charge in May, 1889, succeeding the Rev. Oliver A. Brown, D. D. He was transferred, by Bishop Merrill, from the Genesee Conference to the Newark Conference for that purpose, the church having invited him and he having accepted a few months previously. He came directly from the First Methodist Church of Rochester, N. Y., to Morristown. Dr. Adams is a clever and thoughtful writer. He says himself: " I have done nothing in authorship that is worthy of record. I have only written newspaper and magazine articles occasionally and published a few special sermons. I am fond of writing and have planned quite largely for literary work, including several books, but very exacting parish work has thus far delayed execution."

Some of his sermons published are as follows :

"St. Paul's Veracity in Christian Profession Sustained by an Infallible Test. Text : Romans 1:16. Published in New Brunswick, N. J., 1877."

"The Final Verdict in a Famous Case. A Bible Sermon Preached Before the Monmouth County Bible Society, and published by that Society in 1883."

"The Golden Rule. A Discussion of Christ's Words in Matthew 7:12, in the First Methodist Episcopal Church, Rochester, N. Y. Published in Rochester, 1886."

"Human Progress as a Ground of Thanksgiving. A Thanksgiving Sermon, Preached in Morristown, N. J., 1889, and published by request."

Rev. James Munroe Buckley, D.D., LL. D.

At this point, three theologians and editors present themselves, not occupying definite pulpits, but often taking a place in one or another, as opportunity for usefulness occurs. These are the Rev. James M. Buckley, D. D. and the Rev. James M. Freeman, D. D., of the Methodist Episcopal Church and the Rev. Kinsley Twining, D. D., of the Congregational.

Of the genius of Dr. Buckley, it may be said, it is so all-embracing that it would be difficult to tell what he is *not*, in distinctive literary capacity. First of all certainly, he is a theologian, then editor, orator, scientist, traveler and so on among our classifications. One is led to apply to him the familiar saying that "he who does one thing well, can do all things well."

It is pleasant to note that a man of such keen observation and well balanced judgment as Dr. Buckley, after extensive travel in our own country and abroad can state, as many of us have heard him, that, of all the beautiful spots he has seen in one country and another, none is so beautiful, so attractive and so desirable, in every respect, as Morristown.

Dr. Buckley is a true Jerseyman, for he was born in Rahway, N. J., and educated at Pennington, N. J. Seminary. He studied theology, after one year at Wesleyan University, at Exeter, N. H., and joined the New Hampshire Methodist Episcopal Conference on trial, being stationed at Dover in that state. In 1864 he went to Detroit and in 1866 to Brooklyn, N. Y. In 1881, he was elected to the Methodist Ecumenical Conference in London and also in that year was elected editor of the New York *Christian Advocate*, which position he has held to the present time. The degree of D. D. was conferred upon him by Wesleyan University in 1872 and LL. D. by Emory and Henry College, Virginia.

As a traveler, Dr. Buckley is represented by his work on "The Midnight Sun and the Tsar and the Nihilist" being a book of "Adventures and Observations in Norway, Sweden and Russia". This book is full as we might expect of information communicated in the most entertaining manner, full of very graphic descriptions, original comments, spices of humor, with a clever analysis of the people and conditions of life around the author—all of which characteristics give us a feeling that we are making with him this tour of observation. In the chapters on "St. Petersburg" and "Holy Moscow", we see these qualities especially evidenced. Here is a short paragraph quite representative of the author, who is writing of the Cathedral of the Assumption, Moscow, an immense building in the Byzantine style of architecture, in which a service of the Greek church is going on :

"The monks sang magnificently, but there was not a face among them that exhibited anything but the most profound indifference. Some of the young monks fixed their eyes upon the ladies who accompanied me from the hotel, and kept them there even while they were singing the prayers, which they appeared to repeat like parrots, without any internal consciousness or recognition of the meaning of the words, but in most melodious tones." Again, the author visits a Tartar Mosque where he and his party are told "with oriental courtesy, that they may be permitted to remain outside the door, looking in, while the service progresses:"

"Here," he says, "I was brought for the first time in direct contact with that extraordinary system of religion which, without an idol, an image, or a picture, holds one hundred and seventy million of the human race in absolute subjection, and whose power, after the lapse of twelve hundred years, is as great as at the beginning."

Of the summoning of the people to prayers from the minaret, he writes:

"Dr. J. H. Vincent for many years employed at Chatauqua the late A. O. Van Lennep, who went upon the summit of a house at evening time, dressed in the Turkish costume, and called the people to prayer.

"I supposed when I heard him that he was overdoing the matter as respects the excruciating tones and variations of voice which he employed, or else he had an extraordinary qualification for making hideous sounds, whereby he out-Turked the Turks, and sometimes considered whether Dr. Vincent did not deserve to be expostulated with for allowing such frightful noises to clash with the ordinary sweet accords of Chatauqua. Worthy Mr. Van Lennep will never appear there again, but I am able to vindicate him from such unworthy suspicion as I cherished. He did his best to produce the worst sounds he could, but his worst was not bad enough to equal the reality. With his hands on his ears, the Mohammedan priest of the great mosque of Moscow emitted, for the space of seven minutes or thereabouts, a series of tones for which I could find no analogy in anything I had ever heard of the human voice. There seemed occasionally a resemblance to the smothered cries of a cat in an ash-hole ; again to the mournful wail of a hound tied behind a barn ; and again to the distant echo of a tin horn on a canal-boat in a section where the canal cuts between the mountains. The reader may think this extravagant, but it is not, and he will ascertain if ever he hears the like."

Dr. Buckley's published writings are, besides his great work as editor of *The Christian Advocate*, in editorials and in many directions,—and besides the book we have already mentioned, "The Midnight Sun, the Tsar and the Nihilist"; "Oats versus Wild Oats"; "Christians and the Theatre"; "Supposed Miracles", and " Faith Healing, Christian Science, and Kindred Phenomena", published

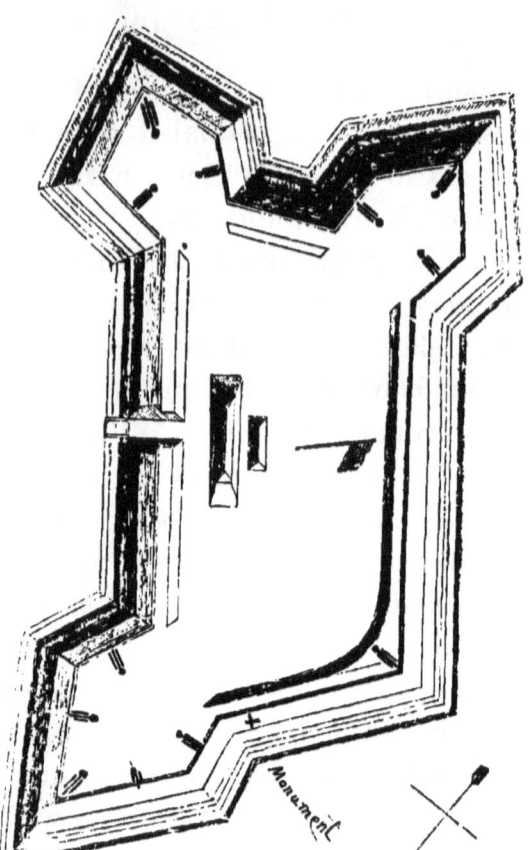

PLAN OF FORT NONSENSE.
FROM PEN AND INK SKETCH BY MAJOR J. P. FARLEY, U. S. A.

quite recently (in October, 1892). Among magazine articles, may be especially mentioned "Two Weeks in the Yosemite", and in pamphlet form have appeared some letters worthy of mention, about "A Hereditary Consumptive's Successful Battle for Life".

As a philanthropist, Dr. Buckley is widely interested in all questions concerning humanity, and he responds continually with his time and thought to the appeals made to him from one direction and another. Our own State Charities Aid Association of New Jersey owes much to Dr. Buckley for his warm and earnest co-operation in its early struggles in Morristown for existence, and in its work, since then.

As an orator, all who have heard Dr. Buckley feel that he has what is called the magnetic power of controlling and carrying with him his audience, and a remarkable capacity for mastering widely different subjects. The beautiful spring day (April 27, 1888), will long be remembered, when the people of Morristown had the opportunity of hearing his eloquent address at the unveiling of the Soldiers Monument on Fort Nonsense.

In Dr. Buckley's last book on "Faith Healing; Christian Science and Kindred Phenomena," published by the Century Company, quite lately, (October, 1892), the subjects of Astrology, Coincidences, Divinations, Dreams, Nightmares and Somnambulism, Presentiments, Visions, Apparitions and Witchcraft are treated. Papers have been contributed by him on these subjects at intervals for six years with reference to this book, but the contents of the latter are not identical, *i. e.* they have been improved and added to. From this we give the following extract :

EXTRACT FROM "FAITH HEALING, CHRISTIAN SCIENCE AND KINDRED PHENOMENA."

The relation of the Mind Cure movement to ordinary medical practice is important. It emphasizes what the most philosophical physicians of all schools have always deemed of the first importance, though many have neglected it. It teaches that medicine is but occasionally necessary. It hastens the time when patients of discrimination will rather pay more for advice how to live and for frank declarations that they do not need medicine, than for drugs. It promotes general reliance upon those processes which go on equally in health and disease.

But these ethereal practitioners have no new force to offer ; there is no causal connection between their cures and their theories.

What they believe has practically nothing to do

with their success. If a new school were to arise claiming to heal diseases without drugs or hygiene or prayer, by the hypothetical odylic force invented by Baron Reichenbach, the effect would be the same, if the practice were the same.

Recoveries as remarkable have been occurring through all the ages, as the results of mental states and nature's own powers.

*   *

The verdict of mankind excepting minds prone to vagaries on the border-land of insanity, will be that pronounced by Ecclesiasticus more than two thousand years ago :

"THE LORD HATH CREATED MEDICINES OUT OF THE EARTH ; AND HE THAT IS WISE WILL NOT ABHOR THEM. MY SON, IN THY SICKNESS BE NOT NEGLIGENT ; BUT PRAY UNTO THE LORD AND HE WILL MAKE THEE WHOLE. LEAVE OFF FROM SIN AND ORDER THY HANDS ARIGHT, AND CLEANSE THY BREAST FROM ALL WICKEDNESS. THEN GIVE PLACE TO THE PHYSICIAN, FOR THE LORD HATH CREATED HIM ; LET HIM NOT GO FROM THEE, FOR THOU HAST NEED OF HIM. THERE IS A TIME WHEN IN THEIR HANDS THERE IS GOOD SUCCESS. FOR THEY ALSO SHALL PRAY UNTO THE LORD, THAT HE WOULD PROSPER THAT WHICH THEY GIVE FOR EASE AND TO PROLONG LIFE."

Rev. James M. Freeman, D. D.

Dr. Freeman is the second of the trio of theologians and editors, whose homes are in Morristown. For the last twenty years, he has been associate editor of "Sunday School Books and Periodicals and of Tracts" of the Methodist Episcopal Church. His Biblical studies are well known. His "Hand-Book of Bible Manners and Customs" was compiled with great care after years of research and published in 1877. This "Hand-Book" has been invaluable to Bible students and in it a large amount of information is given in small space, and in an interesting and entertaining manner.

Another important volume is "A Short History of the English Bible". Both these works are in the Morristown Library, presented by the author.

Many years ago, Dr. Freeman published, under the name of Robin Ranger, some charming story-books "for the little ones", in sets of ten tiny volumes. This work has placed him already in our group of *Story-Writers*.

Besides these, there are two Chautauqua Text-books, viz., "The Book of Books" and "Manners and Customs of Bible Times", also "The Use of Illustration in Sunday School Teaching".

The "Hand-Book of Bible Manners and Customs", in particular, and the "Short History of the English Bible" are books which one can not look into without desiring to own. In the former, the author says in his short but admirable preface :

"Though the Bible is adapted to all nations, it is in many respects an Oriental book. It represents the modes of thought and the peculiar customs of a people who, in their habits, widely differ from us. One who lived among them for many years has graphically said : 'Modes, customs, usages, all that you can set down to the score of the national, the social, or the conventional, are precisely as different from yours as the east is different from the west. They sit when you stand ; they lie when you sit ; they do to the head what you do to the feet ; they use fire when you use water ; you shave the beard, they shave the head ; you move the hat, they touch the breast ; you use the lips in salutation, they touch the forehead and the cheek ; your house looks outwards, their house looks inwards ; you go *out* to take a walk, they go *up* to enjoy the fresh air ; you drain your land, they sigh for water ; you bring your daughters out, they keep their wives and daughters in ; your ladies go barefaced through the streets, their ladies are always covered'.

"The Oriental customs of to-day are, mainly, the same as those of ancient times. It is said by a recent writer that 'the Classical world has passed away. We must reproduce it if we wish to see it as it was.' While this fact must be remembered in the interpretation of some New Testament passages, it is nevertheless true that many ancient customs still exist in their primitive integrity. If a knowledge of Oriental customs is essential to a right understanding of numerous Scripture passages, it is a cause of rejoicing that these customs are so stereotyped in their character that we have but to visit the Bible lands of the present day to see the modes of life of patriarchal times."

Therefore, the author undertakes and undertakes with remarkable success, to illustrate the Bible by an explanation of the Oriental customs to which it refers.

Rev. Kinsley Twining, D. D., LL. D.

Rev. Dr. Twining, up to 1879, devoted his time and attention entirely to the ministry and charge of two large city Congregational churches, one in Providence, R. I. While in the latter city, he published a book of "Hymns and Tunes", for his church there, which was acceptable and popular among the people, and contributed largely to develop the hearty congregational singing for which end it was compiled. While in this charge, he was for some time abroad, and mingled considerably in the literary life of Germany, and also in the musical life of that country. Hence, he is a fine theorist in music.

Since 1879 he has been literary editor of *The Independent*, and during these years he has written enough valuable editorials and reviews to fill many books. Many of his lectures, addresses, essays and other writings have appeared in magazines and other publications, notably a charming description of an "Ascent of Monte Rosa" in the *American Journal of Science and Arts*, of May, 1862. We find in a book entitled "Boston Lectures, 1872", a chapter given to one on "The Evidence of the Resurrection of Jesus Christ, by Rev. Kinsley Twining, Cambridge, Mass.", in which the argument is, as might be expected, keen and clear. One of his more recent published papers was read by him at one of the Literary Reunions at Mr. Bowen's in Brooklyn, N. Y., and attracted much attention. It has since been given in Morristown : subject, "The Wends, or a Queer People Surviving in Prussia".

Dr. Twining has made a special study of Shakespeare and holds a high rank as a Shakesperian critic and scholar.

With regard to editorial work, it may be said an editor has a maximum of influence, the minimum of recognition,—for nobody knows who does it. It is certain that powerful editorials sometimes turn the tide of public opinion or actually establish certain results which affect the progress of the world, and at least make a mark in the world's advance. Who, indeed, can compute or measure the power of the press at the present day ?

We choose for Dr. Twining, some paragraphs from his editorial which has already acquired some celebrity in *The Independent* of Sept. 15, 1892, on John Greenleaf Whittier. The death of the poet occurred on the 7th of the same September and he had been one of the earliest and most regular contributors to that paper since 1851.

FROM EDITORIAL ON JOHN GREENLEAF WHITTIER.

It has been said that every man of genius makes a class distinct by himself, out of relation and out of comparison with everybody else. At all events poets do, the first born in the progeny of genius ; and of none of them is this truer than of the four great American poets, Bryant, Longfellow, Lowell and Whittier. In what order of merit they stand in their great poetic square, the distinct individuality of genius bestowed on each makes it needless to inquire. They have been our lights for half a century, and now that they have taken their permanent place in the galaxy of song, will continue to shine there, to use the phrase which Whittier himself invented for Dr. Bowditch's sun-dial, as long as there is need of their "light above" in our "shade below."

*   *   *

Whittier is the ballad-master and legend singer of the American people. Had he known the South and the West as he knew New England, he would have sung their legends as he has sung those of New England. The meaning of all this is that he is the minstrel of our people. This he has been, and this he will remain. Whether it is in the solemn wrath of the great ballad, "Skipper Ireson's Ride," one of the greatest in modern literature, in the high patriotic strain of "Barbara Frietchie," in the pathos of "The Swan Song," of "Father Avery," "The Witch's Daughter," or in the grim humor of "The Double-Headed Snake of Newberry."

"One in body and two in will,"
it matters little what the subject is, or from whence it comes, the poem has in it some reflection of the common humanity, and as such speaks and will speak to the hearts of men.

It has been the fashion to write of Victor Hugo as the poet of democratic humanity. We shall not dispute his claim. There is a certain epic grandeur in his work which entitles him to a seat alone. But to those who believe the world is moving toward a democracy whose ideals are the realization of the

Sermon on the Mount, whose essence is ethical, and whose laws are gentleness, usefulness and love, Greenleaf Whittier will be the true democratic poet whose heart beats most nearly with the pulses of the democratic age, and who best represents the principles which are to give it permanence.

Rev. Theodore Ledyard Cuyler, D.D.

The Rev. Dr. Cuyler should immediately follow the group of editors and theologians, as he has been a regular writer for the religious press, as well as for the secular, for many years. To the former he has contributed more than 3,000 articles, many of which have been republished and translated into foreign languages.

In reply to a request for certain information, Dr. Cuyler, in a letter dated from Brooklyn, January 13, 1890, and written "in a sick room, where he was laid up with the 'Grip'", a disease of the present day which we hope may become historic,—replies to the author of this book as follows:

"Probably no American author has a *longer* association with Morristown than I have; for my ancestors have laid in its church-yards for more than a century.

"My great-great-grandfather, Rev. Dr. Timothy Johnes, preached in the 1st Presbyterian Church for 50 years and administered the Communion to General Washington.

"My great-grandfather, Mr. Joseph Lewis, was a prominent citizen of Morristown and an active friend and counsellor of Washington.

"My grandmother, Anna B. Lewis, was born in Morristown.

"My mother, Louisa F. Morrell, was also born in Morristown (in 1802) in the old family "Lewis Mansion" in which Mr. William L. King now lives.

"I was at school in Morristown in 1835 and it was my favorite place for visits for *many, many* years. I have often preached or spoken there.

"The man most familiar with my literary work is Dr. J. M. Buckley, the editor of the *Christian Advocate*—who now resides in Morristown."

This letter was signed with his name, as "Pastor of Lafayette Avenue Presbyterian Church." Less than a month later he announced to his astonished congregation, his intention of resigning his charge among them on the first Sabbath of the following April, when it would be exactly thirty years since he came to a small band of 140 members, which then composed his flock. At the close of his remarks on that occasion he said: "It only remains for me to say that after forty-four years of uninterrupted ministerial labors it is but reasonable to ask for some relief from a strain that may soon become too heavy for me to bear."

During the celebration of the twenty-fifth anniversary of his pastorate, in 1885, he told his congregation that during that time he had preached over 2,300 discourses, had made over 1,000 addresses, officiated at about 600 marriages, baptized 800 children, received into the church 3,700 members, of whom about 1,600 were converts, and had lost but one Sunday for sickness. Probably few men are more widely known for their literary and oratorical powers and extended usefulness both in the pulpit and out of it. Few, if any, have accomplished more in the same number of years or made a wider circle of warm and earnest friends both at home and abroad. Among the latter is the Hon. Wm. E. Gladstone, and was, the late John Bright. In his sermons and addresses, the personality of Dr. Cuyler is so marked that to hear him once is to remember him always. In England he has been especially popular as a preacher and temperance advocate. The latter cause he has espoused most warmly during his entire life.

Dr. Cuyler was born in the beautiful village of Aurora, N. Y., upon Cayuga Lake, of which his great-grand-father, General Benjamin Ledyard, was the founder. He was graduated at Princeton in 1841, and at Princeton Theological Seminary in 1846. Two years later, he was ordained into the Presbyterian Ministry, and was installed pastor of the Third Presbyterian Church of Trenton, N. J., then of the Market St. Reformed Dutch Church of New York City, and in April 1860, of the Brooklyn Lafayette Avenue Presbyterian Church.

Among the author's books are the following, nearly all of which have been reprinted in London and have a very wide circulation in Great Britain. Five or six of them have been translated into Dutch and Swedish :

"Stray Arrows", "The Cedar Christian", "The Empty Crib", a small book published many years ago after the death of one of his children and full of solace and consolation to the hearts of sorrowing parents ; "Heart Life" ; "Thought Hives" ; "From the Nile to Norway"; "God's Light on Dark Clouds"; "Wayside Springs", and "Right to the Point," of the "Spare Minute Series".

Dr. Cuyler himself says that he considered his *chief* literary work to have been the preparation of over 3,000 articles for the leading religious papers of America. There might be added to this the publication of a large number of short and popular tracts.

Here again we find, as in several instances before recorded in this book, a man of long experience and good judgment placing in the highest rank of writings, useful to mankind, those done for the religious or secular newspapers. We give a short passage

FROM, "GOD'S LIGHT ON DARK CLOUDS."

There is only one practical remedy for this deadly sin of anxiety, and that is to *take short views*. Faith is content to live "from hand to mouth," enjoying each blessing from God as it comes. This perverse spirit of worry runs off and gathers some anticipated troubles and throws them into the cup of mercies and turns them to vinegar. A bereaved parent sits down by the new-made grave of a beloved child and sorrowfully says to herself, "Well, I have only one more left, and one of these days he may go off to live in a home of his own, or he may be taken away; and if he dies, my house will be desolate and my heart utterly broken." Now who gave that weeping mother permission to use that word "if"? Is not her trial sore enough now without overloading it with an imaginary trial? And if her strength breaks down, it will be simply because she is not satisfied with letting God afflict her; she tortures herself with imagined afflictions of her own. If she would but take a short view, she would see a living child yet spared to her, to be loved and enjoyed and lived for. Then, instead of having two sorrows, she would have one great possession to set over against a great loss; her duty to the living would be not only a relief to her anguish, but the best tribute she could pay to the departed.

Rt. Rev. Wm. Ingraham Kip, D.D., LL.D.

Bishop Kip, since 1853, Bishop of California, was called to old St. Peter's Church, Morristown, immediately after his taking orders in 1835. "The first time the service of the Protestant Episcopal Church was used in Morristown, so far as known," says our historian, "was in the Summer of 1812. At that time Bishop Hobart of New York was visiting Mr. Rogers at Morristown, and by invitation of the officers of the First Presbyterian Church, he officiated one Sunday in their church, preaching and using the Episcopal service."

For two years, 1820 and '21, the service was held on Sundays, at the house of George P. McCulloch, and finally on Dec. 4th, 1828, the church building was consecrated which has stood until quite recently. Now a superb stone edifice covers the ground of the old church.

In the ancestry of Bishop Kip we have a link with the far off story of France, for he is descended from Ruloff de Kype of the 16th Century, who was a native of Brittany and warmly espoused the part of the Guises in the French civil war between Protestants and Papists. After the downfall of his party, this Ruloff fled to the Low Countries; his son Ruloff became a Protestant and settled in Amsterdam and *his* son Henry made one of the Company which organized in 1588 to explore a northeast passage to the Indies. He came with his family, to America in 1635, but returned to Holland leaving here his two sons Henry and Isaac. Henry was a member of the first popular assembly in New Netherlands and Isaac owned the property upon which now stands the City Hall Park of New York.

In 1831, the young William Ingraham, was graduated at Yale College and after first studying law and then divinity was admitted to orders and at once became the third rector of St. Peter's, at Morristown, remaining from July 13th, 1835, until November of the following year. Columbia bestowed upon him in 1847, the degree of S. T. D. Between the rectorship of St. Peter's and the bishopric of California, he served as assistant at Grace Church, New York, and was rector of St. Paul's, at Albany.

Bishop Kip has published a large number of

THEOLOGIANS. 321

books, many of which have gone through several editions. In addition he has written largely for the *Church Review* and the *Churchman* and several periodicals. Among his books are "The Unnoticed Things of Scripture", (1868); "The Early Jesuit Missions" (2 Vols., 6 editions, 1846); "Catacombs of Rome", (8 editions, 1853); "Double Witness of the Church", (27 editions, 1845); Lenten "Fast", (15 editions, 1845); the last two were published in both England and America as was also "Christmas Holydays in Rome", (1846). Besides these are "Early Conflicts of Christianity", (6 editions); "Church of the Apostles"; "Olden Times in New York"; "Early Days of My Episcopate", (1892).

EXTRACT FROM THE PREFACE OF THE "EARLY JESUIT MISSIONS."

There is no page of our country's history more touching and romantic than that which records the labors and sufferings of the Jesuit Missionaries. In these western wilds they were the earliest pioneers of civilization and faith. The wild hunter or the adventurous traveler, who, penetrating the forests, came to new and strange tribes, often found that years before, the disciples of Loyola had preceded him in that wilderness. Traditions of the "Black-robes" still lingered among the Indians. On some moss-grown tree, they pointed out the traces of their work, and in wonder he deciphered, carved side by side on its trunk, the emblem of our salvation and the lilies of the Bourbons. Amid the snows of Hudson's Bay—among the woody islands and beautiful inlets of the St. Lawrence—by the council fires of the Hurons and the Algonquins—at the sources of the Mississippi, where first of the white men, their eyes looked upon the Falls of St. Anthony, and then traced down the course of the bounding river, as it rushed onward to earn its title of "Father of Waters"—on the vast prairies of Illinois and Missouri—among the blue hills which hem in the salubrious dwellings of the Cherokees and in the thick canebrakes of Louisiana—everywhere were found the members of the Society of Jesus. Marquette, Joliet, Brebeuf, Jogues, Lallemand, Rasles and Marest,—are the names which the West should ever hold in remembrance. But it was only by suffering and trial that these early labours won their triumphs. Many of them too were men who had stood high in camps and courts, and could contrast their desolate state in the solitary wigwam with the refinement and affluence which had waited on their early years. But now, all these were gone. Home—the love of kindred—the golden ties of relationship—all were to be forgotten by these stern and high-wrought men, and they were often to go forth into the wilderness, without an adviser on their way, save their God. Through long and sorrowful years, they were obliged to "sow in tears" before they could "reap in joy."

Rev. William Staunton, D. D.

With this author, the fifth rector of old St. Peter's Church, in Morristown, we go back in association to the ancient city of Chester, England, where he was born and where his grandfather on his mother's side was a leading dissenting minister and the founder of Queen's Street Chapel, Chester. His father, an intellectual man and well read in Calvinistic theology, also affiliated with the Independents, but was often led by his fine musical taste to attend with his son the services of the Cathedral. It was in this Cathedral of Chester, which is noted for the beauty and majesty with which the Church's ritual is rendered, that the boy acquired that love of music which placed him in after life in the front rank of church musicians. One who knew him well has said of him in this respect: "This knowledge of music was profound and comprehensive. He was not simply a musical critic or a composer of hymn tunes and chants, but he had followed out through all its intricacies the science of music. So well known was he for his learning and taste in this department that it was a common thing for professional musicians of distinction to go to him for advice and to submit their compositions to him, before publication. Much of his own music has been published. But his musical accomplishments are best attested by the work which he did as associate editor of Johnson's Encyclopedia." He was in particular, the musical editor of this work and wrote nearly all of the articles relating to music in it. He was also a prolific writer for church reviews and other periodicals. Among his publications in book-form are: "A Dictionary of the Church", (1839) ; "An Ecclesiastical Dictionary", (1861) ; "The Catechist's Manual", a series of Sunday School instruction books; "Songs and Prayers"; "Book of Common Prayer"; "A Church Chant Book", and "Episodes of Clerical and Parochial Life".

Dr. Staunton came with his father and the family, when fifteen years of age, to Pittsburg, Pa. He was closely associated with the Rev. Mr. Hopkins, afterward the Bishop of Vermont. His first ministerial charge was that of Zion Church, Palmyra, N. Y., and it was in 1840 he accepted the rectorship of St. Peter's Church, Morristown, which position he held for seven years. He then organized in Brooklyn, N. Y., a much needed parish, which he named St. Peter's after the parish he had just relinquished.

"Dr. Staunton," says the present rector of St. Peter's, the Rev. Robert N. Merritt, D. D., who took up the work of the parish in 1853, and to whose untiring exertions, the parish and the people of Morristown are largely indebted for the erection of the massive and beautiful stone structure that stands on the site of the church of Dr. Staunton's time,—"Dr. Staunton was no ordinary man, though he never obtained the position in the church to which his abilities entitled him. Besides being above the average clergyman in theological attainments, he was a scientific musician, a good mechanic, well read in general literature, and so close an observer of the events of his time that much information was always to be gained from him. His retiring nature and great modesty kept him in the back ground."

The following interesting reminiscence comes to us, in a letter, from one of the boys who was under his ministration when rector for seven years of old St. Peter's. "I remember", says this parishioner, "Dr. Staunton very distinctly and with much affection as well as regard and gratitude, for the training I had from him in the doctrines and ordinances of the church. He was for those days a very advanced churchman, being among the first to yield to the influence the Oxford movement was exercising and to adopt the advance it inaugurated in the ritual and service of the liturgy informing strictly however himself and teaching his people to recognize the authority of the rubrics. He maintained this, I think, till his death, and was ranked then as a conservative rather than a high churchman, though when he was here, the same attitude made him to be thought by some as almost dangerously ultra.

"He was not eloquent nor what might be called an attractive preacher, but wrote well and accomplished a great deal as a careful and impressive teacher of sound doctrine and christian morality.

"Dr. Staunton was an accomplished scholar in scientific as well as ecclesiastical learning, was skilled as a draughtsman and designed, I remember, the screen of old St. Peter's when the chancel stood at the South street end ; and it was wonderfully good and effective of its kind. He was also a trained musician, and at one time instructed a class of young ladies in thorough-bass, among them being the two Misses Wetmore, my eldest sister, and others, and, in addition to this, he made the choir while he was here, both in the music used and its efficiency, a vast improvement upon what it had been. He was a tall man, fully six feet, of a severe countenance and rather austere manner, leading him to be thought sometimes cold and unsympathetic, though really he was most kind and considerate, and in all respects a devoted and watchful pastor. He published, I think, a church dictionary later in life which is still a standard book and authority.

"These are my impressions of Dr. Staunton received principally as a very young boy, though confirmed by an acquaintance continued till his death, and I retain the most sincere gratitude for the abiding faith in the sound doctrine of the Episcopal Church which he, after my mother, so trained me in that I have accepted them ever since as impregnable ; and for this I am sure there are many others of his pupils and parishioners besides myself to 'call him blessed.'"

Rev. Arthur Mitchell, D. D.

Rev. Dr. Mitchell was the third pastor of the South Street Presbyterian Church, which was the fifth, says our historian, "in our galaxy of churches." The time of his ministration, during which the church was greatly enlarged, both internally and externally, was from 1861 to 1868.

Dr. Mitchell is the son of Matthew and Susan Swain Mitchell, and was born in Hudson, N. Y.

He was graduated at Williams College in 1853, was tutor in Lafayette College, Pa., for one year, and then traveled for a year in Europe and the East. Returning he entered the Union Theological Seminary of New York City and was graduated from there in 1859. In this year he accepted the charge of the Third Presbyterian Church in Richmond, Va., and in Oct. 1861, he became pastor of what was then called, the "Second Presbyterian Church" in Morristown. The first Presbyterian Church of Chicago, Ill., claimed him in 1868 and in 1880 the First Presbyterian Church of Cleveland, Ohio. In 1884, Dr. Mitchell became Secretary of the Foreign Missions of the Presbyterian Church to which position he had been called fifteen years before, but had felt constrained to decline. This important office, which from his intense and life-long interest in the great cause of Christian missions to the heathen world, he was remarkably qualified to fill, he has held to the present time. In all his ministrations, in each individual church which he has served, he has succeeded in imparting his own love of, and interest in, Foreign Missions and his position as Secretary of this department of the church organization has enabled him to stimulate the great congregations and masses of individuals throughout the denomination.

Dr. Mitchell's eloquence in the pulpit and on the platform, is so well-known that it seems hardly worth while to refer to it. Mastering his subject completely as he does, he has the rare power of condensing clearly and giving out his thoughts in language and in tones of voice which hold and attract his audience to the end. He has published no books, only sermons and addresses in pamphlet form and innumerable articles in magazines and newspapers. To the great value of this sort of literary work, several of our distinguished authors have already testified. In the *Church at Home and Abroad*, we find the most exhaustive articles from Dr. Mitchell's pen, on the missions and conditions of the various countries of the earth which he has also recently visited in a trip around the world. These are all written from so large a standpoint that they are about as interesting to the general reader as to the specialist. In the publication, the "Concert of Prayer" many of these valuable papers are found and a considerable number of his addresses, articles, &c., are bound among those of other writers, in large volumes. In the next generation we find a writer also, in Dr. Mitchell's daughter, Alice, who does not desire mention for the reason that her writings are so fragmentary and scattered. Nevertheless, her literary work has been considerable and cannot be easily measured or described. One who knows her well, says: "Not many ladies are better read in missionary annals." In an article of hers, of great interest, published in the *Concert of*

Prayer for Church Work Abroad, and entitled "The Martyrs of Mexico," we come upon the story of the Rev. John L. Stephens, previously mentioned in this book among "Travels", &c., and who, Miss Mitchell tells us, was one of the earliest missionaries of the Congregational church to Mexico.

We have already mentioned that Mr. Matthew Mitchell, the father of our writer, lived in Morristown for many years and married for his second wife, Miss Margaret, the daughter of the good Doctor John Johnes, and the grand-daughter of the good Pastor Johnes.

We give a short passage from the opening of Dr. Mitchell's Memorial Sermon on James A. Garfield, delivered in the First Presbyterian Church of Cleveland, Ohio, on Sunday, Sept. 25, 1881, and published by a number of prominent men who requested the privilege:

FROM THE "MEMORIAL SERMON" ON JAMES A. GARFIELD.

We share, my friends, to-day, the greatest grief America has ever known. It is no exaggeration to say that no one stroke of Providence has ever spread throughout all our land such poignant and universal pain, or has been so widely felt as a shock and a sorrow in every portion of the earth.

I am not using words without care. I do not
forget those dreadful days of April, sixteen years
ago, when the slow procession passed from State
to State, bearing the remains of the beloved Lincoln
to the tomb. But there was one whole section of
our land, it will be remembered, which had never
acknowledged him as their ruler, and had never
viewed him alas! except as their foe. Innumerable
noble hearts there discussed the crime that laid him
low; but although they abhorred the assassin's
crime, around his victim their sentiments of confidence and admiration and loyalty had never been
gathered.

I do not forget the horror which smote the nation when Hamilton fell, the universal pall of sor-.
row of which our fathers tell us,—the metropolis
of the country draped in black, the vast and solemn
cortège, which amidst weeping throngs, followed
Hamilton through its chief avenue to the grave.

And as one heart, the hearts of Americans
mourned for Washington. There were friends of
liberty who wept with them in every part of the
world. But liberty itself had not then so many
friends on earth as now. By one great nation
Washington was held to have drawn a rebel sword.
And against another, our earlier ally, he had un-
sheathed it and stood prepared for war. And even
by the countrymen of Washington it could not be
forgotten that he had nearly fulfilled the allotted

years of man. His work was done. His years of war had won for his country the full liberty she sought. His eight glorious years of Presidential life had organized the Government, established its relations to foreign powers and made its bulwarks strong. At his death it was even said that he had "deliberately dispelled the enchantment of his own great name;" with wonderful unselfishness he himself placed the helm in other hands, looked on for a time at the prosperity which he had taught others to supply, and "convinced his country that she depended less on him than either her enemies or her friends believed." And then he died in the peaceful retirement of his home. It was the death of a venerated father whose work was done.

Rev. Charles E. Knox, D. D.

For six or eight months in the midst of the Rev. Arthur Mitchell's pastorate, a distinguished scholar of the Presbyterian Church, the Rev. Charles E. Knox, D. D., filled Dr. Mitchell's place as pastor of the South Street Church, Morristown, while the latter was absent in Europe and Palestine. This period was from September 1863 to May 1864. When Dr. Mitchell resigned in 1868, the present pastor, Rev. Dr. Erdman, was called at Dr. Knox's suggestion. From 1864 to 1873, Dr. Knox was pastor of the church at Bloomfield, N. J., and since that time has been President of the German Theological School of Newark, which is located in Bloomfield. Dr. Knox says, in writing of his sojourn in Morristown : "I had a happy time with the good South street people and have retained always the liveliest interest in all that belongs to them."

"A Year with St. Paul" had just been published when the charge of this South Street Church was undertaken. It has since been translated into Arabic at Beirut, Syria. "It is in good part," says the author, "a compilation and condensation of Conybeare and Howson's Life and Epistles of St. Paul", (then in two large and expensive volumes), with some original matter. It has a chapter for every Sunday of the year.

Dr. Knox began in Morristown a series of "Graduated Sunday School Text Books,"—Primary Year, Second Year, Third Year, Fourth Year and Senior Year. This was an introduction of the secular graded system into Sunday School Teaching. It introduced the Quarterly Review which has since been followed.

"David the King," a life of David with section

maps inserted in the page and a location of the Psalms in his life, was published later at Bloomfield.

Rev. Albert Erdman, D. D.

The Rev. Dr. Erdman is entitled to honorable mention among Morristown writers. He has been the faithful pastor of the South Street Presbyterian Church since May 1869, following the Rev. Arthur Mitchell, D. D. It was during his ministry that in 1877, the church edifice was totally consumed by fire, and the beautiful new building located on its site, in the late Byzantine style. It is said by one who knows and appreciates Dr. Erdman's work that "few men read more or digest better their reading."

For several years, he has prepared "Notes on the International Sunday School Lessons", for a monthly periodical published in Toronto, Canada.

A number of sermons have been published by request, among them the "Sermon on the Fiftieth Anniversary of the South Street Presbyterian Church".

Addresses on "Prophetic and other Bible Studies" have been printed in Annual Reports of the Bible Conference at Niagara-on-the-Lake, Ontario, and, besides these, many fugitive newspaper articles of value and importance.

Dr. Erdman has been largely interested in the general welfare, and especially the philanthropies, of the town, outside of his immediate church, and by this public spirit, earnestly and fearlessly manifested, in many instances, he has no doubt greatly extended his sphere of influence.

He has been a warm supporter of, and has given much time and personal attention to the establishment of the Morris County Charities Aid Association and of the State Association which followed, carefully studying the questions of pauper and criminal reform for which purpose this organization exists.

In the Semi-Centennial Sermon we find the following remarkable record :

EXTRACT FROM THE SEMI-CENTENNIAL SERMON ON THE 50TH ANNIVERSARY OF THE CHURCH'S ORGANIZATION.

"I must note the unique fact that the history of these fifty years of Church life is the history of uninterrupted prosperity. Even that which seemed at the time to be against us—the destruction by fire of the former house of worship—proved to be, as are all the Lord's afflictions, a blessing in disguise ; for the history of the church since is that of continued and ever-increasing prosperity, if growing numbers and enlarged usefulness be criterion of success. A spirit of harmony and goodwill mark its whole course, and it is, therefore, with unmingled pleasure and gratitude to God, we may recall the past. No roots of bitterness and strife to be covered up, no rocks of offense to be carefully avoided !

*   *   *

How the memories of the past throng around us—the saintly lives of fathers and mothers, the godly service and earnest prayers of pastors and people, the fervent appeals from pulpit and teacher's chair,—surely it would seem there could be no valid reason why any should be still unsaved or unwilling to take up the duties of christian service.

Finally, as we here recall the story of the past and rejoice in the prosperity of the present, and while we look forward to still larger service and blessing in the days to come, let us, with a deep sense of our unworthiness and dependence, say, with the Psalmist : "Not unto us, O Lord, not unto us ; but unto Thy name be all glory."

Rev. Joseph M. Flynn, L. D.

The Roman Catholic Church in Morristown erected its first building in 1847. It was a small wooden structure, with seating capacity for about 300 people and is now used by the parish school. It was in 1871 that the first priest in full charge, Rev. James Sheeran, was stationed here, and at his death in 1881, the Rev. Joseph M. Flynn succeeded, who has continued in charge of the parish to the present time. He was named "Dean of the Catholics in Morris and Sussex Counties" about six years ago.

This author has recently published a book, (Morristown, N. J., 1892), "The Story of a Parish" from the first chapter of which we quote. Also he has written some magazine articles and a brochure on "Lent and How to Spend it." He is now preparing for publication a volume of short sermons.

"The Story of a Parish" is the story of the foundation and development of this parish of the Church of the Assumption, in Morristown.

In the opening chapter, the author says :

"We know that Raphael, Bramante, and Michel Angelo threw into St. Peter's the very heart and soul of their inspiration, to erect to the living God such a temple as the eye of man had never gazed upon.

"But there are other monuments which thrill no less the beholder, and the names of their creators sleep in an impenetrable obscurity. The cross-crowned fane, lifting to the highest heaven the sign of man's redemption, may tell us neither of him whose genius conceived nor of the toilers whose strong arm and cunning eye, in the burning heats of Summer, or in the chilling blasts of Winter, unfolded to the wondering crowds who daily watched their labors, step by step, inch by inch, the beauties whose finished product Time has preserved to us in many a shire of Britain; by the glistening lakes and verdant vales of Erin; in sunny Italy, in fair France, and in the hallowed soil bathed by our own Potomac. To the humble laborer who dug the trenches, to the artist whose chisel carved foliage or cusp or capital, a share in our grateful memory is due."

Rev. George Harris Chadwell.

The group of people who originated the idea of forming a second Episcopal Church in Morristown, perfected their plans in 1852. The following year the church building was erected. The first rector, Rev. J. H. Tyng, assumed his duties in September, 1852. The Rev. W. G. Sumner accepted a call to the parish in 1870. As he is now Professor of Political Economy at Yale University- he will come, with his specialty, into a later group. In 1880, Rev. George H. Chadwell became rector of the parish, coming from Brooklyn where he had been assistant to the Rev. Charles Hall, D. D., rector of Trinity Church of that City.

Mr. Chadwell courageously undertook the removal of the church edifice from the spot where it had stood since 1854, on the corner of Morris and Pine streets, to its present site on South street, on which occasion he delivered one of his important "Addresses" which was published and largely distributed. He lived to see his aim accomplished and not long after gave, in the church again, on what proved to be the last Sunday of his life, a sermon, which was also published under the title of "A Farewell Discourse."

Mr. Chadwell also published a monthly paper during his rectorship, called *The Rector's Assistant*, and wrote in other directions.

In the "Address on the Occasion of the Reopening of the Edifice for Divine service," August 22, 1886, we find a reference to the interesting history of the land on which the building now stands, and its association with many of the old families of Morristown, as follows :

"Originally the ground we are now occupying belonged to the first Presbyterian Church, which at that date constituted the only religious society in the town, and owned all the land on the east side of South street as far down as Pine street. This plot of ours formed a part of what was designated the parsonage lot. The first sale of it took place in November of 1795, the same year the white church on the Green was dedicated and opened for Divine worship. The consideration was one hundred and twenty pounds, money worth about $300 in the currency of the United States. The Trustees whose names appear in the deed are Silas Condict, Benjamin Lindsley, Jonathan Ford, John Mills, Richard Johnson, Jonathan Ogden and Benjamin Pierson — names which are still represented in our community. The purchaser was the Rev. James Richards. This gentleman was at the time the pastor of the First Presbyterian Church, being the third in succession to that office. His ministry covered a period of fourteen years and was remarkably successful.

*　　　　*　　　　*

"On his departure from Morristown Dr. Richards sold the property we are now describing. The price realized was $4,000. From which I infer that there had been erected upon it the house which we propose to convert into a rectory. Otherwise I can not account for so great an increase in the value of the land as took place.   *   *   *   The new owner proved to be the Rev. Samuel Fisher, the successor of Dr Richards in the pastorate of the church.   Mr. Fisher was the son of Jonathan Fisher, a native of this town.   *   *   *   In 1813, under his auspices, the Female Charitable Society of Morristown, our most venerable eleemosynary institution, was founded, Mr. Fisher's wife being elected to the honored position of its first President. *   *   *   It was somewhere about this time that Mrs. Wetmore, the widow of a British officer, opened on this site a private school for girls." (Mrs. Wetmore was the mother of Mrs. James Colles who long lived, in summer, upon the large estate now opened to the city, in streets and avenues, and largely built upon. She was also the mother of Charles Wetmore, the artist who painted the picture of "Old Morristown," in 1815, now in possession of Hon. Augustus W. Cutler, to whose courtesy we are indebted for the privilege of having made from it the fine pen and ink sketch of Miss Suzy Howell, for the frontispiece of this book.)   "From 1814 to 1829, our property passed through the hands successively of Israel Canfield, James Wood and Silas Condict. During this period, or rather a portion of it, one of New Jersey's most promising lawyers resided on this spot. I refer to Mr. William

Miller, an older brother of our late United States Senator, the Hon. J. W. Miller.   *   *   *

A citizen of Morristown who was personally acquainted with him has lately written me: 'The noble character and the brilliant career of this young lawyer, which were cut short by his untimely death, are still remembered with lively interest by some of our oldest inhabitants.'

"In 1829 the property again changed hands, the purchaser being Miss Mary Louisa Mann. Her father was the editor of *The Morris County Gazette* afterwards known as *The Genius of Liberty*, and of *The Palladium of Liberty*, the first newspapers issued in Morristown. He also published in 1805 an edition of the Holy Scriptures, which gained considerable notoriety as 'The Armenian Bible,' from the error occurring in Heb. vi : 4, 'For it is possible for those who have once been enlightened .... if they shall fall away to renew them again unto repentance.' Miss Mann, now Mrs. Lippincott, of Succasunna, together with her sister, Miss Sarah, put up the building which is to serve us hereafter as a Sunday School room and church parlor. It was erected to meet the wants of a female seminary established by them in 1822, and which had grown under their efficient management so popular that its advantages were sought by pupils from all quarters. Since the close of the school the buildings occupied by it have been used as a boarding house. As such their hospitality has been enjoyed by numbers whose names are familiar to us in connection with important features of our national existence, finance, war and art. I mention in particular the Belmonts, the Perrys, the Rogers, the Enningers. And here in the front parlor of this same boarding house in the summer of 1851, when it had been determined to found a new parish, the first meeting of its originators was held. ' In that room,' to quote the language of one present on the occasion, 'the infant Church was christened The Church of the Redeemer, and from that day it lived; very feebly at first, not a very strong child, but tenderly nurtured, always slowly gaining, until now, after thirty-four years, it promises to grow in strength and to have a powerful future.' Our immediate predecessor in the title to the land was Mr. George W. King, who acquired it in 1854 for the sum of $8,000."

Of the character of the church, Rev. Mr. Chadwell says:

"This Church then, I may observe, has always been conservative in its character. Those who founded it gave to it this tone. They were men opposed in mind and temperament to that mediaeval type of theology which had begun to prevail in their day, and which has since become popular in various quarters. They were out of sympathy with the movement which was then aiming, and which has since succeeded in undoing much the reforming divines of the sixteenth century accomplished. They were averse, for example, to everything that savors of sacerdotalism—to the doctrines which convert the ambassador of Christ into a sacrificing priest, the communion table into a veritable altar, and the eucharist into a sacrifice and constant miracle. Elaborate rites and ceremonies, in which some find a delight, and perhaps a help, were distasteful to them. They felt themselves unable to derive edification from these sources. On the other hand, they were in harmony with what may be denominated the protestant tendencies of our Communion. Of the name itself of protestant they had not learned to be ashamed. They believed in the principles of the great Reformation of three centuries ago. They did not judge its promoters deluded men, nor pronounce them to have 'died for a cause not worth dying for.' They honored them as God-enlightened, and venerated them as heroes and martyrs. The changes these effected in dogma and in ritual they regarded not as mistakes, but as advances in the right direction—from error towards truth. They looked to Christ as their only priest, to His cross as their only altar and to his death thereon as the only atonement for their sin. They loved simplicity of worship and cultivated it in their public devotions. In fine, they were content and best satisfied with that plain system of teaching and practice which the Prayer Book as we have it now seems most naturally to favor. At least this is the impression of these men which I have received from reading the record and memorials of themselves they have left behind. So when they organized this parish it was along these lines which I have indicated. And from its inception to the present moment it has retained, with perhaps some unessential modifications, the stamp they gave it."

Rev. William M. Hughes, S. T. D.

The Rev. Dr. Hughes, who succeeded the Rev. George H. Chadwell, in 1887, as rector of the Church of the Redeemer should have followed our little group—within this group—of editors and theologians, except that he has present charge of a parish, which they have not. He was officially on the editorial staff and in the editorial department of *The Churchman* during 1887 and 1888, and has written for editorial and other departments both before and since. For *The Church Journal* also, as well as other, and secular papers, he has written articles and editorials on various topics, from time to time.

Dr. Hughes was born at Little Falls, New York, and losing both parents early in life, removed to Frankfort, Kentucky, among his mother's relatives. From boarding-school in Ohio, he entered Kenyon College, Class of '71. At the end of Freshman year he went to Hobart College and was graduated there at the head of his class in 1871. During 1871-'72, he studied in Berlin, Germany, and was graduated in 1875 from the General Theological Seminary, New York. The same year he became rector of St. John's Church, Buffalo, N. Y., one of the most important parishes of the diocese of Western New York. This charge he resigned in 1883, to accept a position of honor to which he had been unanimously elected, in Hobart College, Geneva, N. Y., namely, the Chaplaincy of the College and Professorship of "Philosophy and Christian Evidences," the latter department having been hitherto held by the President of the College. It was with great regret, that the people of Buffalo as well as the people of St. John's parish, parted with both Dr. and Mrs. Hughes, if we may judge from all that was expressed in the press on the occasion of their departure. "Here," says one writer, "they will be missed, not only by those with whom they were closely associated in church or neighborhood relationship, but more especially by the sick, the humble, the troubled, and the needy, for whose consolation and comfort they have so unselfishly labored, in many parts of the city, during the last seven years. A thousand blessings follow them."

In 1887, Dr. Hughes became an associate editor of *The Churchman* and Rector of the Church of the Redeemer, Morristown. He is a member of the Executive Council of the Church Temperance Society and Corresponding Secretary of the *University Board of Regents* and originator of the scheme.

Among Dr. Hughes' writings is an important brochure on Boys' Guilds, published under the auspices of the Church Temperance Society, and entitled "Hints for the Formation of Bands of Young Crusaders." In this he discusses "one of the most practical questions before the Church, and the one which the busy rector often asks in sheer bewilderment, if not despair: 'What shall be done with the boys of the Church, from the ages of ten to seventeen?'" He also offers the solution in a plan of organization for one, among many works, which may interest and occupy them, thus training them as the boys of the Church to become the men of the Church.

In the *Magazine of Christian Literature* for September 1892, we find the leading article to be from the pen of Dr. Hughes, on "The Convergence of Darwinism and the Bible." "The conclusions here reached," the author tells us, "have been subjected, during the past eight years, to efficient criticism and repeated examinations." It is proposed that these articles shall continue and finally appear in book form. Of this article, a prominent clergyman of the Church, whose opinion weighs for much, and whose words we have asked the privilege of giving, writes Rev. Dr. Hughes, as follows: "I am deeply moved in recognizing the penetration, the sublimity and sweetness of your essay in the September number of the *Magazine of Christian Literature*. I trust No. I. is prophetic of future numbers.

"You have made a great discovery and you disclose it with great power and beauty. How wonderful is this converging witness of Nature and the Spirit, Faith and Science to the approaching Day of the Son of Man. No question, the Day is swiftly coming. Its light is on the hills. The many signs of His approach and His appearing seem to fill the air and make the spirit tremble with holy fear and gladness. The Lord hasten the Day. Let us prepare ourselves with joy to greet Him. Meantime, we may greet one another in the full assurance of faith, as I you, brother, by these presents."

From a Paper in *The Magazine of Christian Literature* of September 1892, on—

"THE CONVERGENCE OF DARWINISM AND THE BIBLE CONCERNING MAN AND THE SUPREME BEING."

Science and religion are in reality dealing with the same phenomena. Immense human and personal interests are involved in them. Neither can be discussed in the absolutely "dry light" of sheer intellectuality.

Consequences of immense import to the individual character, to the social well-being, and to eternal hopes flow directly from each.

If, by scientific methods, which are plainly sound, conclusions are reached that are directly at variance with the religious faith of the vast majority, both a social and an intellectual as well as an ethical revolution is threatening.

Or if by religious methods traditions are established which deny room to the conclusions of progressive human thought, religion inevitably invites scepticism, the casting off of all traditions, and the unfortunate disclaim of that which is forever true in faith.

There are not a few of us to whom our Lord and Saviour Jesus Christ is dearer far than the most acute thinker in the domain of human speculation or the profoundest student of the world as it is.

If it come to an attack or a logical denial of

that which He is and teaches, we do not hesitate to make a personal matter of it.

If Darwinism, e. g., as a system of ultimate postulates demands that we yield up the Lord of Life to be crucified afresh by the powers of the world, Darwinism, as such, will get no quarter. Getting no quarter, it will give none, and it becomes an internecine strife that knows no truce and admits no peace until the one or the other lies dead on the field of contest.

But if, as a matter of fact, such a conflict is really illogical, hasty, and essentially inimical to both modern science, and to the Christian faith, then much is gained not only for peace, but still more for truth.

It is the direct object of this article to demonstrate, so far as demonstration is possible, that the theory of Darwin, instead of antagonizing, tends irresistibly to affirm the most fundamental truths of the Bible as commonly held by the so-called orthodox Christian world. Nay, more, not only to affirm, but to give them greater power.

PUBLIC SPEAKERS
AND
LAWYERS.

At this point, we must confess to a sensation of being overwhelmed with an embarrassment of riches, for what shall we do with the distinguished men who follow, and bring our little book within its covers? That we may have no more continuous extracts from their works, reluctantly we find ourselves compelled to realize.

Hon. Jacob W. Miller.

We are indebted to Edward Q. Keasbey, Esq., grandson of Mr. Miller, for the facts and data of the following brief sketch.

The Hon. Jacob W. Miller was born in November, 1800, in German Valley, Morris County, N. J. He studied law in Morristown with his brother, William W. Miller from 1818 to 1823, when he was licensed to practice as attorney. He was admitted to the bar of the Supreme Court as counsellor in 1826 and in 1837 he was called to the degree of Sergeant at Law and he was one of the last to whom the degree was given. He had a large practice in Morristown and was one of the leading advocates at the circuit in Sussex and Warren as well as Morris Counties. Mr. Elmer in his reminiscences says: "He was distinguished not only as a fervent and impressive speaker, but for patient industry, faithfulness and tact. He was distinguished also for that sound common sense which is above all other sense, and was, by its exhibition in public and private, a man of great personal influence."

In 1838 he was elected a member of the Council, as the State Senate was then called, and in 1840, he was elected by the Whig party to the Senate of the United States. He was elected again in 1846, and remained in the Senate until 1852. He did not speak very often, but when he spoke it was after a careful study of the subject and his words carried the greater weight. He spoke with wisdom and eloquence. A large number of these speeches are published in scattered pamphlets or in volumes among others. They have never been collected. One of the earliest of these important speeches was on the resolutions of the day in favor of a protective tariff. On May 23, 1844, Mr. Miller delivered a speech against the treaty for annexing Texas to the United States. The objections to the treaty as stated by him, are of considerable interest in the present day. He opposed the annexation on the ground that it was using the National Government to give an advantage to the Slave States. "Slavery," he said was "a matter to be regulated and controlled by the States, and neither to be interfered with nor extended by the National Government. New Jersey had abolished slavery herself and did not ask any territory into which to send her slaves." On Feb'y 21, 1850, he spoke upon the "Proposition to Compromise the Slavery Question" and in favor of the admission of California into the Union.

Among others of his speeches, were those "On the Exploration of the Interior of Africa and in favor of the Independence of Liberia", delivered in the Senate of the United States, March 1853; "In Defence of the American Doctrine of Non-Intervention", delivered in the Senate of the U. S. Feb. 26, 1852; "On the Mexican War and the Mode of Bringing it to a Speedy and Favorable Conclusion", Feb. 2, 1847; "On the Ten Regiments Bill", Feb. 8, 1848, against the prosecution of the Mexican War. Mr. Miller worked and spoke earnestly in favor of "Establishing and Encouraging an American Line of

Steamers". On April 22, 1852, he delivered a carefully prepared speech in favor of sustaining the Collins line of Mail Steamers, and advocated the policy of a subsidy for carrying the mails, which was successful then and has now again been adopted, already resulting in the restoration of the American flag to the transatlantic steamers.

Besides these speeches in the Senate, Mr. Miller delivered a good many addresses and orations. Among these was an oration delivered in Morristown on the Fourth of July, 1851. Even then he foreboded the attempt to break up the Union and, speaking of Secession as rebellion, he maintained the power of the Nation under the Constitution to defend the Union. Several addresses were delivered before historical societies and some in the direction of the agricultural interests of the country. Before the New Jersey Historical Society in Trenton, he spoke of "The Iron State. Its Natural Position, Power and Wealth", Jan. 19, 1854. Before the Bristol Agricultural Society at New Bedford, Mass., Sept. 28, 1854, he spoke on "American Agriculture; its Development and Influence at Home and Abroad".

Hon. William Burnet Kinney.

Mr. Kinney, whose wife, Elizabeth C. Kinney and whose grandson, Alexander Nelson Easton, have already been represented among our poets, may be claimed by Morristown, for his associations of boyhood and of many years in later life. A man of unusual culture, no one who knew him could forget the charm of his courtly manners and delightful conversation. He founded *The Newark Daily Advertiser*, in 1833. It was then the only daily newspaper in the State, and uniting with it *The Sentinel of Freedom*, a long established weekly paper, he gave to the journal a tone so high that it was said of him, "his literary criticisms, contained in it, had more influence upon the opinions of literary men than those of any other journalist of the time." He was fortunate in having an accomplished son, Thomas T. Kinney, Esq., of Newark, N. J., to follow in his footsteps and continue the editorial work he had begun in this leading New Jersey paper. From Mr. Thomas T. Kinney we have a few words of reminiscence written in reply to the question of a friend as to what his father's early associations with Morristown might have been.

"My father," he says, "was born at Speedwell, Morris County (in the edge of Morristown). I think it was in the house afterwards owned and occupied by the late Judge Vail, and the same in which his son Alfred lived. He invented the telegraph alphabet of dots and lines, which made Morse's system practicable, and it is still used.

"Speedwell is on a stream upon which there were mill-sites, owned and worked by my father's ancestry and there is a tradition in the family that his uncle in trying to save a mill during a freshet lost his life and the body was afterwards found through a dream by another member of the family. The lake at Speedwell was a picturesque spot and Sully, the artist, painted his great picture of the 'Lady of the Lake' there, the subject being Lucretia Parsons, a beautiful girl whose family came from the West Indies and settled in the neighborhood. Lucretia married a Mr. Charles King who lived at the Park House in Newark and had the original sketch from which Sully painted the head in the picture. My father was intimate in the family and I think that some of his ancestry rest in the burial ground of the old Presbyterian Church at Morristown,—from all of which we may infer that many of his youthful days were passed there."

Mr. Kinney studied under Mr. Whelpley, author of "The Triangle", and subsequently studied under Joseph C. Hornblower, of Newark. In 1820 he began his editorial life in Newark, which he continued with slight interruption until his appointment in 1851, as United States Minister to Sardinia. "In this position of honor," it is said, "he represented his country with rare ability." With Count Cavour and other men of eminence in Sardinia, he discussed the movement for the unification of Italy. For important services rendered to Great Britain, Lord Palmerston sent him a special despatch of acknowledgment and by his own foresight, judgment and prompt action in the case of the exiled Kossuth, he saved the United States from enlisting in a foreign complication. During his life abroad, at the expiration of his term of office as Minister to Sardinia, while residing in Florence, Mr. Kinney became deeply interested in the romantic history of the Medici family. He began a historical work on this subject, to be entitled, "The History of Tuscany", which promised to be of great importance, but although carried far on to completion, it was not finished when his life ended. In Florence Mr. and Mrs. Kinney were constantly in the society of the Brownings, the Trollopes and others of literary distinction.

Mr. Kinney, besides his editorial writing, delivered, by request, a number of important orations which were published. The last of these, "On the Bi-Centennial of the Settlement of Newark", and delivered on the occasion of that celebration, we find in a volume published in 1866, entitled "Collections of the New Jersey Historical Society".

Hon. Theodore F. Randolph.

Theodore F. Randolph was born in New Brunswick June 24, 1826. His father, James F. Randolph, for thirty-six years publisher and editor of *The Fredonian*, was of Revolutionary stock, belonging to the Virginia family, and for eight years represented the Whig Party in Congress. The son received a liberal education and was admitted to the bar in 1848. He frequently contributed articles to his father's paper when still a youth. In 1850 he took up his residence in Hudson County, where he resided twelve years and until he removed to Morristown. In 1852 he married a daughter of Hon. W. B. Coleman, of Kentucky, and a grand-daughter of Chief Justice Marshall. In 1860 he with others of the American party formed a coalition with the Democrats to whom he ever after adhered. In 1861 he was elected to the State Senate for an unexpired term and in the following year he was re-elected and served till 1865. In 1867, he was made

President of the Morris and Essex Railroad and continued to act as such until the lease was made to the Delaware and Lackawanna Company. In 1868, he was elected Governor of the State and proved a most able and independent Chief Magistrate. In January, 1875, he was elected to the United States Senate in which he served a full term of six years. In 1873 he was one of the four who formed and carried out the design of making the Washington Headquarters "a historic place". His sudden death on the seventh day of November, 1883, shocked the whole community in whose affections he filled so large a place.

Gov. Randolph was a man of most genial manner, honorable in all his business transactions and most liberal-minded and fearless as a legislator. Says one who knew him intimately: "He filled well all the duties to which his fellow-citizens called him."

But it is as a writer that his name appears here. His messages to the Legislature while Governor and his speeches in the United States Senate are known of all and bear the impress of his character. These are scattered through numerous public documents and have never yet been collected in book form. His many contributions to the press were mostly political. In 1871, he pronounced an oration at the dedication of the Soldiers' Monument on our public square, which was published in our

County papers, and on July 5, 1875, at the celebration of the National holiday at Headquarters, he made the eloquent address, which is the best specimen of his skill. This address is given, entire, in Hon. Edmund D. Halsey's "History of the Washington Association of New Jersey".

Hon. Edward W. Whelpley.

Chief Justice Whelpley, by the high order of his judicial qualities rose rapidly from the Bar to the Bench. He was the only son of Dr. William A. Whelpley, a native of New England and a practicing physician in Morristown. Dr. Whelpley was a cousin of the Rev. Samuel Whelpley who wrote "The Triangle". The mother of Judge Whelpley was a daughter of General John Dodd of Bloomfield, N. J., and a sister of the distinguished Amzi Dodd, Prosecutor of Morris County. He was graduated at Princeton, with distinction, at the early age of sixteen; studied law with his uncle, Amzi Dodd and began its practice in Newark, N. J. In 1841 he removed to Morristown and became a partner of the late Hon. J. W. Miller. He was first appointed to the position of Associate Justice of the Supreme Court and in a few years became Chief Justice.

The late Attorney-General Frelinghuysen said of him : "Chief Justice Whelpley's most marked attributes of character were intellectual. The vigorous thinking powers of his mother's family were clearly manifest in him. No one could have known his uncle, Amzi Dodd, without being struck with the marked resemblance between them. The Chief Justice was well read in his profession, familiar with books, and yet he was a thinker rather than a servile follower of precedent. He was a first class lawyer. He sought out and founded himself on principles. He did not stick to the mere bark of a subject. He had confidence in his conclusions and he had a right to have it, for they logically rested upon fundamental truths. But while his intellectual characteristics were most marked, he had admirable moral traits. He felt the responsibilities of life and met them. He was no trifler. He had integrity, which, at the bar and on the bench, was beyond all suspicion".

And Courtlandt Parker, his intimate and life-long friend said of him :

"Intellectually, his qualities were rare. He was made for a Judge. Judicial position was his great aim and desire, and when he attained it, his whole mind was devoted to its duties; they were enjoyment to him ; he felt his strength, and was determined not merely to be a judge, but such a judge as would honor his exaltation, and exercise eminently that high usefulness which belongs to that office".

Chief Justice Whelpley may be justly ranked among important writers of the legal profession. His legal opinions found in the Law Reports are characterized by strength, independence and knowledge of the principles of law.

Hon. Jacob Vanatta.

In a city so honored in the number of its distinguished legal minds, it need not be a surprise to find such a man as Jacob Vanatta, but of only a few can it be said as was truly remarked of him : " His practice grew until, at the time of his death, it was probably the largest in the State. His reputation advanced with his practice, and for years he stood at the head of the New Jersey Bar, as an able, faithful, conscientious and untiring advocate and counsel. He may be truly called one of the greatest of corporation lawyers. He was for years the regular Counsel of the Delaware, Lackawanna and Western Railroad Company, of the Central Railroad Company, and more or less of many other corporations, and his engagements have carried him frequently before the highest Courts of New York, Pennsylvania and of the United States Supreme Court".

The Rev. Rufus S. Green, D. D., said, in his beautiful funeral discourse: "Mr. Vanatta died at the age of fifty-four—an old man worn out by overwork". "Be warned", he continues, "by the sad example of him whom to-day you sincerely mourn of an exhausted brain and prematurely enfeebled body. Take needed rest, cessation from labor, and frequent holidays".

The character of Mr. Vanatta's talent was wholly different from that of Judge Whelpley. The one rose brilliantly and suddenly, driven out by the force of an inborn genius, the other attained to what he was through untiring industry and plodding labor.

"More than any man I have ever known, from his clerkship to his death", says Mr. Theodore Little, into whose office Mr. Vanatta entered a student in the year 1845, "he seemed to have engraved on his very heart the motto, '*Perseverantia vincit omnia*,' and in that sign he conquered and achieved his success".

Mr. Vanatta's published writings are mostly

articles on political questions and many speeches and addresses, which were often reprinted. One of these in particular, made a profound impression. It was delivered at Rahway, when our civil war was threatening, and contained a strong argument and appeal for the Union.

Hon. George T. Werts.

Our present Governor of New Jersey, Hon. George T. Werts, was born at Hackettstown, N. J., March 24th, 1846, and was admitted to the bar in 1867. He was Recorder of Morristown from May 1883 to 1885, and was elected Mayor in May 1886, again in 1888 and in 1890. During the session of the State Senate in 1889, he served as President of the Senate, and was re-elected Senator in the same year. During his time as Senator, he served on many of the most important Committees and the new Ballot Reform Law and the new License Law were both drafted by him; laws which embrace, perhaps, the most radical change of any recently enacted.

While Mayor of Morristown some of the most

important ordinances of the city were of his drafting; indeed while Mayor, he paid particular attention to every ordinance drafted.

Early in 1892 he was appointed Judge of the Supreme Court of New Jersey, resigning the offices of State Senator and Mayor of Morristown to accept this honor, and he resigned the position of Judge to accept that of Governor, to which office he was elected in November, 1892.

Many speeches and addresses of Governor Werts have been published in the metropolitan and State papers, and in pamphlet form. Several are scattered through large volumes containing the speeches and addresses of others. These are mostly political, but some are on other subjects, and have been delivered before juries and at reunions, in the Senate, and on other occasions. Among these published papers are also opinions and decisions while Judge of the Supreme Court.

Joseph Fitz Randolph.

Mr. Randolph has issued a valuable work, known to us as "Jarman on Wills", 1881 and 1882, being the fifth American edition by Mr. Randolph and Mr. William Talcott. This work adds a third volume to a famous two-volume English book.

In 1888, was issued "Randolph on Commercial Paper", which work is of three volumes and contains 3,300 pages on bills, notes, &c., and is considered by the legal profession to be quite exhaustive of the subject. "These", says the author, "are legal monsters into which lawyers dig and delve and which settle knotty questions no doubt, but which probably will not be thoroughly investigated by women, until Fashion or Famine shall drive them into the legal profession".

Again we may quote the author's words, when he says in his usual happy vein of humor, about all his important legal productions, that "they are a necessary nuisance to the maker's friends and the unwilling buyers, that there is no end of making many such, and that they might be written down in line, on a heavy page with some of his brother writers on other abstruse subjects and set in a minor key".

Edward Q. Keasbey.

In one of the large New York dailies of August 1892, we read the following: "Mr. Keasbey, the well known New Jersey lawyer, has some hundred pages on 'Electric Wires in Streets and Highways,' a new subject of growing importance." This refers to a law book published by Mr. Keasbey entitled "The Law of Electric Wires in streets and Highways", Callaghan and Co., Chicago. Mr. Keasbey has also edited *The New Jersey Law Journal* since 1879 and *The Hospital Review* since 1888.

SCIENTISTS.

Samuel Finley Breese Morse, LL. D.

Nothing could be more romantic than the story of the Telegraph, the practical application of which began in Morristown, for it is morally certain that without the enthusiastic confidence in its success generously manifested by Alfred Vail, the young inventor, and his father Judge Stephen Vail, who freely contributed of his means to the experiments of Professor Morse, this great gift to the world would have been indefinitely delayed.

Morse was poor. He had exhausted his means by the necessary time and thought given to the development of his conception, when the value of this work was realized by these two men. It was as an artist, that Morse went first to Speedwell, on October 29, 1837, to observe the progress of his new machinery which was being prepared there at the Speedwell Iron Works belonging to Judge Vail, by

SPEEDWELL IRON WORKS,
AS REPRESENTED ON AN ANCIENT INVOICE.

Alfred Vail and his assistant, William Baxter. Morse had accepted a commission, doubtless given him as a means of relieving his pecuniary stress, to paint the portraits of several members of Judge Vail's household. It will be remembered, that besides his great invention, Professor Morse was an artist of considerable reputation, as well as an author. In his youth, it is said, he was more strongly marked by his fondness for art than for science. He was a pupil of Washington Allston, a member of the Royal Academy, and studied with Benjamin West. He painted the portraits of many distinguished men, among them the then President of the United States, James Monroe, for the city of Charleston ; and, later, Fitz Greene Halleck and Chancellor Kent, now in the Astor Library, and the full length portrait of Lafayette for the city of New York. He was one of the founders and was first President of the National Academy of Design, and it was on his return from the pursuit of his renewed study of art abroad that he met with the remarkable experience which turned his attention from art to invention and gave him his life work. In a letter written to Alfred Vail by Professor Morse, and given in Mr. Vail's book on " The American Electro-Magnetic Telegraph", (page 153), we find the following account :

"In 1826, the lectures before the New York Atheneum, of Dr. J. F. Dana, who was my particular friend, gave to me the first knowledge ever possessed of electro magnetism, and some of the properties of the electro magnet; a knowledge which I made available in 1832, as the basis of my own plan of an electro telegraph. I claim to be the original suggestor and inventor of the electric magnetic telegraph, on the 19th of October, 1832, on board the packet ship Sully, on my voyage from France to the United States and, consequently, the inventor of the first really *practicable telegraph on the electric principle.* The plan then conceived and drawn out in all its essential characteristics, is the one now in successful operation."

Professor Morse had more honors and medals than perhaps any American living. He belonged to a distinguished literary family. His two brothers founded *The New York Observer* in 1823. This is now the oldest weekly in New York and the oldest religious paper in the State. As an author, he wielded the pen of a ready writer. He not only published controversial pamphlets concerning the telegraph, but contributed articles and poems to many magazines and edited the works of Lucretia Maria Davidson, accompanying them by a personal memoir. He published in 1835, a book entitled, "Foreign Conspiracy against the Liberties of the United States; Imminent Dangers to the Free Institutions of the United States through Foreign Immigration and the Present State of the Naturalization Laws, by an American". Later were published "Confessions of a French Catholic Priest, to which are added Warnings to the People of the United States, by the Same Author", (edited and published with an introduction, 1837), and "Our Liberties Defended, the Question Discussed, is the Protestant or Papal System most favorable to Civil and Religious Liberty".

Alfred Vail.

To Alfred Vail belongs a place of honor, as the author of a valuable book on "The American Electro-Magnetic Telegraph", and a place of honor, also, as having been the man to perceive, at a critical moment, the importance to the world of the great invention of Professor Morse. He was among the spectators who witnessed the first operation of the electro-magnetic telegraph at the New York University and saw then, for the first time, the apparatus. Of this occasion he writes as follows: "I was struck with the rude machine, containing, as I believed, the germ of what was destined to produce great changes in the condition and relations of mankind." Again, he says, "I rejoiced to carry out the plans of Professor Morse. I promised him assistance, provided he would admit me to a share of the invention,—to which proposition he assented. I returned to my rooms, locked my door, threw myself upon the bed and gave myself up to the reflections upon the mighty results which were certain to follow the introduction of this new agent in serving the wants of the world". With this intense conviction, young Vail communicated his enthusiasm to his father, Judge Stephen Vail, who owned the Speedwell Iron Works and who generously supplied the means by which the plans for the electric telegraph were put into successful operation. It is an interesting fact that these same Speedwell Iron Works are variously connected with the history of the country, for " here was forged the shaft of the *Savannah*, the first steamship that crossed the Atlantic and here were manufactured the tires, axles and cranks of the first American locomotives."

In *The Century* for April 1888, is a most interesting article, entitled "The American Inventors of the Telegraph, with Special Reference to the Services of Alfred Vail". This is exhaustive of the subject, was written by Franklin Leonard Pope, and was supervised by Mrs. Alfred Vail, as she tells us, and the statements fortified by documents, correspondence and designs. To *The Century* editors and to Mr. James Cummings Vail, of Morris

Plains, son of Alfred Vail, we are indebted for the use of the plate of the Speedwell Iron Works, redrawn from an ancient invoice, the age of which is not known. The illustration of the "Factory" in which the first successful trial and, afterwards, the first public exhibition, of the electric telegraph took place, is from a photograph of the building as it stands at the present day, on the lot in which stands the homestead house, now occupied by Mrs. Lidgerwood.

"I have always understood", says Mr. J. C. Vail, (Jan'y 5, 1893), "that the room in which my father and Baxter (his young assistant) worked and called the 'work shop', was in an old stone building within the Iron Works enclosure, between the bridge and Morristown and is still standing, and is the only stone building within that enclosure."

Of these buildings and associations, Mrs. John H. Lidgerwood, the grand-daughter of Judge Vail, now living on the place, at Speedwell, writes as follows, Dec. 12, 1892:

"My grand-father makes but three entries in his diary:

"'1838, January 6th. Dr. Gale came this morning. They (Prof. Morse, Alfred Vail, and the Dr.) have worked the Tellegraph in the Factory this evening for the first time.'

"'10th. Mr. Morse and Alfred are working and showing the Tellegraph.'

" ' 11th. A hundred came to see the Tellegraph work.'

"The old house", continues Mrs. Lidgerwood, " in which my grandfather then lived, still remains near the foot of the hill nearest the town. The interior has been entirely changed and I never knew the room occupied by Professor Morse.

"The shop, in which the machine was constructed, and which was called the 'work shop', has also been rebuilt. Its four walls are all that are left of the original building. The floor of that room was taken away to make a one story building and the windows were put in the roof. It is now entirely vacant and stands on the side of the dam opposite the saw mill, the gable end of the old shop facing the road. One end of the foundation was partly torn away by the freshet that destroyed the old bridge. The experiments were made in a building called 'The Factory', which is at the foot of our lawn. It was built for a Cotton Factory, but only used for making buttons, owing, I believe, to some fault in its construction.

"My grandfather has told me frequently that the machine was placed on the first floor, and about three miles of copper wire, insulated by being wound with cotton yarn, was wound around the walls of the second story. There are some hooks still in the side walls but I do not know if they are the same. I have still a small portion of the original wire used in the experiments. I do not know the age of any of these buildings. The works were probably here long before the Revolution. I have heard my grandfather say there was a forge here at that time."

The machine used on the occasion to which Judge Vail refers in his diary, and on which he himself had sent the first message of all, "a patient waiter is no loser," is now loaned by the family to the Smithsonian Institute, Washington, D. C.

From the time the first telegraphic message was sent by Alfred Vail from the "Factory" at Speedwell and received by Professor Morse two miles away, and the next experiment when Morse and Vail operated with complete success through ten miles of space,—to the final triumph at Washington, many and great were the perils and moments of anguish through which the inventors passed. It was on the 24th of May, 1844, when the supreme test of the telegraph was made at Washington and the message was sent to Mr. Vail in Baltimore, in the words selected by Miss Annie G. Ellsworth and taken from Numbers xxiii : 23, "What hath God wrought."

During these years Alfred Vail, it is claimed, had "not only become a full partner in the ownership of the invention, but had supplied the entire resources and facilities for obtaining patents and for constructing the apparatus for exhibition at Washington ; and more than this, he had introduced essential improvements not only in the mechanism, but in the fundamental principles of the telegraph." Vail felt that Morse had not acknowledged, as he expected, his (Vail's) part in the invention or fully recognized his rights of partnership. Of this, the Hon. Amos Kendall, the friend and associate of both, has said: "If justice is done, the name of Alfred Vail will forever stand associated with that of Samuel F. B. Morse in the history and introduction into public use of the electro-magnetic telegraph."

Mr. Vail's book, which has place in most of the prominent libraries of Europe and America, was published in 1845 and is entitled "The American Electro-Magnetic Telegraph with the Reports of Congress and a description of all Telegraphs known, employing Electricity or Galvinism". It is illustrated by eighty-one wood engravings.

William Graham Sumner, LL. D.

Professor Sumner is a New Jersey man, born at Paterson. He inherited from his father, Thomas Sumner, who came to this country from Eng-

land in 1836, several important qualities which those who know the son will recognize. Thomas Sumner, we are told, was a man of the strictest integrity, of indefatigable industry, of sturdy common sense and possessing the courage of his convictions. Two of Professor Sumner's early teachers in Hartford, one of them Mr. S. M. Capron, in the classical department, had also great influence upon his character. He was graduated from Yale College in 1863. In the summer of that year, he went abroad, studied French and Hebrew in Geneva, after which he spent two years at the University of Göttingen, in the study of ancient languages, history, especially church history, and biblical science. Here, he tells us, he was "taught rigorous and pitiless methods of investigation and deduction. Their analysis was their strong point. Their negative attitude toward the poetic element, their indifference to sentiment, even religious sentiment, was a fault, seeing that they studied the Bible as a religious book and not for philology and history only ; but their method of study was nobly scientific, and was worthy to rank, both for its results and its discipline, with the best of the natural science methods."

Mr. Sumner went to Oxford in 1866, with the intention and desire of reading English literature on the same subjects which he had pursued at Göttingen. "I expected," he says, " to find it rich and independent. I found that it consisted of secondhand adaptation of what I had just been studying."

Returning to this country, while tutor in Yale College, in 1866, Mr. Sumner published a translation of Lange's "Commentary on Second Kings". In 1867, he was ordained deacon in the Protestant Episcopal Church, and two years later, he received full ordination in New York and became assistant to Rev. Dr. Washburn at Calvary Church, New York, under whom he was made editor of a broad church paper. In September, 1870, he became rector of the Church of the Redeemer at Morristown, N. J., from which event he claims our attention as an author.

With regard to the course of his young ministry in this parish he says: "When I came to write sermons, I found to what a degree my interest lay in topics of social science and political economy. There was then no public interest in the currency and only a little in the tariff. I thought that these were matters of the most urgent importance, which threatened all the interests, moral, social and economic, of the nation, and I was young enough to believe that they would all be settled in the next four or five years. It was not possible to preach about them, but I got so near to it that I was detected sometimes, as, for instance, when a New Jersey banker came to me, as I came down from the pulpit, and said : 'There was a great deal of political economy in that sermon.'"

In September, 1872, Mr. Sumner accepted the chair of Political and Social Science at Yale College, in which he has so highly distinguished himself. Of this he says : "I had always been very fond of teaching and knew that the best work I could ever do in the world would be in that profession ; also that I ought to be in an academical career. I had seen two or three cases of men who, in that career, would have achieved distinguished usefulness, but who were wasted in the parish and pulpit".

In 1884, Prof. Sumner received the degree of LL. D. from the University of Tennessee. A distinguished American economist well acquainted with Prof. Sumner's work has given to a writer from whom we quote, the following estimate of his method and of his position and influence as a public teacher : "For exact and comprehensive knowledge Prof. Sumner is entitled to take the first place in the ranks of American economists ; and as a teacher he has no superior. His leading mental characteristic he has himself well stated in describing the characteristics of his former teachers at Göttingen ; namely, as 'bent on seeking a clear and comprehensive conception of the matter "or truth" under study, without regard to any consequences whatever,' and further, when in his own mind Prof. Sumner is fully satisfied as to what the truth is, he has no hesitation in boldly declaring it, on every fitting occasion, without regard to consequences. If the theory is a 'spade', he calls it a spade, and not an implement of husbandry."

Professor Sumner has published, besides Lange's "Commentary on the Second Book of Kings", the "History of American Currency"; "Lectures on the History of Protection in the United States"; "Life of Andrew Jackson", in the American Statesmen Series; "What Social Classes Owe to Each Other"; "Economic Problems"; "Essays on Political and Social Science"; "Protectionism"; "Alexander Hamilton", in the Makers of America Series, (1890); "The Financier (Robert Morris) and the Finances of the American Revolution", (1891); besides a large number of magazine articles on the same line of subjects.

Elwyn Waller, Ph. D.

Three writers now present themselves, each of whom is distinguished in his department, one of Chemistry, one of Mining and Metallurgy, and one of Mathematics. The Author's Club would exclude these brilliant men from recognition, but here the clause of our title, "and Writers", saves us. Prof. Waller amusingly expresses the position when he says. "I supposed that reference in your book would be made to those who had achieved more or less distinction in what has sometimes been termed 'polite literature.' While I am not ready to admit that the literature of my profession (chemistry) is 'impolite', it probably is too technical to come within the scope of your work."

Like many of our residents, Dr. Waller's time is divided between New York and Morristown, being Professor of Analytical Chemistry at Columbia School of Mines, New York. He has written much of value; innumerable pamphlets and articles for various magazines, for chemical periodicals and Sanitary Reports and for journals far and wide, both technical and general in character, among which are *The Century* and *The Engineering and Mining Journal*. He has written certain articles for Johnson's Encyclopaedia and has edited articles in other books all of which are to be reckoned as technical, but valuable contributions to current chemical literature. He has completed a book on "Quantitative Chemical Analysis", from the MSS. of one of his Colleagues, which was left unfinished in 1879 and he is now engaged in revising and practically re-writing the same work. Besides, he has written gossipy letters for *The Evening Post*, and *The Evening Mail*, of New York, from various far-off islands and inland points, where he has usually made one of a scientific party. One series of letters was written while a member of the U. S. St. Domingo Expedition.

George W. Maynard, Ph. D.

Another scientific man, ranking high in his department of Mining and Engineering, is Professor George W. Maynard, who is just now principally engaged in Colorado, passing back and forth between that State and his home in Morristown. He has had extensive travels over our own country and continent, and abroad. He is a close observer and many of us are familiar with his graphic descriptions of the scenes which he has witnessed, notably in Mexico, also with the illustrated lectures on these and other subjects, which he has generously given from time to time.

Professor Maynard is a graduate of Columbia College, New York, and was Demonstrator in Chemistry in that College for a year. He then studied abroad at Göttingen, Clousthal and Berlin, and was for four years Professor of Mining and Metallurgy in the Rensselaer Polytechnic Institute, of Troy, N. Y. His published writings, which have mostly been of a technical character, have appeared in various technical journals and in the "Transactions of the American Institute of Mining Engineers", and in *The Journal* of the Iron and Steel Institute of Great Britain. Of the above mentioned societies, he is an active member and also of the New York Academy of Sciences.

Emory McClintock, LL. D.

The third of our group of specialists is Dr. Emory McClintock, whom one of his brother scientists warns us we should "not forget to mention as he is one of the most eminent mathematicians in the United States". As associated with Morristown, in his beautiful home on Kemble Hill, high overlooking the Lowantica valley and scenes full of memories of the Revolution, we claim him with pride, in spite of his saying that his writings have all been records of scientific researches and not literary in any sense and that he has never written a book, big or little, nor even a magazine article. It remains, that his many writings are of great value as published in pamphlet form or in periodicals of technical character, such as *The Bulletin of the New York Mathematical Society*, which is "A Historical and Critical Review of Mathematical Science"; or, *The American Journal of Mathematics* from which a large pamphlet is reprinted on *The Analysis of Quintic Equations*, or, in the direction of his art or specialty as a life insurance actuary, where appears, among other writings, a large pamphlet on *The Effects of Selection*—being "An Actuarial Essay," in which we find very interesting matter for the general reader.

Andrew F. West, LL. D.

Professor West, of Princeton College, is well remembered as a resident of Morristown for two years, (1881-1883). He was at that time, the predecessor of Mr. Charles D. Platt, at the Morris Academy, and mingled largely in the literary, social and musical circles of the city. He, like Dr. McClin-

:tock, is a Pennsylvanian, and was born at Pittsburg.

Since Mr. West accepted a professorship at Princeton College, which was the occasion of his leaving Morristown, he has written largely on classical and medieval subjects.

His last book, just published, by Charles Scribner's Sons, New York, 1892, is entitled "Alcuin and the Rise of the Christian Schools." It appears in the Series of "The Great Educators", edited by Nicholas Murray Butler. It is a volume of 205 pages, and contains a sketch of Alcuin at York and at Tours, also treating of his educational writings, his character, his pupils, and his later influence.

Various literary, philological and educational articles in reviews have been contributed by Professor West, and two books additional to the one mentioned, have been published by him. These are, "The Andria and Heauton Timorumenos, of Terence," edited with introduction and notes, and published by Harper and Brothers (1888); and "The Philobiblon of Richard de Bury," edited from the manuscripts, translated and annotated. The latter is in three volumes : I., The Latin Text ; II., The English Version ; III., Introduction and Notes Printed by Theodore De Vienne for the Grolier Club of New York. (1889).

José Gros.

From the shores of Spain, has come to us one of our advanced thinkers and writers, Señor José Gros. He is a disciple of Henry George and, on one occasion, introduced that distinguished man to a Morristown audience, in our Lyceum Hall, giving, to a large number of people assembled, the opportunity of listening to his own exposition of the views about which so wide and warm a controversy has raged.

Señor Gros was born and educated in Spain. He has traveled extensively through Italy, France, Germany, England, and a portion of our own country, finally taking a position in a commercial house in New York, in 1859, in which he remained until 1870, when he retired to Morristown. Since then, in his own words, he has "dedicated most of his time to the study of history and science, more especially social science," for which he has been writing articles for western magazines and journals and also for one or more of our local papers.

In the *Locomotive Firemen's Magazine*, of Terre Haute, Indiana, a large number of these articles have appeared. They go with this magazine to all the States and Territories of the Union, to parts of Canada and Mexico, and they are connected with over 500 Labor Clubs. The subject of one series of these papers is "Civilization With its Problems". Other subjects are, "The Struggle for Existence"; "Confusion in Economic Thought"; "Governments by Statics or Dynamics"; "Congested Civilizations"; "Social Skepticism", and a series on "To-day's Problems". In all his arguments, Señor Gros considers as vital to advance in Social Science the principles of the Christian religion. "No system," he says, "can save us from disasters without clear perceptions of duty on what I call 'Christian citizenship.'"

MEDICAL AUTHORS
AND
WRITERS.

Condict W. Cutler, M. S., M. D.

Dr. Cutler, claims through his father, the Hon. Augustus W. Cutler, as ancestor, the Hon. Silas Condict, one of the most renowned patriots of the Revolution, and his childhood and boyhood was spent in the house which was built, in 1799, by this great-great-grandfather and occupied by him. It has been owned and occupied since then, and is now, by Hon. Augustus W. Cutler. The old house, in which Silas Condict previously lived, is still standing about a mile west of the present Cutler residence. Many historic incidents and traditions cluster about this place.

Dr. Cutler has done credit to this ancestor's

memory in his exceptionally successful career. A member of many societies, and associate editor of *The New York Epitome of Medicine*, he has written largely for journals and magazines, besides publishing three books, which are entitled "Differential Medical Diagnosis"; "Differential Diagnosis of the Diseases of the Skin", and "Essentials of Physics and Chemistry." These, say the medical and surgical critics, are prepared with care and thoroughness and show a wise use of standard textbooks and the exercise of critical judgment guided by practical experience.

Many may think that the books belonging to Materia Medica, being of technical character, do not come directly within our province, but we may say *everything* in the line of authorship is within our broad range, and we are glad to say emphatically that nothing, not even theological questions, concern mankind more deeply than just this great question upon which Dr. Cutler has expended so much thought and labor and which too is the result of his experience as a medical man,—namely, the Differential Diagnosis of Disease. When we take into consideration the fact, that no disease can be successfully treated until it is *known* and as it cannot be known without being properly diagnosed, and as successful diagnoses depend upon just such principles and relations as Dr. Cutler demonstrates, we can see the value of the work even though we may not belong to the medical fraternity. More than all, we can see the benefit which such a work confers upon mankind at large and not alone upon the healers of diseased and afflicted humanity. Let any one go into the houses of the poor; the streets and the alleys, and into the overflowing hospitals and witness the immensity of the evil of that terrible phase of disease, "The Skin Diseases" of which Dr. Cutler treats, and he will realize what earnest thanks we owe to a man whose life work is to devote his time and brains to the alleviation of this type of human suffering.

Phanet C. Barker, M. D.

Dr. Barker, of Morristown, has for twenty-five years past written more or less, from time to time, for medical journals published in New York and Philadelphia. The majority of these contributions have been of a practical character and consequently rather brief. Some of them have been formal studies of practical questions, such as "The Vaccination Question", questions connected with Sanitary

Science, &c. Of the latter, one we would mention in particular, entitled, "The Germ Theory of Disease and its Relations to Sanitation". In this the writer tells us: "The germ theory of disease is destined to hold a place in literature as the romance of medicine, and if it stands the test of time, and the scrutiny which is certain to be bestowed upon it, the theory will mark an epoch for all time to come. The present century has been distinguished in many and various ways, which need not be alluded to in this connection. Among the discoveries and improvements of the age, Sanitary Science occupies an important, a commanding position, that can hardly be exaggerated. Indeed it has contributed more to civilization and to the well-being of the human race than steam, electricity or any other scientific or economic discovery." Then the writer refers to the condition of Englishmen who lived in the fourteenth century, and traces the ravages of the Black Death to the people's mode of living. He sketches the epidemics that have prevailed in the world at various periods, and asserts that even "chronology has been changed and the fate of great and powerful peoples like those of Athens, of Rome and of Florence, has been sealed by the direct or indirect effects of what we now term preventible diseases."

Such contributions as Dr. Barker has made to general literature have had relation to economic questions generally, although the preparation of a few papers on "Popular Astronomy", "Meteorological Observations" and "Fishing in Remote Canadian Waters" have served, as he says, "to rest and refresh his mind, when harassed by anxieties incident to the practice of his profession." These papers have been published,—the former in New York City or in our local papers, and the latter in *The Forest and Stream.* One of the pamphlet publications on popular astronomy is unusually attractive and is entitled "The Stars and the Earth"..

Horace A. Buttolph, M. D., LL. D.

Dr. Buttolph, whose professional life, as connected with the care and treatment of the insane in three large institutions, in New York and New Jersey, covering a period of forty-two years, although devoted so exclusively to administrative, professional and personal details, that little time was left to engage in writing for the press, beyond the preparation of the usual annual Reports of such institutions, has, nevertheless turned that little time to good account.

The State Asylum for the Insane at Morristown was under the superintendence of Dr. Buttolph from its opening in August 1876 to the last day of the year 1884, when he tendered his resignation. Previous to this he had been in charge of the Trenton Asylum from May 1848 to April 1876, making a period of unbroken service in New Jersey of more than thirty-seven years, during which time these buildings were organized on his plan, and that of Morris Plains, with its extensive machinery, was mostly planned by him. One specialty in the line of machinery in both institutions, in use for many years,—that of making aerated or unfermented bread, which is most cleanly, healthful and economical, is probably not in use in any institution in the world, outside of New Jersey.

Dr. Buttolph was born in Dutchess County, N. Y., and was graduated from the Berkshire Medical Institution at Pittsfield, Mass., in 1835. Having been early attracted to the study of insanity, he made it a specialty and accepted a position in the new State Lunatic Asylum, at Utica, N. Y., in 1843. This he retained until 1847 when he went as Medical Superintendent to the State Lunatic Asylum near Trenton, N. J. During the previous year, while still attached to the Utica Asylum, he went abroad to study the architecture and management of other institutions and visited thirty or more of the principal asylums in Great Britain, France and Germany. At this time very few institutions for the insane had been established in this country and all sorts of problems had to be worked out. Dr. Buttolph soon came to be a very high authority and, in that recognized capacity, he was chosen to direct the Asylum at Morris Plains, which is the largest in the United States and one of the best equipped in the world. It was a matter of very great regret to his large circle of friends in Morristown, and out of it, when he found it impossible to remain longer in the charge he had filled so faithfully and well.

Dr. Buttolph's writings have been on insanity or mental derangement ; also on the organization and management of hospitals for the insane ; the classification of the insane with special reference to the most natural and satisfactory method of their treatment, etc. These writings have been published in many magazines and journals, and a large number in pamphlet form. Also addresses, delivered on important occasions or before societies, have been published in pamphlet form. Of these, one is widely known, given before the Association of Medical Superintendents of American Institutions for the Insane, at Saratoga, N. Y., June 17, 1885, on "The Physiology of the Brain and its Relations in Health and Disease to the Faculties of the Mind."

AUTHORS AND WRITERS
ON
ART.

Thomas Nast.

Mr. Nast, who has for so long been identified with Morristown, may be designated both as artist and bookmaker. In the true sense of the term, author, he may then be fairly presented, as probably no living man has wielded a greater influence through his power of expression. Many readers of this sketch will remember the consternation that prevailed upon the revelation of the Tweed Ring scandals and at the question of Tweed himself as he defied the City of New York,—"What are you going to do about it?" They will remember how Mr. Nast with wonderful courage and grasp of the situation, came to the front and at great personal risk to himself and family, threw with steady aim, the stone which killed that Goliath of Gath and put to rout the Philistines. They will remember Tweed's exclamation : "I can stand anything but those pictures!" Mr. Nast, then, is a hero in our history, and the fact cannot be forgotten.

When the Washington Headquarters was first purchased from the Ford family, the original owners, by a few gentlemen who organized the Washington Association to preserve the historic building and grounds, for a national possession, many will remember how Mr. Nast entered into the spirit of the Centennial Celebration there in 1875, when so many of the prominent men and women of Morristown took part, wearing the dress of the Revolution and working hard to accomplish the end of fitting up the building by the proceeds of the entertainment. All were astonished by the result in sales of tickets, collation, and little hatchets, of between eleven and twelve hundred dollars in one single afternoon and evening ; so much, that the amount was divided between the Headquarters and the "Library" of Morristown, then in its beginning. Mr. Nast had much to do with this success. He worked early and late at the decorations and filled one of the largest rooms with his immense and humorous cartoons of scenes in the Revolution and the stories of George Washington.

The book published by Mr. Nast is now in our

library, "Miss Columbia's Public School", and is a clever satire on the Northern and Southern boy and the general condition of Miss Columbia's pupils in the time of our Civil War. It was issued in 1871.

Another charming publication of Mr. Nast was brought out by the Harper Brothers for Christmas, 1889, under the title of "Thomas Nast's Christmas Drawings for the Human Race". Of this says one of the critics of the time : "His Santa Claus, jolly vagabond that he is, seems to radiate a warmth more genial than tropic airs, and a gayety that overbears the sadness of experience. 'What a mug' does he show us on the title page,: so kindly, so roguish, so venerable, so comical, so shrewd, so pugnaciously cheerful ! How seriously he takes himself, and yet what a wink in those twinkling eyes, as who should say, 'Confidentially, of course, we admit the fraud, but mum's the word where the children are concerned !'"

Thomas Nast came from Bavaria, with his father, at the age or six, and at fourteen was a pupil for a few months of Theodore Kaufmann, soon after beginning his career, as draughtsman on an illustrated paper. In 1860, as special artist for a New York weekly paper, he went abroad and while there, followed Garibaldi in Italy, making sketches for London, Paris and New York illustrated papers. His war sketches appeared in *Harper's Weekly* on his return in 1862. The political condition of national affairs gave him opportunity for manifesting his peculiar gift for representing in condensed form, a powerful thought. His first political caricature established his reputation. It was an allegorical design which gave a powerful blow to the peace party.

Besides the *Harper's Weekly* sketches, Mr. Nast has contributed to other papers and has illustrated books in addition to those mentioned, in particular Petroleum V. Nasby's book. For many years, he brought out "Nast's Illustrated Almanac".

In the principal cities of the United States, Mr. Nast has lectured, illustrating his lectures with rapidly executed caricature sketches, in black and white, and in colored crayons. It is said by a contemporary writer that "in the particular line of pictorial satire, Thomas Nast stands in the foremost rank."

Rev. Jared Bradley Flagg, D. D.

The Rev. Dr. Flagg, recently a resident of Morristown, has just published a delightful and important book on the "Life and Letters of Washington Allston", Scribner's Sons, November, 1892. It is illustrated by reproductions from Allston's paintings. Many remember the very striking full length portraits of Wm. H. Vanderbilt, Mr. Evarts and others, which were shown in Dr. Flagg's gallery in Morristown, on the occasion of a reception given at his residence here, a few years ago.

In addition to the book above mentioned, Dr. Flagg has written a great deal as a clergyman. He belongs to an artistic family, of New Haven, Conn. His brother, George, was considered in his youth a prodigy and his pictures and portraits attained celebrity. His style resembles the Venetian School, like that of his uncle, Washington Allston, with whom he studied. Dr. Flagg studied with both his brother and his uncle, and began as an artist at an early age, painting professionally and earning a living at sixteen. At twenty, "his love of letters, and fear of Hell," as he says, led him to connect himself with Trinity College, Hartford, Conn., and to study for the church. After an active ministry of ten years, during eight of which he was rector of Grace Church, Brooklyn Heights, his health broke down, and he devoted what strength he had left to artistic and literary pursuits, in which he is still engaged and in which, he tells us, he finds increasing interest with declining years.

Rev. J. Leonard Corning, D. D.

Dr. Corning has already been represented, in our group of poets. He has passed much of his life abroad and has made a special study of art, upon which he is an authority. He was for several years a regular contributor to *The Independent* and *The Christian Union* on art subjects, and wrote for *The Manhattan Magazine*, a series of articles, among them, on the "Luther Monument at Worms", "William Lübke" and " Women Artists of the Olden Time". The fruits of his art study have largely been put into the form of popular lectures, which he has delivered in many of the large American cities.

It is remembered that some years ago, during his residence in Morristown, Dr. Corning gave a series of art lectures with illustrations, for the benefit of the Morristown Library. The proceeds were devoted to the purchase of books on art and the volumes thus added were selected by Dr. Corning. In this way, the library is indebted to him for very valuable additions.

George Herbert McCord, A. N. A.

Mr. McCord, of the National Academy, is best known to us as an artist, bringing before us, with his magic brush, historic scenes of England, picturesque views of Canada, on the St. Lawrence and elsewhere, and many of our own country, among them spots of beauty about Morristown, which other eyes perhaps have not discovered until shown to them by him. But, he is also an art critic and one of those writers of out of door life, who find, like Hamerton, both rest and recreation among the scenes which he transfers to his canvas. Often he contributes to our papers and magazines current news from the art world to which he so essentially belongs. Sometimes, in his contributions to *The Richfield News*, for which he writes, he gives us a bit of word painting that is scarcely less poetic than the creations of his canvas. More than all, Mr. McCord is not a croaker. He never comes before us with that chronic wail of the neglect of American art. On the contrary, he tells us cheerfully that the most prominent dealers in foreign art productions are buying and selling works of American art. We like such cheerful summer writers, bringing bright visions of the future to our world of art.

Mr. McCord's beautiful picture, "The Old Mill Race", transfers to canvas a scene on the Whippany River. It also makes a fine addition to a little collection of "Choice Bits in Etching", published by Mr. Ritchie.

DRAMATIST.

William G. Van Tassel Sutphen.

Mr. Sutphen, who is now permanently engaged in journalism, is no less a successful dramatist and, from the first, has shown those most attractive and rare qualities which are essentially requisite to reach dramatic success. A list of his more important published works will show that he is no idler, and includes several bright clever farces contributed to *Harper's Bazar*, among them, "The Reporter"; "Hearing is Believing"; "Sharp Practice", and "A Soul Above Skittles". Not long ago appeared a romantic opera entitled "Mary Phillipse; An Historical and Musical Picture, in Four Scenes." This is founded on certain events in the history of the city of Yonkers, Westchester County, New York, between the years 1760 and 1776. It was set to music by George F. Le Jeune, and produced with marked success, June 30, 1892, at Yonkers and on succeeding dates. "Hearing is Believing" was performed twice in Morristown in the same winter.

Mr. Sutphen has only lately published in the July number of *Scribner's Magazine* (1892), a poem entitled "To Trojan Helen" and containing some fine verses. This is worthy of high place in Mr. Sutphen's intellectual work. Another poem of merit, "Insciens", appeared also in *Scribner's Magazine*. In addition to these, miscellaneous verses and sketches have been contributed to *Puck*, *Life*, *Time* and other periodicals, and in most cases, anonymously. For the past eight years, Mr. Sutphen has had charge of the weekly edition of *The New York World*. While at Princeton College he was one of the editors of the *Nassau Literary Magazine*, and one of the founders and first editor of the *Princeton Tiger*, an illustrated weekly, modeled on the *Harvard Lampoon*. "Condensed Dramas" and "Latterday Lyrics" should also be mentioned, a series of light sketches and verses contributed to *Time* during the existence of that periodical.

It is, however, by his dramatic talent, that we wish to represent Mr. Sutphen, and for this reason we expected and would be glad to give in full, were it possible, "The Guillotine ; a Condensed Drama", which first appeared in *The Argonaut*, a San Francisco Journal. This is an extremely clever and witty comedy, perhaps the best of his dramatic writings, to which an extract will hardly do justice. We are thankful to Mr. Sutphen for contributing a little of the laughter element to the condensed mass, included in this volume, of theology, history, philosophy, poetry, romance, mathematics, medicine, art and science.

EXTRACT FROM "THE GUILLOTINE."

Scene : The Public Square in a French Town. In the centre of the square is seen a guillotine. Enter venerable gentleman of scientific aspect reading a newspaper.

(In the first scene the professor, finding himself alone with the guillotine and seeing a notice of an execution to take place three hours later, is impelled to examine the instrument. He adjusts the axe and works the spring until he masters the mechanism, and finds the spring on the right releases the knife, spring on the left, the head. Finally he decides to put his own head on the block to try the sensation. Horrible! he cannot remember which is his right hand and which his left. While in this position, a party of tourists come along, armed with Baedekers and accompanied by a guide.)

GUIDE (*gesticulating*) Zare, ladies and gentlemans. Ze cathedral! Ah! ciel! Look at him.

Magnifique! (*Chorus of "ahs" from tourists and general opening of Baedekers.*)

GUIDE—Ze clock-tower ees of a colossity excessive. It elevates himself three hundred and eighty-six feet. (*Immense enthusiasm.*) At ze terminality of ze wall statue ze great Charlemagne. Superbe! Chuck-a-block to him, Dagobert, Clovis and Voila! (*Catching hold of elderly tourist.*) Le bon Louis. (*The tourists take notes with painful accuracy and minuteness.*)

ELDERLY TOURIST—Very interesting. Rose, my child, have you got all that down. How old is the cathedral, guide?

GUIDE—It has seven hundred and feefty-six years.

SPINSTER AUNT (*Severely*)—Baedeker says seven hundred and fifty-five.

GUIDE (*politely*)—It ees hees one mistaké. (*An exclamation from Rose. Everybody turns.*)

ROSE (*pointing to guillotine*)—Oh, do look there!

SPINSTER AUNT—It looks as though an execution were in progress. Baedeker says—

ELDERLY TOURIST (*eagerly*)—Is it really so, guide?

GUIDE (*indifferently*)—Yes, but zare ees no fee and zarefore no objection in seeing it. It ees modern—vat you call him—cheap-John. We will now upon ze clock-tower upheave ourselves. Zare are two hundred and one steps.

ELDERLY TOURIST—But we want to see the execution.

GUIDE—You enjoy ze ferocity! Bah! you shall have him. For one franc zare ees to see picture S. Sebastian—ver' fine, all shot full wiz burning arrows.

ELDERLY TOURIST—Never mind, we will wait. Do you think, guide, I would have time to go back and get my wife. I am sure she would enjoy it?

www.ingramcontent.com/pod-product-compliance
Lightning Source LLC
Chambersburg PA
CBHW051727300426
44115CB00007B/490